Essential Steps to College Success

Review this list, and work to complete each of these tasks in your first few weeks of college. These are important first steps to assure that you will get off to a good start in college.

❑ Meet your academic adviser. Make sure your adviser is someone you feel comfortable with.

❑ Figure out how to access your campus e-mail, learning management systems, and any other technology tools that you'll be expected to use in your classes or across campus.

❑ Be sure you know important deadlines such as those for dropping or adding courses, your first exams, and upcoming quizzes and paper due dates. Write them down in your planner or add them to your electronic calendar.

❑ Create a weekly schedule that includes time for study, recreation, and sleep.

❑ Purchase all your textbooks, and keep up with reading assignments.

❑ Find an upper-level student you can talk to and ask for advice.

❑ Make an appointment to talk to one or more of your instructors outside of class.

❑ Find a quiet place to study. You might need to negotiate with a roommate or family members for dedicated study space and time.

❑ Find a club or organization you would be interested in joining.

❑ Learn about academic support available on your campus, and make an appointment to visit the academic support center.

❑ Create a budget, and monitor it regularly to make sure you're sticking to it.

❑ Join or form a study group, especially for your most challenging courses.

❑ Get some exercise every day.

❑ Check back over this list weekly, and knowing yourself as you do, add other items that are necessary for your success.

Step by Step
to College and Career Success

Sixth Edition

John N. Gardner

President, John N. Gardner Institute for Excellence in Undergraduate Education
Brevard, North Carolina
Distinguished Professor Emeritus, Library and Information Science
Senior Fellow, National Resource Center for The First-Year Experience
  and Students in Transition
University of South Carolina, Columbia

Betsy O. Barefoot

Senior Scholar
John N. Gardner Institute for Excellence in Undergraduate Education
Brevard, North Carolina

Bedford/St. Martin's

Boston • New York

For Bedford/St. Martin's

Vice President, Editorial, Macmillan Higher Education Humanities: Edwin Hill
Publisher for College Success: Erika Gutierrez
Senior Executive Editor for College Success: Simon Glick
Developmental Editor: Jennifer Jacobson, Ohlinger Publishing Services
Senior Production Editor: Deborah Baker
Senior Production Supervisor: Dennis J. Conroy
Senior Marketing Manager: Christina Shea
Associate Editor: Bethany Gordon
Copyeditor: Arthur Johnson
Indexer: Mary White
Photo Researcher: Sue McDermott Barlow
Director of Rights and Permissions: Hilary Newman
Senior Art Director: Anna Palchik
Text Design: Jerilyn Bockorick, Cenveo® Publisher Services
Cover Design: William Boardman
Cover Photo: Students sitting on bench © Commercial Eye/Getty Images
Composition: Cenveo® Publisher Services
Printing and Binding: RR Donnelley and Sons, Willard

Manufactured in the United States of America.

9 8 7 6 5
f e d c b

For information, write: Bedford/St. Martin's, 75 Arlington Street, Boston, MA 02116   (617-399-4000)

ISBN 978-1-4576-7251-4

Brief Contents

01 Starting Out on the Right Foot 1

02 Managing Your Time 13

03 Understanding How You Learn 31

04 Getting the Most Out of Class 51

05 Reading for Success 67

06 Taking Exams & Tests 85

07 Thinking Critically 105

08 Developing Information Literacy 119

09 Communicating Clearly 135

10 Connecting with Others in a Diverse World 149

11 Managing Money 167

12 Staying Healthy 183

13 Considering Majors & Careers 197

Contents

Preface   xiii

01 Starting Out on the Right Foot   1

What You Need to Know about This Course and Your Book   3

Why Should I Take This Course?   3

Aren't All the Topics in This Book Common Sense?   3

What Will I Get Out of This Course?   3

TRY IT! FEELING CONNECTED ▷ Finding Your Niche on Campus   4

Making a Successful Transition to College   5

Different Worlds: High School and College   5

TRY IT! FEELING CONNECTED ▷ Get to Know Your Instructors   5

Advantages of a College Education   6

Returning Students versus Traditional Students   6

Office Hours   7

Setting Goals for Success   8

TRY IT! MAKING DECISIONS ▷ This Way or That   8

Getting Started   8

TRY IT! SETTING GOALS ▷ Plan for the Future   9

Chapter Review   11

02 Managing Your Time   13

Time—Your Most Valuable Resource   15

Setting Goals   15

TRY IT! MAKING DECISIONS ▷ Your Ten-Year Plan   16

Getting Your Priorities in Order   17

TRY IT! SETTING GOALS ▷ "I've Got to Get My Priorities in Order!"   17

A Balancing Act   17

R-E-S-P-E-C-T   18

Time-Management Pitfalls   19

Don't Put It Off! Beating Procrastination   19

Dealing with Distractions   20

Ask Yourself the Tough Questions   20

When You're Spread Too Thin   22

Maintaining Motivation   22

Get Smart about Organizing Your Days, Weeks, Tasks, and More   23

Using a Daily or Weekly Planner   23

Scheduling Your Time Week by Week   23

At the Top of My To-Do List Is "Make a To-Do List"!   25

Thinking about Your Class Schedule   26

TRY IT! FEELING CONNECTED ▷ Compare Your Class Schedules   26

Maximizing Study and Review Time   27

Going from Here to There — Using Travel Time Wisely   28

Chapter Review   29

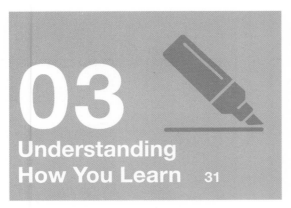

03 Understanding How You Learn 31

Why Be an Engaged Learner? 33

TRY IT! SETTING GOALS ▷ Engage in Learning 33

Collaborative Learning Teams 34

Making Learning Teams Productive 34

TRY IT! MAKING DECISIONS ▷ Group Study — Give It a Chance 35

Eight Great Uses for Learning Teams 35

Is There *Really* More Than One Way to Learn? 36

The VARK (Visual, Aural, Read/Write, and Kinesthetic) Learning Styles Inventory 36

The VARK Questionnaire (Version 7.1, 2011) 36

Scoring the VARK 38

TRY IT! FEELING CONNECTED ▷ Connect with VARK "Buddies" 39

Using VARK Results for Success 40

TRY IT! SETTING GOALS ▷ Developing Study Strategies That Match How You Learn 40

Know Thyself — Understanding Emotional Intelligence 41

What Is Emotional Intelligence? 41

Identifying Competencies 42

Emotional Intelligence Questionnaire 43

How Emotions Affect Success 44

TRY IT! SETTING GOALS ▷ Emotional Reactions Have Consequences 45

How to Improve Your Emotional Intelligence 45

Learning with a Learning Disability 46

Attention Disorders 46

Cognitive Learning Disabilities 46

TRY IT! FEELING CONNECTED ▷ Prepare for a Learning Disability to Touch Your Life 47

A Learning Disability = Learning Difference 48

Chapter Review 49

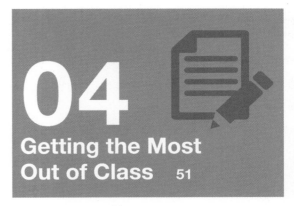

04 Getting the Most Out of Class 51

Preparing for Class 53

TRY IT! SETTING GOALS ▷ Do All of Your Assigned Reading before Class 53

Pay Attention! Listening, Participating, and Note Taking 54

Listening Critically 55

Step by Step to Becoming a Critical Listener 55

Step by Step to Becoming an Active Class Participant 55

TRY IT! FEELING CONNECTED ▷ Work Up the Nerve 55

Taking Notes 56

Approaches to Note Taking 57

Cornell Format 57

Outline Format 58

Paragraph Format 59

List Format 60

Taking Notes in Class 61

Make Adjustments for Different Classes 61

Strategies for Note Taking in Quantitative Courses 62

Keep It Fresh by Reviewing Your Notes 63

Class Notes and Homework 64

TRY IT! MANAGING TIME ▷ Review Your Notes before Class 64

Chapter Review 65

05 Reading for Success 67

Four-Step Plan for Active Reading 69

Step 1: Previewing 69

Map It! 70

Step 2: Reading and Marking 71

TRY IT! SETTING GOALS ▷ Practice Marking a Chapter 72

Step 3: Reading with Concentration 72

TRY IT! FEELING CONNECTED ▷ Two (or More) Are Better Than One 73

Get the Most Out of Your Textbook 73

Step 4: Reviewing 74

Different Courses — Different Kinds of Textbooks 75

Reading Math Textbooks 75

Reading Science Textbooks 76

TRY IT! MAKING DECISIONS ▷ Weighing the Pros and Cons of Tablets and E-readers 76

Reading Social Science and Humanities Textbooks 77

The Value of Primary Source Material 77

TRY IT! MANAGING TIME ▷ Planning Out Your Reading Assignments 78

Improving Your Reading 79

Developing Your Vocabulary 79

What to Do When You Fall Behind in Your Reading 80

If English Is Not Your First Language 81

Chapter Review 82

06 Taking Exams & Tests 85

Preparing for Tests 87

Work with Instructors, Peers, and Tutors 87

TRY IT! FEELING CONNECTED ▷ Tutoring and Study Groups 89

Prepare for Math and Science Exams 89

TRY IT! SETTING GOALS ▷ Be at Your Best for the Next Test 90

Prepare Physically and Emotionally 90

Study to Make It Stick 91

Help Your Memory Help You 91

Review Sheets, Mind Maps, and Flash Cards 92

Summaries 93

Tips for Nailing Your Test Prep 94

Taking Tests and Exams 95

Be Ready for Every Kind of Pitch 95

TRY IT! MANAGING TIME ▷ Time Flies — Even When You're Taking an Essay Test 96

Fear Not the Online Test 98

Academic Honesty and Misconduct 99

Cheating 99

Plagiarism 100

TRY IT! MAKING DECISIONS ▷ Ignorance Is No Excuse 100

Consequences of Cheating and Plagiarism 100

Reducing the Likelihood of Academic Dishonesty 100

Guidelines for Academic Honesty 101

Chapter Review 102

07
Thinking Critically 105

Becoming a Critical Thinker 107

Ask Questions 107

TRY IT! SETTING GOALS ▷ Make Up Your Own Mind 108

Consider Multiple Points of View 108

Draw Conclusions 108

TRY IT: MAKING DECISIONS ▷ Study Groups: Pros and Cons 108

Collaboration and Critical Thinking 109

Faulty Reasoning: Logical Fallacies 110

TRY IT! FEELING CONNECTED ▷ True Confessions 110

TRY IT! MAKING DECISIONS ▷ I Can't Believe I Fell for That! 111

Bloom's Taxonomy 112

Bloom's Six Levels of Learning 112

Bloom's Taxonomy and Your First Year of College 112

Critical Thinking in College and in Life 114

Challenge Assumptions 115

Thinking Critically about Arguments 116

Examine the Evidence 116

Chapter Review 117

08
Developing Information Literacy 119

Understanding Information Literacy 121

Choosing, Narrowing, and Researching a Topic 123

Check Your Engine 124

Using the Library 125

TRY IT! FEELING CONNECTED ▷ A Library Is a Terrible Thing to Waste 125

The 20-Minute Rule 126

TRY IT! MAKING DECISIONS ▷ Put the 20-Minute Rule to the Test 126

Scholarly Articles and Journals 126

Periodicals 127

Books 127

TRY IT! SETTING GOALS ▷ Cozy Up to Your College Library 127

Evaluating Sources 128

Relevance 128

Research Wisely 129

Authority 130

Bias 130

Synthesizing Information and Ideas 131

TRY IT! MANAGING TIME ▷ Be the Early Bird 131

Chapter Review 132

09 Communicating Clearly 135

Understanding the Basics of Writing 137

Steps to Good Writing 137

TRY IT! MANAGING TIME ▷ The Importance of Time in the Writing Process 139

Know Your Audience 140

E-mail Etiquette 140

Citing Your Sources 142

Citations: Why and How? 142

About Plagiarism 142

TRY IT! MAKING DECISIONS ▷ Facebook through an Employer's Eyes 143

Speaking 144

Guidelines for Successful Speaking 144

TRY IT! SETTING GOALS ▷ Seek Out Chances to Speak 146

Chapter Review 147

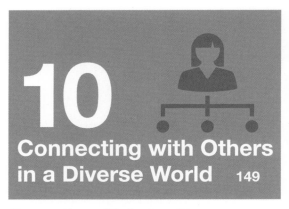

10 Connecting with Others in a Diverse World 149

Connecting with Instructors 151

What Your Instructors Expect from You 151

What You Can Expect from Your Instructors 151

Maximizing the Learning Relationship 152

So What *Is* Academic Freedom? 153

Handling Conflict between You and an Instructor 153

Personal Relationships 154

Roommates 154

Romantic Relationships 154

Breaking Up Is Hard to Do 154

Relationship No-Nos 154

The Ties That Bind: Family 155

Marriage and Parenting during College 155

Relationships with Parents 156

Communicating in a Digital Age 157

Thriving in Diverse Environments 159

Stereotyping: Why We Believe What We Believe 159

TRY IT! MAKING DECISIONS ▷ Resist Prejudice 160

Other Differences You Will Encounter in College 160

TRY IT! SETTING GOALS ▷ Make a New and Different Friend 162

Creating a Welcoming Environment on Your Campus 162

Connecting through Involvement 163

TRY IT! MANAGING TIME ▷ How Involved Is Too Involved? 163

Working 163

Community Service 164

Chapter Review 165

11 Managing Money 167

Living on a Budget 169

Creating a Budget 169

TRY IT! MAKING DECISIONS ▷ Miscellaneous Expenses 170

Cutting Costs 170

TRY IT! SETTING GOALS ▷ Develop a Personal Budget 171

Understanding Financial Aid 172

Types of Aid 172

Navigating Financial Aid 173

Qualifying for Aid 174

How to Keep Your Funding 174

Steps to Qualify for Financial Aid 174

TRY IT! SETTING GOALS ▷ Exhaust All Avenues 175

Achieving a Balance between Working and Borrowing 176

Advantages and Disadvantages of Working 176

TRY IT! MANAGING TIME ▷ Be Realistic 176

Student Loans 176

TRY IT! FEELING CONNECTED ▷ Search Party 177

Plan for the Future 177

Managing Credit Wisely 178

Understanding Credit 178

Debit Cards 179

Frequently Asked Questions about Credit Cards and Identity Theft 180

Chapter Review 181

12 Staying Healthy 183

Managing Stress 185

Evaluate Your Diet and How Much You Exercise 185

TRY IT! SETTING GOALS ▷ Are You Losing It? 186

TRY IT! MANAGING TIME ▷ It's All in Your Hands 187

Get Enough Sleep 187

Take Control 187

Paying Attention to Nutrition and Weight Management 188

Eating Disorders 189

Maintaining Sexual Health 190

Avoiding Sexually Transmitted Infections 190

Communicating about Safe Sex 190

Using Birth Control 190

Protecting against Sexual Assault 191

Using Alcohol Responsibly 192

TRY IT! FEELING CONNECTED ▷ Sharing and Comparing Experiences 193

Tobacco — the Other Legal Drug 193

Chapter Review 194

13 Considering Majors & Careers 197

Careers and the New Economy 199

Building the Right Mind-Set for the Future 200

Working with an Academic Adviser 200

Self-Exploration in Career Planning 203

Values 203

Skills 203

Aptitudes 204

Personality 204

TRY IT! SETTING GOALS ▷ No Time Like the Present to Plan for the Future 204

Life Goals and Work Satisfaction 204

Interests 204

Exploring Your Interests 204

TRY IT! FEELING CONNECTED ▷ Where Do You Fit in the Holland Model? 206

Planning for Your Career 207

Diving into Industry Research 208

Getting Experience 209

Experiential Learning Opportunities 209

Working in College 210

TRY IT! MAKING DECISIONS ▷ College Jobs and Your Career 210

Job Search Strategies 211

Market Yourself 211

Build a Résumé 211

Write a Cover Letter 212

Know How to Interview 212

Skills Employers Seek 214

Content Skills 214

Job Candidate Skills/Qualities Ranked as Very Important by Employers 214

Transferable Skills 215

Staying on the Path to Success 216

Chapter Review 217

Index 220

Preface

Anyone who teaches beginning college students knows how much they have changed in recent years. Today's students are increasingly job-focused, technologically adept, and concerned about the future. We are seeing diverse students of all ages and backgrounds enrolling in both two- and four-year institutions, bringing with them the hopes and dreams that a college education can help fulfill. This textbook is designed specifically to give *all* students the practical help they need to set goals, succeed, and stay in college so that those hopes and dreams can become realities.

We remain devoted to our students and their success. We have written this text for students of any age at any type of college. We present comprehensive and helpful information on every aspect of the college experience for a variety of student audiences, from students straight out of high school to returning adult learners, from commuters to residents at all higher education institutions. We aim to convey respect and admiration for our students in our writing while recognizing their continued need for challenge and support. Our text is grounded in the growing body of research on student success and retention. Simply put, we do not like to see students fail. We are confident that if students both read and heed the information herein, they will become engaged in the college experience, learn, and persist to graduation.

Our briefest text, *Step by Step to College and Career Success* is written to be to the point, yet comprehensive in coverage. We've pared away extras to focus on the most crucial skills and the most important choices that students make in order to succeed in college and beyond. The sixth edition covers pressing topics that affect students' lives and how they learn, such as active learning, time management, test taking, career preparation, relationships, and technology, and we have expanded on the book's themes of motivation, persistence, resilience, and decision-making. The sixth edition features a new, compelling design sure to keep students engaged. Each new copy of the text can be packaged with LearningCurve, an adaptive, online assessment tool.

We also want to ensure that students think about long- and short-term goals so that they're able to take the steps necessary to do well in this course, their other courses, and their careers. In addition, this text covers a broad range of academic and life skills, including time management, learning styles, critical thinking, listening and taking notes, reading, communication, testing, money management, diversity, health, and majors and careers.

Engaging and retaining today's students are also challenges we know many of you face. To help you meet these challenges, we created a package of support materials, including an *Instructor's Manual and Test Bank*, PowerPoint slides, and videos. The *Instructor's Manual and Test Bank* includes in-class, group, and video exercises; a Guide to Teaching with YouTube; sample syllabi; capstone projects; teaching objectives, chapter outlines, and lesson plans; an expanded question pool with more than 600 questions that test key concepts; midterm and final exams; and student self-assessments. The *Instructor's Manual and Test Bank* is available online.

Whether you are considering this textbook for use in your first-year seminar or have already made a decision to adopt it, we thank you for your interest, and trust that you will find it to be a valuable teaching aid. We also hope that this book will guide you and your campus in understanding the broad range of issues that can affect student success.

New to the Sixth Edition

Powerful LearningCurve online assessment system available with every new book.

When it comes to retaining new information, research shows that self-testing with small, bite-sized chunks of information works best. *LearningCurve for College Success*, a new adaptive online quizzing program, helps students focus on the material they need the most help with. With LearningCurve, students receive as much practice as they need to master a given concept and are provided with immediate feedback and links back to online instruction. A personalized study plan with suggestions for further practice gives your students what they need to thrive in the college success course, in their college career, and beyond!

Quizzes open and close each chapter.

Chapter-opening "How Do You Measure Up?" quizzes get students thinking about how key topics in the chapter relate to them. A "Now . . . How Do You Measure Up?" quiz at the end of the chapter prompts students to consider what they have learned after the chapter has presented new ways of thinking.

A great new design and expanded art program engage students.

The book's new design is fresh, colorful, and open, and was created to make information easy to find and understand. The art program has been expanded and updated, with more images of current students and pop culture to help students feel comfortable and connected.

A fun, streamlined, and compelling approach.

The text has been streamlined and focused to make it as readable as possible. New pull-out "articles" address important, real-world topics of pressing concern to students and to their success such as making and using to-do lists (Chapter 2), using commuting time wisely (Chapter 2), improving emotional intelligence (Chapter 3), nailing test preparation (Chapter 6), knowing and following guidelines for academic honesty (Chapter 6), understanding the connection between collaboration and critical thinking (Chapter 7), working with an academic adviser (Chapter 13), doing industry research (Chapter 13), and many more.

Extensive coverage of technology and online learning.

Technology continues to transform aspects of the college experience and students' lives, and *Step by Step* is staying on the cutting edge. Coverage of technological tools and skills has been integrated into every chapter in the book, and included as new, discrete articles. Topics include using electronic tools for planning and time management, and guidelines on communicating successfully through e-mail, texts, and social media in school, in life, and on the job.

Expanded Try It! boxes in each chapter get students involved.

Focusing on four themes—managing time, feeling connected, setting goals, and making decisions—each Try It! box explains a specific action for students to try, the benefit of doing so, and first steps to get started. They can be used for student self-direction or as assignments inside or outside the classroom. Examples include Feeling Connected: Get to Know Your Instructors (Chapter 1); Setting Goals: "I've Got to Get My Priorities in Order!" (Chapter 2); Setting Goals: Emotional Reactions Have Consequences (Chapter 3); Feeling Connected: Two (or More) Are Better Than One (Chapter 5); Making Decisions: I Can't Believe I Fell for That! (Chapter 7); Managing Time: Be the Early Bird (Chapter 8); and Making Decisions: College Jobs and Your Career (Chapter 13).

A new Chapter 10, "Connecting with Others in a Diverse World."

This new chapter helps students think about different types of relationships and encourages students to enrich their college experience by seeking out and getting to know people who can expand their horizons. The chapter incorporates topics such as connecting with instructors, managing family and romantic relationships in college, connecting through involvement, and—in an exciting new section, "Communicating in a Digital Age"—gaining insights into how to become more competent in various types of online communication.

Streamlined chapter-ending sections.

Elements include a Steps to Success checklist which reviews the key action steps in the chapter; an Applying What You've Learned section with application opportunities; and a Create Community section where students are encouraged to go to peers (online or in person), use social media, use office hours, study groups, campus resources, and references like books, and Web sites to take initiative in answering different kinds of common questions and solving different kinds of problems.

Resources for Instructors

LearningCurve for College Success is an online, adaptive, self-quizzing program that quickly learns what students already know and helps them practice what they don't yet understand. LearningCurve motivates students to engage with key concepts before they come to class so that they are ready to participate, and offers reporting tools to help you discern your students' needs. To package *LearningCurve for College Success* for **free** with the text, use ISBN 978-1-319-01295-3. To order LearningCurve standalone, use ISBN 978-1-4576-7999-5.

The *Instructor's Manual and Test Bank* includes chapter objectives, teaching suggestions, a sample lesson plan for each chapter, and various case studies that are relevant to the topics covered. It also includes test questions for each chapter, a midterm, and a final exam. New to this edition are sample syllabi, final capstone projects for the end of the course, and an expanded question pool with new scenario-based questions which asks students to apply key concepts to real-life situations. The *Instructor's Manual and Test Bank* is available online.

The *Computerized Test Bank* includes a mix of fresh, carefully crafted multiple-choice, fill-in-the-blank, and short-answer questions. The questions appear in Microsoft Word format and in easy-to-use test bank software. This allows instructors to add, edit, resequence, and print questions and answers. Instructors can also export questions into a variety of formats, including Canvas and Blackboard. The number of multiple-choice has been doubled from the prior edition. The *Computerized Test Bank* contains more than 600 multiple-choice, true/false, short-answer, and essay questions designed to assess students' understanding of key concepts. An answer key is included.

French Fries Are Not Vegetables is a comprehensive instructional DVD featuring three different resources for class and professional use. ISBN: 978-0-312-65073-5.

- **A 30-minute documentary** that follows five students through the life-changing transition of the first year of college. Their honest, funny, and intense observations shed light on everything from eating habits to concerns about grades and finances.

- *Conversation Starters* offers sixteen very brief videos combining student and instructor interviews on the most important topics taught in first-year seminar courses, including money management, diversity, emotional intelligence, and critical thinking.

- *Teaching Ideas and Conversations*, a forty-five-minute documentary, features fifteen expert instructors giving advice on what makes a successful first-year course.

The **CS Select** custom database allows you to create a textbook for your College Success course that reflects your course objectives and uses just the content you need. Start with one of our core texts, and then rearrange chapters, delete chapters, and add additional content — including your own original content — to create just the book you're looking for. Get started by visiting **macmillanhighered.com /csSelect**.

The **Custom Solutions** program allows Bedford/ St. Martin's Custom Publishing to offer the highest-quality books and media, created in consultation with publishing professionals who are committed to the discipline. Make *Step by Step to College and Career Success* more closely fit your course and goals by integrating your own materials, including only the parts of the text you intend to use in your course, or both. Contact your local Macmillan Education sales representative for more information.

Resources for Students and Packaging Options

LearningCurve for College Success is an online, adaptive, self-quizzing program which quickly learns what students already know and helps them practice what they don't yet understand. For more information, see the section on Resources for Instructors. To package *LearningCurve for College Success* for **free** with the text, use ISBN 978-1-319-01295-3. To order LearningCurve standalone, use ISBN 978-1-4576-7999-5.

The **College Success companion site** offers a number of tools to use in class including videos with quizzing, downloadable podcasts, flash cards of key concepts, and links libraries for students to access further online resources. From the companion Web site, you can also access instructor materials whenever you need them. Go to **macmillanhighered.com /collegesuccess/resources**.

VideoCentral for College Success is a premier collection of video content for the college success classroom. The site features the 30-minute documentary *French Fries Are Not Vegetables and Other College Lessons: A Documentary of the First Year of College*, which follows five students through the life-changing transition of the first year of college. It also includes access to

- Sixteen brief *Conversation Starters* that combine student and instructor interviews on the most important topics taught in first-year seminar courses

- Sixteen accompanying video glossary definitions with questions that bring these topics to life

Learn more at **macmillanhighered.com /videosuccess/catalog**.

Free Bedford Coursepacks We know that it's not enough to build digital products that work in the classroom—we have to make sure that you can plug into your course-management system, whether you use Blackboard, Angel, Desire2Learn, Canvas, Moodle, or Sakai. The content of our student sites is available as downloadable coursepacks that can plug into multiple course-management systems. Learn more at **macmillanhighered.com /aboutcoursepacks**.

Bedford e-Books for *Step by Step* For roughly half the cost of the print book, **Bedford e-Books** offer an affordable alternative for students. For more on Bedford e-Books, visit **macmillanhighered .com/aboutebooks**.

E-Book Choices You can also find PDF versions of our books when you shop online at our publishing partners' sites: CourseSmart, Barnes & Noble NookStudy, Kno, CafeScribe, or Chegg.

Bedford/St. Martin's Insider's Guides are concise and student-friendly booklets on topics critical to college success and are a perfect complement to your textbook and course. Bundle one with any Bedford/St. Martin's textbook at no additional cost. Topics include:

- **New!** *Insider's Guide to College Etiquette*, Second Edition

- **New!** *Insider's Guide for Returning Veterans*

- **New!** *Insider's Guide to Transferring*

- *Insider's Guide to Academic Planning*
- *Insider's Guide to Beating Test Anxiety*
- *Insider's Guide to Building Confidence*
- *Insider's Guide to Career Services*
- *Insider's Guide to College Ethics and Personal Responsibility*
- *Insider's Guide to Community College*
- *Insider's Guide to Credit Cards*, Second Edition
- *Insider's Guide to Getting Involved on Campus*
- *Insider's Guide to Global Citizenship*
- *Insider's Guide to Time Management*, Second Edition

For more information on ordering one of these guides free with the text, go to **macmillanhighered.com/collegesuccess**.

The Bedford/St. Martin's Planner includes everything that students need to plan and use their time effectively, with advice on preparing schedules and to-do lists, along with blank schedules and calendars (monthly and weekly) for planning. Integrated into the planner are tips and advice on fixing common grammar errors, note taking, and succeeding on tests; an address book; and an annotated list of useful Web sites. The planner fits easily into a backpack or purse, so students can take it anywhere. To package *The Bedford/St. Martin's Planner* for **free** with the text, use ISBN 978-1-319-01290-8. To order the planner stand-alone, use ISBN 978-0-312-57447-5.

Journal Writing: A Beginning Designed to give students an opportunity to use writing as a way to explore their thoughts and feelings, this writing journal includes a generous supply of inspirational quotes placed throughout the pages, tips for journaling, and suggested journal topics. ISBN 978-0-312-59027-7.

TradeUp allows you to bring more value and choice to your students' first-year experience by packaging *Step by Step to College and Career Success* with one of a thousand titles from Macmillan publishers at a 50 percent discount off the regular price. Contact your local Macmillan Education sales representative for more information.

About the Authors

John N. Gardner brings unparalleled experience to this authoritative text for first-year seminar courses. John is the recipient of his institution's highest award for teaching excellence. He has twenty-five years of experience directing and teaching in the most respected and most widely emulated first-year seminar in the country, the University 101 course at the University of South Carolina. John is universally recognized as one of the country's leading educators for his role in initiating and orchestrating an international reform movement to improve the beginning college experience, a concept he coined as "the first-year experience." He is the founding executive director/president of two influential higher education centers that support campuses in their efforts to improve the learning and retention of beginning college students: the National Resource Center for The First-Year Experience and Students in Transition at the University of South Carolina (www.sc.edu/fye), and the John N. Gardner Institute for Excellence in Undergraduate Education (www.jngi.org), based in Brevard, North Carolina. The experiential basis for all of his work is his own miserable first year of college on academic probation, an experience he hopes to prevent for this book's readers. Today, as a much happier adult, John is married to fellow author of this book, Betsy Barefoot.

Betsy O. Barefoot is a writer, researcher, and teacher whose special area of scholarship is the first year of college. During her tenure at the University of South Carolina from 1988 to 1999, she served as codirector for research and publications at the National Resource Center for The First-Year Experience and Students in Transition. She taught University 101, in addition to special-topics graduate courses on the first-year experience and the principles of college teaching. She conducts first-year seminar faculty training workshops around the United States and in other countries and is frequently called on to evaluate first-year seminar outcomes. Betsy currently serves as senior scholar at the John N. Gardner Institute for Excellence in Undergraduate Education in Brevard, North Carolina. In this role she led a major national research project to identify institutions of excellence in the first college year. She currently works with both two- and four-year campuses in evaluating all components of the first year.

Acknowledgments

Although this text speaks with the voices of its two authors, it represents contributions from many others. We gratefully acknowledge these contributions and thank these individuals, whose special expertise has made it possible to introduce new college students to their college experience through the holistic approach we deeply believe in.

We are indebted to the following reviewers who offered us thoughtful and constructive feedback on this edition:

Erin Barnett, Eastern Kentucky University

Audra Cooke, Rock Valley College

Peggy Dunn, New River Community College

Gina Floyd, Shorter University

Darby Johnsen, Oklahoma City Community College

Tony Jones, Milligan College

Christopher Lau, Hutchinson Community College

Stacey Murray, Sonoma State University

Rick Robers, Virginia Western Community College

Michelle Van de Sande, Arapahoe Community College

Peggy Whaley, Murray State University

Mike Wood, Missouri State University

We would also like to acknowledge and thank the numerous colleagues who have contributed to this book in its previous editions: Catherine Andersen, Gallaudet University; Katheryn Arrington, Baton Rouge Community College; Elaine Barry, Central Maine Technical College; Michelle Murphy Burcin, University of South Carolina at Columbia; Tom Carskadon, Mississippi State University; Audra Cooke, Rock Valley College; Michael Dunn, Radford University; Jerry Eddy, Sinclair Community

College; Juan Flores, Folsom Lake College; Philip Gardner, Michigan State University; Britta Gibson, University of Pikeville; Chris Gurrie, University of Tampa; Jeanne L. Higbee, University of Minnesota, Twin Cities; Nancy Hunter, Maysville Community College; Natala Kleather (Tally) Hart, Ohio State University; Jonathan Long, Central Missouri State University; Tawana Mattox, Athens Area Technical Institute; Eileen McDonough, Barry University; Mary Ellen O'Leary, University of South Carolina at Columbia; Adenike Oloyede, Lake Michigan College; Richard Robers, Virginia Western Community College; Rajon Shore, Blue Ridge Community College; Kate Trombitas, Ohio State University; Lenora White, Baton Rouge Community College;

Michael Wood, Missouri State University; and Edward Zlotkowski, Bentley College.

As we look to the future, we are excited about the numerous improvements to this text that our creative Bedford/St. Martin's team has made and will continue to make. Special thanks to Edwin Hill, Vice President of Editorial, Humanities; Erika Gutierrez, Publisher for College Success; Simon Glick, Senior Executive Editor for College Success; Jennifer Jacobson, Development Editor at Ohlinger Publishing Services; Bethany Gordon, Associate Editor; and Christina Shea, Senior Marketing Manager.

Most of all, we thank you, the users of our book, for you are the true inspiration for this work.

01

3
What You Need to Know about This Course and Your Book

5
Making a Successful Transition to College

8
Setting Goals for Success

Starting Out on the Right Foot

Redberry/Shutterstock.

Congratulations! You are going to college—you have made a choice to change your life for the better. You may have been a star student in high school, or you may have struggled with some of your classes. Your parents may be paying your tuition and giving you spending money, or you may have a job or loans. No matter your age, background, academic skills, or economic circumstances, whether you succeed in college will depend on your commitment and your willingness to take advantage of all that your institution has to offer.

This book is a step-by-step guide to college success. Reading, remembering, and practicing the information and strategies in each chapter will help you accomplish your goals and avoid the kinds of problems that sometimes trip up even the best students in their first year. What you learn from this book will also be valuable to you throughout your college experience and in life.

Don't forget that college life is more than just academic work. It is also about making the most of new and continuing relationships and finding your niche on campus. During your first term, investigate opportunities for becoming involved in a campus group or organization. Meeting others who share your talents or interests will help you feel at home in this new environment. While it might be tempting to restrict your relationships to people who look like you or have the same worldviews as you do, your college experience will be more meaningful if you branch out and meet some people whom you might never encounter in your hometown.

You're on an exciting journey. Use this book as your roadmap, and you will achieve more in college and in your career than you might have dreamed possible. This road will take you to new places and introduce you to new ideas and new people. You will also learn about how to harness your own strengths to achieve the goals you have always had and those you may discover.

How do you measure up?

1. I am excited to be in this college success course because I know I will get information and learn strategies to succeed in college.
   ○ Agree
   ○ Don't Know
   ○ Disagree

2. I am motivated to stay focused and put in the time and effort college requires.
   ○ Agree
   ○ Don't Know
   ○ Disagree

3. I know how to set short-term goals for my academic success.
   ○ Agree
   ○ Don't Know
   ○ Disagree

4. I have thought about how my college experience will relate to what I want to do after I graduate.
   ○ Agree
   ○ Don't Know
   ○ Disagree

Review the items you marked "Don't Know" or "Disagree." Pay special attention to these topics in this chapter—you will develop a better understanding of why they are important to your success in college.

The "Aha!" Moment— Linking What You Enjoy to a Major

△ **Shawn Mosley**

solominviktor/Shutterstock.

"Here's the thing: I'm not planning to stay in college," I tell my academic adviser, Dr. Beene, at our first meeting. "I'm just here for a year to get my parents off my back. College is a big deal for them: They were the first ones in their families to go, and my dad's always regretted dropping out before he got his degree. So, it really doesn't matter to me what I take. Why don't you just pick some courses for me?"

"What are your interests?" Dr. Beene asks. He looks surprised when I say sports—especially rock climbing—and girls and cars, which are pretty typical for a nineteen-year-old, in my opinion. "Well, there's room in your schedule for a humanities elective, so how about a women's studies class?" he says. "And you've got a lab science requirement, so I suggest geology." The fact that I never even took geology in high school doesn't faze him. "You might as well know something about those rocks you're climbing, right?"

Cut to the end of the first term: I'm back in Dr. Beene's office. "Remember how you forced me to take geology?" I say. "Well, our field trips turned out to be pretty cool. The professor was this genius *Man vs. Wild* type and really made me think about the environment in a new way. And I ended up making some good friends."

"So what now?" asks Dr. Beene. "Still planning to drop out?"

"No," I say. "I lined up a work-study position in the geology department next spring, and now I *definitely* want to major in geology. I brought a list of the required courses and a few courses I think would be great electives. Can you help me work these into my schedule?"

What do you think about what led Shawn to begin college? How do his reasons for being in college compare with yours? What seems to be the motivation behind Shawn's interest in geology? What steps should he take before committing to his decision that geology is the right major for him or even that college makes sense for him right now?

What You Need to Know about This Course and Your Book

Since you're reading this textbook, it's likely you are enrolled in a first-year seminar or college success course. Both the course—possibly the most important course you will take—and this textbook—possibly the most important textbook you will read—are about improving your chances for success in college and beyond. However, before you start reading, you probably have some questions.

Why Should I Take This Course?

Research conducted by colleges and universities has found that first-year students are far more likely to be successful if they participate in courses and programs designed to teach them how to succeed in college. This course is designed to help you avoid some of the pitfalls—both academic and personal—that trip up many beginning students.

Aren't All the Topics in This Book Common Sense?

In college, issues such as relationships and personal health become even more important when you're living on your own, away from home. Even if you're living with your family or have a family of your own, college will challenge you to manage your time, feel comfortable interacting with professors, and study effectively. Though some of the information in this textbook may seem like common sense, much of it is based on research and the experiences of thousands of students and college educators. Therefore this book will provide new insights and information to help you make decisions that will lead to success. And in case you are wondering whether the topics discussed in this book were already covered in high school, the answer is no. We find that many college success strategies cannot be properly presented or understood until students are actually in college and have an immediate "need to know."

What Will I Get Out of This Course?

Although your classmates might not say it out loud, many of them share your concerns, doubts, and fears about being in college. This

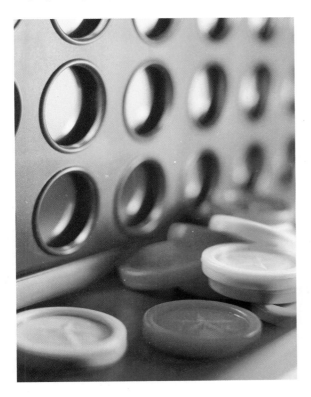

◁ **"Four Across—I Win!"**
In your first weeks in college you may feel eager to make new friends and find your place. Your college offers many ways for you to connect with other students, including organizations ranging from astronomy club to yoga club. Believe it or not, some colleges even have clubs dedicated to specific games like Connect Four. Check out your college's Web site or look for postings in common areas to find kindred spirits with whom you can play your favorite board game or participate in activities like dodgeball, soccer, community outreach, choir, line dancing, a club linked to your major, or whatever! You'll also find information on how to start a club yourself. © Lai Leng Yiap/Alamy.

FEELING CONNECTED ▷ **Finding Your Niche on Campus**

Many students discover that becoming involved in campus organizations significantly eases the transition to college. They also find that campus involvement helps them make connections with other students, faculty, and staff members and prepares them for the world of work.

Search your school's Web page for information on campus organizations and groups.

- Which ones dovetail with some of your present interests and talents?
- Which ones focus on activities and programs that are new to you but that you are interested in exploring?
- List the groups and organizations that catch your attention, along with their contact information, and take steps to learn more about them.

course will provide a supportive environment in which you can share your successes and your frustrations, get to know others who are beginning college, develop lasting relationships with your instructor and other students, and begin to think about your plans for life after college.

As college professors, researchers, and administrators with many years of experience working with first-year students, we are well aware that starting college can be challenging. We also know that if you apply the ideas in this book to your everyday life, you are likely to enjoy your time in college, graduate, and achieve your life goals. In this first chapter we'll discuss how you fit into the whole idea of college. We'll also help you to explore the purposes of college—many that your college might define for you—and to set goals for your college experience. More important, we'll help you to define your purposes for being here and offer strategies to help you succeed. ■

Making a Successful Transition to College

Why do so many college students have problems in the first year? For those of you fresh out of high school, your newfound freedom may be a major challenge. Your college instructors are not going to tell you what, how, or when to study. If you live on campus, your parents aren't there to wake you in the morning, see that you eat well and get enough sleep, monitor whether or how carefully you do your homework, and remind you to allow enough time to get to class. Getting everything done now depends on you.

For returning students, the opposite is true: Most experience an overwhelming lack of freedom. Work, family, and other commitments and responsibilities compete for the time and attention necessary for those students to do their best or even simply to stay in school.

Whichever challenges you are facing, you also must wrestle with a lot of questions: What will motivate you to stay focused? And what about the enormous investment of time and money that getting a college degree requires? Are you convinced that the investment will pay off? Have you selected a major, or is that on your list of things to do after you arrive? Do you know where to go when you need help with a personal or financial problem? If you are a minority student on your campus, are you concerned about how you will be treated? If you are attending a community college, do you understand the transfer process? These are all common concerns, fears, and questions that the college success course can help you with. You are not alone!

Different Worlds: High School and College

The differences between high school and college can also make starting college difficult. You may attend a college far from home, one in which you are part of a larger or more diverse student body than that of your high school.

Your classes also may be larger and may meet for longer periods of time. Because college classes meet on various days, managing your time and juggling other commitments will be a challenge. Most colleges offer hundreds of courses to choose from, and you will be expected to do academic work out of class, including your own original research.

Your class experience will also be different. Tests are given less frequently in college than you might be used to, but you will probably do more writing than you did in high school. And while high school courses tend to be textbook focused, you may find that your college instructors rarely focus on the textbook and instead use a variety of sources to prepare their lectures.

TRY IT!

FEELING CONNECTED ▷ **Get to Know Your Instructors**

Developing relationships with your course instructors is important in helping with your transition to college. The basis of such relationships is mutual respect. Instructors who respect students treat them fairly and are willing to help them both in and out of class. Students who respect instructors come to class regularly and take their work seriously. Make it a priority to get to know your instructors each term. The relationships you develop with instructors will be valuable to you both now and in the future. To start, do an Internet search for one or more of your instructors.

- Do any of your instructors have a biography on the campus Web site, a Facebook page, or a LinkedIn profile?
- What can you learn online about your instructor(s)?
- Make an appointment with an instructor whose background interests you.
- Get in the habit of visiting your instructors during office hours when you have a question or a problem with a class assignment.

Advantages of a College Education

According to the Carnegie Commission on Higher Education, being a college graduate will benefit you in many ways:

- You will have a more stable job history.
- You will earn more promotions.
- You will likely be happier in your work.
- You will be less likely than a non-graduate to become unemployed.
- Not only will you earn more with a college degree, but you also will find it easier to get a job and hold on to it.

Of course, college will affect you in other ways. A well-rounded college education will expand life's possibilities for you. As a result:

- You will learn how to work independently and discover new knowledge.

- You will encounter the cultural, artistic, and spiritual dimensions of life and learn more about how to appreciate them.
- You will learn more about how to seek appropriate information before making a decision.
- You will grow intellectually through learning about and interacting with cultures, languages, ethnic groups, religions, nationalities, and socioeconomic groups other than your own.

One of the best aspects of college is that you will have the opportunity to meet people who are different from you and to make many new friends, some of whom may be your friends for life.

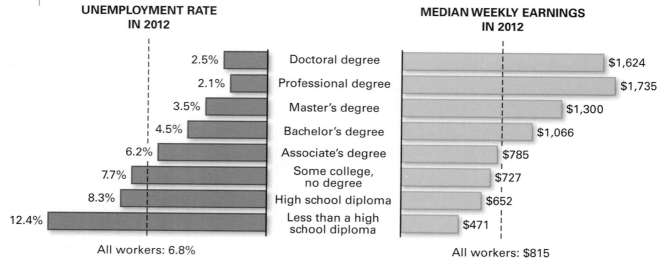

UNEMPLOYMENT RATE IN 2012

Doctoral degree	2.5%
Professional degree	2.1%
Master's degree	3.5%
Bachelor's degree	4.5%
Associate's degree	6.2%
Some college, no degree	7.7%
High school diploma	8.3%
Less than a high school diploma	12.4%

All workers: 6.8%

MEDIAN WEEKLY EARNINGS IN 2012

Degree	Median Weekly Earnings
Doctoral degree	$1,624
Professional degree	$1,735
Master's degree	$1,300
Bachelor's degree	$1,066
Associate's degree	$785
Some college, no degree	$727
High school diploma	$652
Less than a high school diploma	$471

All workers: $815

Figure 1.1 △ Education Pays
Source: U.S. Department of Labor, Bureau of Labor Statistics, Current Population Survey, 2012.

Returning Students versus Traditional Students

Returning students must deal with major life changes when they begin college. Sometimes going to college while working can be stressful, but reexploring higher education can also be exciting and invigorating. Parents whose grown children have moved away may find college to be a new beginning, a stimulating challenge, or a path to a new career. Generally speaking, returning students tend to take their studies more seriously and work harder than some younger students. Therefore they earn higher grades. Age brings with it a wealth of wisdom and experience that can help returning students achieve, and even exceed, their goals. ■

Office Hours

What are office hours?

Instructors are required to be available to their students during defined office hours. Check with your instructor to find out if you need to make an appointment before coming to his or her office.

When are office hours?

Instructors usually post their office hours on or beside their office doors. You can also ask your instructor, check the syllabus, ask the department secretary, or look online.

Why should you visit your instructor during office hours?

You might be able to ask your instructor a quick question before or after class, but you will be able to get far more help by actually visiting his or her office. By taking advantage of office hours, you will also let the instructor know that you are serious about learning.

What should you ask your instructor during office hours?

You can ask the instructor for direct help with any question or misunderstanding that you have. You might also want to ask some questions about the instructor's educational career and particular research interests.

Read more about the importance of building relationships with instructors in Chapter 10, "Connecting with Others in a Diverse World."

Setting Goals for Success

How do you define success? Is success about money, friendship, or power? Is it about achieving excellence in college and beyond, or about finding a sense of purpose in your life? For most people, success is a combination of all of these factors and more. While luck or "who you know" may play a role, success will first and foremost be the result of intentional steps that you take. So, in your quest for success, where do you begin? First, it is important to establish goals—goals for today, this week, this year, and beyond. Students who prefer to "go with the flow" and let life happen are more likely to flounder and less likely to achieve success in college or in a career. So instead of simply reacting to what college and life present, think instead about how you can take more control over your decisions and choices that lay the foundation for the achievement of future life goals. Making vague plans for the future is easy, but you need to determine which short-term steps are necessary if those plans are to become a reality.

> ## While luck or "who you know" may play a role, success will first and foremost be the result of intentional steps that you take.

As you plan your college experience and life goals, think about the kind of life you want to live. What is most important to you—having a family, pursuing a demanding career, working in service to others, making a lot of money, or something else? If your career choice aligns with your basic values and interests, you will be more likely to find satisfaction in your life beyond college.

Then consider your personal strengths. For instance, do you like to talk, deal with conflict, and stand up for yourself? Are you a good reader? If your answer to both questions is yes, then you may want to consider a career in the legal profession. Or if you excel at science and enjoy working with your hands, you might think about pursuing dentistry. Do you have fond memories of grade school, and do you like to work with children? A career as an elementary or middle school teacher may be the best choice for you. Your campus career center can help you discover your unique strengths, which, combined with your interest and values, can inform the direction you should take as you explore career choices.

TRY IT!

MAKING DECISIONS ▷ This Way or That

Do you make snap decisions, or is your process of deciding between alternatives difficult and slow? Different people have different ways of decision making, and there is no one right way to go about it. When you're making decisions about your major and your life goals, remember that college gives you lots of opportunities to try out different options. You can decide to explore a major by taking an introductory course in that academic area. If you discover that the major isn't going to be a good fit for you, you'll have plenty of time to choose another major. Most colleges won't require you to make a decision about your major right away. But at some point, even if the decision is hard, you'll have to choose. Decide now to use your first year to gather more information about major and career possibilities. Then you'll be ready to choose the best major when you have to make that final decision.

Getting Started

College is an ideal time to begin setting and fulfilling short- and long-term goals. A short-term goal might be something simple, like reading twenty pages from your history text

twice a week to prepare for an exam that will
cover the first hundred pages of the book. A
long-term goal might be to create a two- or
four-year academic plan that will help you
prepare for your career.

Thinking about a career might seem unrelated
to some of the general education courses you are
required to take in your first year. Sometimes
it's hard to see the connection between a history
or literature course and what you want to do
with the rest of your life. If you're open to learning, though, you may discover potential areas of
interest that you never considered before—areas
of interest that may lead you to discover a new
career path.

It's okay if you don't know which career to pursue yet; in fact, it's perfectly normal. While many
students declare a major when they enter college, more than 60 percent of them will change
majors at least once, often because they discovered a match between their strengths and a
potential career field they had never considered before.

Follow these guidelines to set some short-term
goals, and consider how they fall within the
framework of setting SMART goals—goals that
are *specific*, *measurable*, *attainable*, *relevant*, and
anchored to a *time* period.[1]

1. **Specific.** Be specific about what you want to
   achieve and when.

2. **Measurable.** State each goal in measurable
   terms. For instance, you might set a goal to
   exercise at least one hour, three times a
   week, for the 16 weeks of the first term—a
   total of forty-eight hours. You can measure
   your actual time spent exercising as a
   percentage of your forty-eight-hour goal.

TRY IT!

SETTING GOALS ▷ Plan for the Future

Before working toward any long-term goal, it's
important for you to be realistic and honest with
yourself.

- Is this *your* goal—one that you value and want
  to pursue—or is this a goal that a parent or
  friend argued was "right" for you?
- Given your abilities and interests, is the goal
  realistic? Remember that dreaming up long-
  term goals is the easy part.
- Be very specific and systematic about the steps
  you will take today, this week, and throughout
  your college experience to reach your goals.
- Use the information in Figure 1.1 (p. 6) and in
  "Advantages of a College Education" (p. 6) as
  motivation for making the most of college. The
  more education you have, the more likely you
  are to be employed after finishing college, and
  the higher your earnings will be.

[1] T. Doran, "There's a S.M.A.R.T. Way to Write Management's Goals
and Objectives," *Management Review* 70, no. 11 (1981): 35–36.

3. **Attainable.** Be sure that each goal is attainable—that you can actually achieve it. Allow enough time to pursue it. If you don't have the necessary skills, strengths, and resources to achieve a goal, make adjustments so that it is more appropriate for you. Be sure you really want to reach the goal. Don't set out to work toward something only because you want to please others.

4. **Relevant.** In other words, be sure that each goal applies to your life and that you can know why the goal matters. Your goals should help your larger plan and give you a sense of moving forward.

5. **Time period.** Be sure each goal is achievable within the desired time frame. Consider the difficulties you might encounter, and plan for ways you might deal with them. Decide which goal comes first. How will you begin? Create steps and a time line for reaching your next goal.

As an example, let's assume that you are thinking about working in an underdeveloped country after you graduate, perhaps spending some time in the Peace Corps. What are some short-term goals that would help you reach this long-term objective? One goal might be to take courses focused on different countries or cultures. But that goal isn't very specific, nor does it state a particular time period. A much more specific goal would be to take one course each year that would help you build a body of knowledge about other countries and cultures. An even more specific goal would be to review the course catalog and identify the courses you want to take and list them on a personal time line. You could also look for courses that will give you the opportunity to engage in service learning. Course-based service activities will give you a taste of the kind of work you might be doing later in an underdeveloped country.

You might also want to gain some actual experience before making a final decision about working in other countries. Thus another intermediate goal could be to travel to other countries or to combine the earning of college credits with performing service abroad through an international organization such as the Partnership for Service Learning. Your goal for this week could be to do an Internet search or visit your campus study-abroad office to research your options for international travel or service work. ■

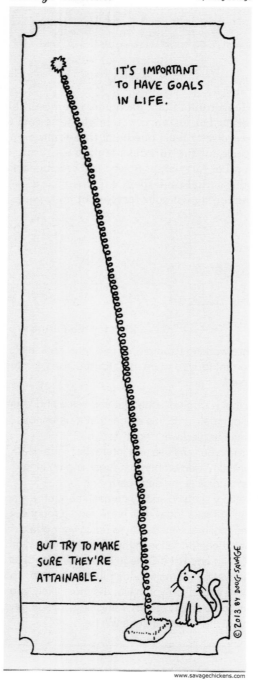

Savage Chickens
by Doug Savage

IT'S IMPORTANT TO HAVE GOALS IN LIFE.

BUT TRY TO MAKE SURE THEY'RE ATTAINABLE.

© 2013 BY DOUG SAVAGE

www.savagechickens.com

◁ **The Sky's the Limit?**

Aiming high is admirable, but setting yourself up to fail isn't productive. If you want to be a nurse but find that most medical procedures make you queasy, consider other professions within the allied health fields. If you dream of owning a restaurant but do not like taking financial risks, explore other ways to enter this field. Set goals that you have the skills, strengths, and resources to achieve. © Doug Savage.

Chapter Review

Steps to Success:
Starting Out on the Right Foot

○ **Set both short-term and long-term goals.** You will be far more likely to succeed in college if your goals for today, tomorrow, and four years from now are clear and if your expectations are realistic.

○ **Stay motivated.** Understand what learning opportunities at your institution excite and interest you. If your motivation is lagging, it may be time for a change. Your academic adviser or counselor can help you sort out the reasons and design a plan of action if you occasionally feel unmotivated.

○ **Become engaged in campus activities.** Visit the student activities office, join a club or an organization that interests you, or participate in community service.

○ **Meet with your instructors outside of class** during office hours or by appointment.

○ **Use the academic skills center, library, and campus career center.** These essential services can help you be a better student and plan for your future.

○ **Keep up with your weekly schedule and do your work on time.** Get a paper calendar or download a calendar app and use it consistently to keep track of assignments and appointments.

○ **Improve your study habits.** Find the most effective methods for reading textbooks, listening, taking notes, and studying.

○ **Explore this textbook for a wealth of strategies for success.**

Applying what you've learned . . .

Now that you have read and discussed this chapter, consider how you can apply what you have learned to your academic and personal lives. The following prompts will help you reflect on the chapter material and its relevance to you both now and in the future.

1. Review "Advantages of a College Education" on page 6. While landing a lucrative career is probably high on your list of goals after college, take a look at the other possible advantages of obtaining a college degree. List the three advantages from this section that you relate to the most. If you think of an advantage that is not noted in the chapter, add it to your top three. Why are these advantages important to you?

2. College students often feel the stress of trying to balance their personal and academic lives. Life's ups and downs are inevitable, but we can control our choices and attitudes. As a first-year student, you will want to begin developing a personal strategy for bouncing back after a particularly difficult time. Your strategy should include at least three steps you can take to get back on track and move forward.

Create Community

Becoming familiar with the resources available to you will prove handy when obstacles present themselves. Resilience comes from knowing how to handle the various situations that will arise while you're in college. Your institution offers the following services that can help you learn to manage your time. Acquaint yourself with them, and as you get to know your peers and meet the people who staff these offices, you will feel your sense of community grow.

GO TO ▷ Your academic adviser or counselor; or consult your college's catalog, phone book, or Web site; or call or visit student services or student affairs: If you need help finding college support services.

GO TO ▷ The academic advisement center: If you need help choosing courses and understanding degree requirements.

GO TO ▷ The academic skills center: If you need help finding tutors and improving your memory and study skills.

GO TO ▷ The adult reentry center: If you need help learning about programs for returning students, finding child care, and making contact with other adult students.

GO TO ▷ The career center: If you are interested in learning more about careers, finding job and internship listings, and assessing your fit with a particular career.

GO TO ▷ Commuter services: If you need help finding off-campus housing options, information about your community, transportation information, or possible roommates.

GO TO ▷ The computer center: If you need help improving your computer skills and are looking for information on campus computer resources.

GO TO ▷ The counseling center: If you need help managing personal issues or stress.

NOW . . . How do you measure up?

1. I am excited to be in this college success course because I know I will get information and learn strategies to help me succeed in college.
   - ○ Agree
   - ○ Don't Know
   - ○ Disagree

2. I am motivated to stay focused and put in the time and effort college requires.
   - ○ Agree
   - ○ Don't Know
   - ○ Disagree

3. I know how to set short-term goals for my academic success.
   - ○ Agree
   - ○ Don't Know
   - ○ Disagree

4. I have thought about how my college experience will relate to what I want to do after I graduate.
   - ○ Agree
   - ○ Don't Know
   - ○ Disagree

Review the items you marked "Don't Know" or "Disagree." How do your answers here compare to your responses to the quiz you took at the start of the chapter? Which sections of this chapter left a strong impression on you? College can be an amazing, once-in-a-lifetime adventure. In your first year, explore your interests and what motivates you to do your best. Take advantage of all that your institution has to offer and begin creating a life plan by setting goals for this month, this term, and this year.

15
**Time—Your Most
Valuable Resource**

19
**Time-Management
Pitfalls**

23
**Get Smart about Organizing
Your Days, Weeks, Tasks,
and More**

27
**Maximizing Study
and Review Time**

Managing Your Time

How often do you find yourself saying, "I don't have time"? Once a week? Once a day? Several times a day? The next time you find yourself saying it, stop and ask yourself whether it is really true. Do you really not have time, or have you made a choice, consciously or unconsciously, not to make time for that particular task or activity? Once you recognize that you can control and change how you use your time, you'll want to assess your time-management strengths and then set time-management goals and priorities.

The first step in this assessment is to acknowledge that you have control over how you use your time. You have control over many of the commitments you choose to make. You also have control over many small decisions that affect your time-management success, such as what time you get up in the morning, how much sleep you get, what you eat, how much time you spend studying, and whether you exercise. All these small decisions have a big effect on your success in college and in life.

Being in control means that you make your own decisions and take responsibility for your actions. If you're a recent high school graduate, you'll find that two ways in which college differs significantly from high school are students' increased autonomy, or independence, and greater responsibility. If you're a returning student, you most likely have already experienced a higher level of independence, but returning to school creates responsibilities above and beyond those you already have, whether they include employment, family, community service, or other commitments. Whichever type of student you are, making the transition into college might lead to some unanticipated demands on your time, demands that will require new strategies for time management. You'll find these strategies in this chapter as well as tools to help you set time-management goals, get organized, recognize and avoid common time-management problems, and make your schedule work for you.

How do you measure up?

1. I set academic and personal goals to guide how I prioritize my time.
   - ○ Always
   - ○ Occasionally
   - ○ Never

2. I am able to focus on the task at hand instead of procrastinating or getting distracted.
   - ○ Always
   - ○ Occasionally
   - ○ Never

3. I use a daily or weekly planner, to-do lists, or other planning devices to keep track of my commitments.
   - ○ Always
   - ○ Occasionally
   - ○ Never

4. I am able to balance my social life and my need for personal time with my academic requirements.
   - ○ Always
   - ○ Occasionally
   - ○ Never

Review the items you marked "Don't Know" or "Disagree." Pay special attention to these topics in this chapter—you will find motivating strategies for developing in these areas.

Getting Out of a Jam

△ **Nicoleta Larsen**

On the first day of class, my English instructor spent more time talking about deadlines than books. "Review the syllabus and enter all your upcoming tests and papers in your datebook," Professor Hughes said. So, okay, I typed everything into my iPhone. But I was also thinking about my job, my next class, and my band's show on Saturday, and it's sort of hard to think about the future when your here-and-now is packed.

"Your final research paper should be at least fifteen pages and will count for 25 percent of your final grade," Professor Hughes added. "Find a topic and start gathering resource materials *now*." I jotted down a couple of ideas and figured I'd go to the library later in the week to get help. As the term went on, I did a pretty good job of keeping up with assignments and tests, but I didn't make much headway on my final paper.

Cut to three weeks before the deadline: I still hadn't made it to the library, and panic was starting to set in. I decided to come clean with Professor Hughes and ask for some help. He referred me to the chapter in my college success textbook on information literacy, and we walked over to the library together so that I could connect with a librarian. I knew that I would have to make some tough choices about my priorities for the rest of the term, but I felt determined to make myself and Professor Hughes proud.

What could Nicoleta have done differently to stay out of this jam? What would you do if you were in her position? What time-management techniques do you hope to get from this chapter that you could apply to a situation like this?

Time—Your Most Valuable Resource

The way you spend your time should align with your most important values. To begin connecting your use of time with your values, first set some goals for the future. What are your goals for the coming decade? If you're like most students reading this book, one of your goals is probably to earn a two-year or four-year degree or technical certificate. Maybe you've already decided on the career that you want to pursue. Or perhaps you plan to go on to graduate or professional school. As you look to the future, you may see yourself buying a new car, owning a home, starting a family, owning a business, or retiring early. Achieving these things will take a lot of your *time*. Time management is one of the most effective tools to assist you in meeting such goals.

When considering all the things you'll need to do and the limited time you have, start with this question: How do you approach time? Because people are innately different and come from many different cultures, they tend to view time in different ways. The way you look at time may also have to do with your basic personality. For example, if you're a natural organizer, you probably enter all due dates for assignments, exams, and quizzes on your calendar as soon as you receive each course syllabus, and you may be good at adhering to a strict schedule. On the other hand, if you are more laid-back, you may prefer to be more flexible, or to "go with the flow," rather than follow a daily or weekly schedule. You may excel at dealing with the unexpected, but you may also be a procrastinator. If this sounds like you, find time-management techniques that feel comfortable but still help you keep on track. You may have to stretch a bit, but your efforts can have a significant payoff.

Setting Goals

More than likely, one goal you will set or have already set is to find a good job when you complete your degree, or a job that is

△ **Sold!**
Many people dream of owning their own home. How you spend your time is directly related to how you spend your money. When planning a significant purchase, consider carefully how much money you need to earn and save before you can make the purchase. How much time will it take to make this happen? © Ariel Skelley/Blend Images/Corbis.

significantly better than the one you have now. You might be working on identifying just what that "good job" looks like—what it pays, where the best opportunities to get that job are, what the hours are likely to be, and so on. You might already be taking steps to make yourself a competitive candidate in a job search or to find an internship in a related field.

In a job search, good grades and a college degree may not be enough to distinguish you. When setting goals and objectives for allocating your time, consider the importance of having a well-rounded résumé when you graduate. What would such a résumé look like? It might show that you participated in extracurricular activities, gained leadership experience, engaged in

TRY IT!

MAKING DECISIONS ▷ **Your Ten-Year Plan**

Life is full of decisions. Some are made for us, and some we make for ourselves. If asked where you see yourself five or ten years from now, how would you respond? Use the worksheet below to help you through this thought process. Think of two goals you hope to accomplish. List at least three important decisions you will have to make toward achieving each goal, and then below each decision, write down something you need to learn about yourself as you approach that decision. Then write down the biggest challenge or challenges you foresee to making the decision.

Goal 1: _____

Decision 1: _____

Something I need to learn about myself as I approach this decision: _____

_____

Challenge(s) to making this decision: _____

Decision 2: _____

Something I need to learn about myself as I approach this decision: _____

_____

Challenge(s) to making this decision: _____

Decision 3: _____

Something I need to learn about myself as I approach this decision: _____

_____

Challenge(s) to making this decision: _____

Goal 2: _____

Decision 1: _____

Something I need to learn about myself as I approach this decision: _____

_____

Challenge(s) to making this decision: _____

Decision 2: _____

Something I need to learn about myself as I approach this decision: _____

_____

Challenge(s) to making this decision: _____

Decision 3: _____

Something I need to learn about myself as I approach this decision: _____

_____

Challenge(s) to making this decision: _____

This list will help you focus on your own path and goals. Refer to it a few times each term to check your progress.

community service, took advantage of internship or co-op opportunities, developed job-related skills, kept up-to-date on technological advances, or pursued relevant part- or full-time employment while attending classes.

When it is time to look for a permanent job, you want to demonstrate that you have used your college years wisely. Doing so will require planning and effective time-management skills, which are highly valued by employers. Your college or university's career center can help you arrange for an internship, a co-op program, or community service that will give you valuable experience and strengthen your résumé.

Getting Your Priorities in Order

Once you have established goals and objectives, your next step is to prioritize your time. Which goals and objectives are the most important to you? For example, is it more important to study for a test tomorrow or to attend a job fair today? Keep in mind that ignoring long-term goals in order to meet short-term goals isn't always a good idea. In fact, the more time and thought you devote to setting your long-term goals, the easier

it becomes to know how to spend your time in the short term. Using good time management, you can study during the week before a test so that you can attend a job fair the day before the test. One way that skilled time managers establish priorities is to create a to-do list (discussed in more detail later in this chapter), rank the items on the list, and then determine a schedule and deadline for each task. These tasks can be related to your long- or short-term planning.

A Balancing Act

Another aspect of setting priorities in college is to find an appropriate way to balance an academic schedule, family life, your social life, and time for yourself. Social activities are an important part of the college experience. Being involved in campus life can enhance your satisfaction with college and thus boost your achievement level and your determination to continue in college. However, if you never have time alone or time to study and think, you might feel overwhelmed. And employment, family, and community obligations are also important and time consuming and aren't "optional." For many students, the greatest challenge of prioritizing is to balance college with these other valuable dimensions of life.

◁ **Set Priorities Like a Pro**
Professional coaches help their teams thrive by setting effective priorities, whether that means making a plan for the next play, the next game, or the entire season. In setting your own priorities, take a lesson from an NFL coach like Pete Carroll, coach of the 2014 Super Bowl champion Seattle Seahawks: If you prioritize your long-term plans while making smart play-by-play decisions every day, success can be yours. Jeff Gross/Getty Images.

Many decisions you make today are reversible. You may later decide to change your major, and your career and life goals may shift as well. But the decision to take control of your life—to establish your own goals for the future, to set your priorities, and to manage your time accordingly—is an important one for the present and the future.

Successful people frequently say that staying focused is a key to their success. To help you stay focused, make a plan. Begin with your priorities, and then think about the necessities of life. Finish what needs to be done before you move from work to pleasure. ∎

R-E-S-P-E-C-T

How does time management relate to respect? Think of the last time you made an appointment with someone who either forgot the appointment entirely or was very late. Were you upset or disappointed with the person for wasting your time? In college, if you repeatedly arrive late for class, you are breaking the basic rules of politeness. You are intentionally or unintentionally showing a lack of respect for your instructors and your classmates.

At times what instructors perceive as inappropriate or disrespectful behavior may result from a cultural misunderstanding. All cultures view time differently. In American academic culture, punctuality is a virtue. Being strictly on time may be a difficult adjustment for you if you grew up in a culture that is more flexible in its approach to time, but it is important to recognize the values of the new culture you are encountering.

Here are a few basic guidelines for respectful behavior in class and in other interactions with instructors:

- Be in class on time. Arrive early enough to remove outerwear and have your assignments, notebook or computer, and writing tools ready to go.
- Avoid behavior in class that is disrespectful to the instructor and other students. This includes answering your cell phone, texting, or checking Facebook; doing homework for another class; falling asleep; and whispering or talking.
- Manage your time when participating in class discussions. Don't "hog the floor"; give others the opportunity to express their ideas.
- Be on time for scheduled appointments with your instructors and advisers and be prepared with good questions. This will show how much you appreciate their time and the help they can give you.

Time management is a lifelong skill. To secure and succeed at a good job after college, you will have to manage your own time and possibly that of other people you supervise. If you go to graduate or professional school, time management will continue to be essential to your success. Time management is also important as a way in which you show respect for others—your friends, your family, and your college instructors.

Time-Management Pitfalls

If you're human, which of course you are, you likely procrastinate from time to time or even a lot, which makes it harder to manage your time. In fact, procrastination is one of the biggest challenges for college students, so we're going to tackle it right away, along with the other most common time-management pitfalls.

Don't Put It Off! Beating Procrastination

To procrastinate means to put off doing something or to be slow or late about doing a task that should be done. Dr. Piers Steel, who specializes in researching procrastination and motivation, writes that procrastination is on

Procrastination is one of the biggest challenges for college students.

the rise, with 80–95 percent of college students spending time procrastinating.[1] According to Steel, half of all college students report that they procrastinate on a daily basis, spending as much as one-third of their time in activities solely related to procrastination. These numbers,

[1]Piers Steel, "The Nature of Procrastination: A Meta-Analytic and Theoretical Review of Quintessential Self-Regulatory Failure," *Psychological Bulletin* 133, no. 1 (2007): 65–94.

△ **Take the Bite Out of Time-Management Problems**
Avoid procrastination, distractions, and getting spread too thin. Learn and apply the effective time-management techniques presented in this chapter and stay out of trouble. © Paul Souders/Corbis.

plus widespread acknowledgment of the negative effects of procrastination, provide evidence of a serious issue that trips up many otherwise capable people.

The good news is that, of those people who procrastinate on a regular basis, 95 percent want to change their behavior.[2] An important first step toward change is to understand why people procrastinate. According to Steel, even people who are highly motivated often fear failure, and some people even fear success (though that might seem counterintuitive). Consequently, some students procrastinate because they are perfectionists; not doing a task might be easier than having to live up to their own very high expectations or those of their parents, teachers, or peers. Many procrastinate because they are easily distracted, they have difficulty organizing and regulating their lives, or they have difficulty following through on goals that seem far in the future. They might find an assigned task boring or irrelevant or consider it unimportant "busy work."

Changing how you think about and approach less enjoyable assignments is key to overcoming procrastination and increasing your success

[2]Ibid.

in college. For instance, simply disliking an assignment is not a good justification for putting it off; that's an *excuse*, not a valid *reason*. Life is full of tasks you won't find interesting, and in many cases you won't have the option to ignore them. Whether it is cleaning your house, filing your taxes, completing paperwork, or responding to hundreds of e-mails, tedious tasks will always be there, and you will have to figure out strategies to complete them. When you're in college, procrastinating can signal that it's time to reassess your goals and objectives and your readiness for academic work at this point in your life. A counselor or academic adviser can help you sort that out.

Dealing with Distractions

Distractions are another common pitfall when it comes to time management. Some students use distractions as excuses to procrastinate. Others don't want to be distracted, and they need coping strategies to help them focus on tasks at hand and resist distractions.

Consider the types of distractions you encounter, and when and where you are most often distracted. For instance, where should you study?

Ask Yourself the Tough Questions

Why are you in college here and now? Why are you in this course? What is really important to you? Is what you value important enough to forgo some short-term fun or laziness and get down to work? Are your academic goals really your own, or were they imposed on you by family members, your employer, or societal expectations? Think about your answers to these tough questions—are you motivated to get busy? Which of the following strategies for beating procrastination can help?

- Think about ways to make less enjoyable classes and assignments relevant to your interests and goals.
- Remind yourself of the possible consequences if you do not begin your work. Then get started.
- Create a to-do list. Check off items when you finish them. Use the list to focus on the tasks that aren't getting done. Move them to the top of the next day's list. Working from a list will give you a feeling of accomplishment.
- Break down big jobs into smaller steps. Tackle short, easy-to-accomplish tasks first.
- Promise yourself a reward for finishing each task, such as watching your favorite TV show or going out with friends. For more substantial tasks, give yourself bigger and better rewards.
- Find a place to study that's comfortable and that doesn't allow for distractions and interruptions. If you study in your room, close your door.
- Say no to friends and family members who want your attention; agree to spend time with them later.
- Don't talk on the phone, text, or surf the Web during planned study sessions.

Some students find it's best to avoid studying in places associated with leisure, such as at the kitchen table, in the living room, or in front of the TV. Similarly, it might not be wise to study on your bed because you might drift off to sleep. Instead, find quiet places, both on campus and at home, where you can concentrate each time you sit down to do your work.

Accurately predicting the distractions you will face is especially important. For instance, if you have children at home, assume that they will always want your attention no matter how much others try to help out. It's a good idea to develop strategies for minimizing distractions while you study. Let's look at the examples in the table below:

Table 2.1 ▽ Strategies for Minimizing Distractions

Distraction	Solution
You're tempted to text or to check Facebook.	Turn off all devices; put them in another room or leave them in another location.
Your children want your attention.	Study away from home.
You keep falling asleep when you're studying.	Sit upright at your desk or worktable; avoid studying in bed or on the couch; try to get more rest.

List some distractions that you face and come up with solutions to avoid them.

Distraction	Solution
_____	_____
_____	_____
_____	_____
_____	_____
_____	_____

When You're Spread Too Thin

Being overextended is a primary source of stress for college students and another pitfall to managing time. Often, students underestimate how much time it will take to do well in college and overschedule themselves with work and other commitments.

Prioritize and focus on what you can manage. Learn to say no.

The best advice is to prioritize and focus on what you *can* manage. If you do not have enough time to carry your course load and meet your commitments, drop a course before the drop deadline so that you won't have a low grade on your permanent record. Keep in mind, however, that if you receive financial aid, you must be registered for a minimum number of credit hours to maintain your current level of aid. Learn to say no.

If dropping a course is not feasible and if other activities are not that important, let go of one or more nonacademic commitments. *Learn to say no.* Saying no can be difficult, especially if you think that you are letting other people down. However, it is far more preferable to respectfully excuse yourself from an activity than to fail to come through at the last minute.

Maintaining Motivation

Motivation is the feeling of enthusiasm or interest that makes you determined to do something. You've probably met students who have a strong sense of purpose—students who are enthusiastic and motivated to do their best in college. (You might recall the highly motivated monster Mike Wazowski from the first chapter of your textbook!) You may have met others who seem to have little interest in being in college. Motivation is an essential component of setting and achieving your academic and life goals, and the absence of motivation is a major pitfall. Forcing yourself to do something in which you have no interest is almost impossible. Think about yourself, and consider what motivates you in determining your goals for college and for life. What areas of study or career paths excite you the most? Over time, you may find different areas of interest, and any decision you make in the first year of college is reversible. However, if you have lost interest in your academic or career path—if you feel unmotivated—it may be time to consider a change. Talk with an academic adviser or counselor about how to refocus your purpose for being in college and regain your motivation.

Many students of all ages question their decision to attend college and sometimes feel overwhelmed by the additional responsibilities that being in college brings. Prioritizing, rethinking some commitments and letting some things go, and weighing the advantages and disadvantages of attending college part-time versus full-time can help you work through this adjustment period. Make a plan that begins with your priorities: attending classes, studying, working, and spending time with the people who are important to you. Then think about the necessities of life: sleeping, eating, exercising, and relaxing. Leave time for fun things such as talking with friends, checking out Facebook, watching TV, and going out, but finish what *needs* to be done before you move from work to pleasure. Also, don't forget about personal time. If you live in a residence hall or share an apartment with other students, talk with your roommates about how to coordinate your class schedules so that each of you has some privacy. If you live with your family, particularly if you are a parent, work with them to create special family times as well as quiet study times.

Don't let this early adjustment period become a pitfall for you. It's a normal part of the transition to college that all students experience. Take control by developing a plan to manage your time. ■

Get Smart about Organizing Your Days, Weeks, Tasks, and More

As you begin your first year of college, how far ahead are you in making plans and developing a schedule? Your academic year will be divided into chunks of time or set terms—either semesters, which are fourteen to sixteen weeks long, or quarters, which are about twelve weeks long. You will quickly discover the temptation to plan only for today or tomorrow, but begin by taking a long view. Think of the time between now and when you plan to graduate. Do you have a good idea of which courses you will have to take and when? Work with your academic adviser to make sure that you stay on track and get in all of your requirements for graduation. If you plan to transfer, make sure that the new institution will accept the credits for the courses you are taking now. Seek help from your academic adviser and from an adviser at the college or university to which you plan to transfer.

If you are a parent or are working off campus, the whole idea of planning ahead may seem futile. We all know how often "life gets in the way," and the best-laid plans may have to be adjusted to meet last-minute emergencies. You'll be more likely to manage your life and juggle your responsibilities, though, if you create a term-length calendar as you begin your college experience.

Many techniques and tools, both paper and electronic, are available to help you manage your time. Which system you use doesn't really matter. What matters is that you select a tool and use it every day.

Using a Daily or Weekly Planner

In college, as in life, you will quickly learn that managing your time is a key not only to survival but also to success. Consider buying a week-at-a-glance organizer for the current year. Your campus bookstore may sell one designed just for your college or university, with important dates and deadlines already provided. If you prefer to use an electronic planner, that's fine—your computer, smart phone, or tablet comes equipped with a calendar.

Carry your planner with you at all times and continue to enter all due dates as soon as you know them. Write in meeting times and locations, scheduled social events, study time for each class, and so forth. Add phone numbers and e-mail addresses, too, in case something comes up and you need to cancel plans with someone. Get into the habit of using a planner to help you keep track of commitments and maintain control of your schedule. Choose a specific time each day to check your notes for the current week and the coming week. Making certain that you aren't forgetting something important takes just a moment, and it helps relieve stress!

Scheduling Your Time Week by Week

Use the following steps to schedule your time for each coming week:

- Begin by entering all of your commitments for the week—classes, work hours, family commitments, and so on—on your schedule.

- Track your activities for a full week by entering into your schedule everything you do and how much time each task requires. Use this record to help you estimate the time you will need for similar activities in the future.

- Try to reserve at least two hours of study time for each hour spent in class. This 2-for-1 rule

SEPTEMBER

Time	MONDAY 3	TUESDAY 4 First Day of Classes	WEDNESDAY 5	THURSDAY 6	FRIDAY 7	SATURDAY 8	SUNDAY 9
5 am							
6 am							
7 am							
8 am							
9 am	Work	Psychology	Work	English			
10 am					Work	Work	
11 am							
12 pm							
1 pm			Math				
2 pm		Work		Work	Mom's doctor's appointment		Math: Review Notes
3 pm							
4 pm							
5 pm							
6 pm							Party at Susan's [235-523-6898]
7 pm							
8 pm		Psychology: Read Ch. 1	Math HW 1	English: Read Ch. 1		Math HW 1	
9 pm					Psychology: Review Notes	English: Read Ch. 1	
10 pm							
11 pm							
12 pm							

Figure 2.1 △ Weekly Timetable
Using your class schedule for the term and your list of work, social, and family commitments, create your own weekly timetable using an app like iCal or LifeTopix. You can also find blank schedule templates on the College Success Student Site at bedfordstmartins.com/collegesuccess/resources.

reflects many faculty members' expectations for how much work their students should do to master the material in their classes. So, for example, if you are taking a typical full-time class load of fifteen credits, you should plan to study an additional thirty hours each week. Think of this forty-five-hour-per-week commitment as comparable to a full-time job.

- Taking into consideration your body clock, your obligations, and potential distractions, decide whether you will study more effectively in the day or in the evening, or by using a combination of both. Determine whether you are capable of getting up early in the morning to study, or whether (and how late) you can stay up at night and still wake up for morning classes.

- Estimate how much time you will need for each assignment, and plan to begin your work early. A good time manager frequently plans to finish assignments before actual due dates to allow for emergencies.

- Set aside time for research and other preparatory tasks. For example, instructors may expect you to be computer literate, but they usually don't have time to explain how to use a word processor, spreadsheet, or statistical computer program. Most campuses have learning centers or computer centers that offer tutoring, walk-in assistance, or workshops to assist you with computer programs, e-mail, and Internet searches.

- Schedule at least three aerobic workouts per week. (Walking to and from classes doesn't count.) Taking a break for physical activity relaxes your body, clears your mind, and is a powerful motivator.

At the Top of My To-Do List Is "Make a To-Do List"!

Keeping a to-do list can help you avoid feeling stressed or out of control. If to-do lists become part of your daily routine, you'll be amazed at how they help you keep up with your activities and responsibilities. You can keep a to-do list on your cell phone—download a to-do list app such as Errands—or in a notebook or memo pad, or you can post it on your bulletin board or refrigerator. Some people start a new list every day or once a week. Others keep a running list and only throw a page away or clear the contents of the list when everything on the list is done. Use your to-do list to keep track of all the tasks you need to remember, not just your academic commitments.

Develop a system for prioritizing the items on your list, and as you complete each task, cross it off your list. Experiment with color—make your lists in black and cross out items in red, or use highlighters or colored ink. You can also rank your to-do items by marking them with one, two, or three stars or with the letters A, B, C, and so on. Use your to-do list in conjunction with your planner. You will feel good about how much you have accomplished, and this positive feeling will help you to stay motivated.

Figure 2.2 ▷ Daily and Weekly To-Do Lists
Almost all successful people keep a daily to-do list. The list may be in paper or electronic form. Get in the habit of creating and maintaining your own daily list of appointments, obligations, and activities.

Thinking about Your Class Schedule

If you are a first-year student, you may not have had much flexibility in determining your current course schedule; by the time you could register for classes, some sections of your required courses may have been closed already. You also may not have known whether you would prefer taking classes back-to-back or having a break between classes.

Building a schedule that works for you will set you up for success—you have to consider a lot of factors to get the right schedule. How early in the morning are you willing to start classes? Do you prefer evening classes? What impact do work or family commitments have on scheduling decisions? What times of day are you more alert? Less alert? How many days a week can you or do you want to attend classes? Over time, have you found that you prefer spreading your classes over five or six days of the week? Or have you discovered that you like to go to class just two or three days a week, or only once a week for a longer class period? (At some institutions you can go to school full-time by attending classes exclusively on Saturday.) Your attention span as well as your other commitments may influence your decisions about your class schedule. Before you register for the next term, think long and hard about how to make your class schedule work for you. ■

TRY IT!

FEELING CONNECTED ▷
Compare Your Class Schedules

Are you happy or unhappy with your class schedule? Do you have enough time to get from one class to another? Are any classes too early or too late for your preference? In a small group, share your current class schedules. Exchange ideas on how to handle time-management problems and the challenges you see in your schedules. Discuss how you would arrange your schedule differently for the next term. Go online and check your college's days and times of classes for next term. See if you can get the courses you want within the schedule that you prefer.

Maximizing Study and Review Time

Studying effectively means that you need to consider the time of day or night when you study best, where you can study with the least distractions, and how to actually learn while you study. Here are some strategies you can use to get the most benefit from your study time:

- **Find your space.** Use the same study area regularly, and make sure it is free of distractions and quiet enough so that you can focus. The library is usually the best choice. Try empty classrooms and study halls on campus, too. Bring essential supplies to your study area. Make sure you have everything you need.

- **Stick to a study routine.** The more firmly you have established a specific time and a quiet place to study, the more effective you will be in keeping up with your schedule.

- **Break down large tasks.** By taking on one thing at a time, you will make steady progress toward your academic goals.

- **Set realistic goals for your study time.** Assess how long it takes to read a chapter in different types of textbooks and to review notes in your courses, and then schedule your time accordingly. Allow adequate time to review and then test your knowledge when preparing for exams. Online classes often require online discussions and activities that take the place of face-to-face classroom instruction, so be prepared to spend additional time on these tasks.

- **Review when the material is fresh.** Schedule time to review immediately after class or as soon as possible; you will remember more of what you learned in class. Invest in tools (note cards, digital recorders, flash card apps, etc.) to convert less productive time into study time.

- **Time and attention.** Know your best times of day to study, and routinely assess your attention level. Schedule activities such as doing laundry, responding to e-mail, and seeing friends or family for those times of day when you have difficulty concentrating. Also, use waiting time (on the bus, before class, before appointments) to review.

- **Study difficult or boring subjects first,** when you are fresh. (Exception: If you are having trouble getting started, it might be easier to begin with your favorite subject.)

- **Divide study time into 50-minute blocks.** Study for 50 minutes and then take a 10- or 15-minute break; then study for another 50-minute block. Try not to study for more than three 50-minute blocks in a row, or you will find that you are not accomplishing 50 minutes' worth of work in each block. (In economics, this drop-off in productivity is known as the "law of diminishing returns.") If you have larger blocks of time available on the weekend, take advantage of them to review or to catch up on major projects.

- **Script your study sessions.** Break extended study sessions into a variety of activities, each with a specific objective. For example, begin by reading, then develop flash cards by writing key terms and their definitions or key formulas on note cards, and finally test yourself on what you have read.

- **Avoid multitasking.** Although you may be good at juggling many tasks at once, or at least may *think* that you are, the reality is (and research shows) that you will study more effectively and retain more if you concentrate on one task at a time.

You will study more effectively and retain more if you concentrate on one task at a time.

- **Dis distractions!** Turn off the TV, your DVD player, the radio, your iPod, etc., unless the background noise truly helps you concentrate or drowns out bigger distractions. Put your worries aside and don't let personal concerns interfere with studying. Restrict distracting and time-consuming tasks such as texting to a certain time; don't text every hour, and certainly not each time your phone beeps—mute it!

- **Let others help.** Find an accountability partner to help keep you on track. If you struggle with keeping a regular study schedule, find a friend, relative, or classmate to keep

you motivated and on course. If you have children, plan daily family homework times and encourage family members to help you study by taking flash cards wherever you go.

- **Be flexible!** You cannot anticipate every disruption to your plans. Build extra time into your study schedule so that unexpected interruptions do not prevent you from meeting your goals.

- **Reward yourself!** Develop a system of short- and long-term study goals as well as rewards for meeting those goals. Doing so will keep your motivation high. ■

Going from Here to There—Using Travel Time Wisely

Consider how you might best work with travel time, be it on campus or commuting to and from your school. If you live on campus, you may want to create a schedule that situates you near a dining hall at mealtimes or allows you to spend breaks between classes at the library. Or you may need breaks in your schedule for relaxation, like spending time in a student lounge or at the campus center. You may want to avoid returning to your residence hall room to take a nap between classes if a nap will make you feel lethargic or make you oversleep and miss later classes. Also, if you attend a large college or university, be sure that you allow adequate time to get from building to building. If you are a commuting student, or you work off campus, you may prefer scheduling your classes together in blocks without breaks. *Block scheduling,* which means enrolling in back-to-back classes, allows you to cut travel time by attending classes one or two days a week, and it may provide more flexibility for scheduling employment or family commitments.

In spite of its advantages, block scheduling can also have drawbacks. If you become ill on a class day, you

could fall behind in all your classes. You might also become fatigued from sitting in class after class. Having a last-minute study period immediately before a test will be difficult when one class immediately follows another because you likely will have no more than a 15-minute break between classes. Finally, remember that for

back-to-back classes, several exams might be held on the same day. Scheduling classes in blocks might work better if you have the option of attending lectures at alternative times in case you are absent, if you alternate classes with free periods, and if you seek out instructors who are flexible about due dates for assignments.

△ **Do You Have One of These?**
You don't have a limo at your disposal like they do, so plan ahead and be on time! Make the most of waiting for and riding public transportation by reading, studying, and doing homework during that time. Alan Chapman/FilmMagic/Getty Images.

Chapter Review

Steps to Success:
Managing Your Time

○ **Make sure that the way you use your time supports your goals for being in college.** All your time doesn't have to be spent studying, but remember the "two hours out of class for each hour in class" rule. Also, plan some intentional out-of-class activities that support your goals.

○ **Identify and address common time-management problems before they spiral out of control.** Be aware of issues with procrastination, distractions, overscheduling, and motivation. As you notice them happening, take stock and make changes. If any of these issues becomes a serious problem, seek help from your campus counseling center.

○ **Get organized by using a calendar or planner.** Choose either an electronic format or a paper calendar. Your campus bookstore or Web site will have a campus-specific version that includes exam dates, campus events, and deadlines you will need to know.

○ **Devise a weekly timetable of activities and then stick to it.** Be sure to include special events or responsibilities in addition to recurring activities such as classes, athletic practice, or work shifts.

○ **Create and use day-by-day paper or electronic to-do lists.** Crossing off those tasks you have completed will give you a real sense of satisfaction.

○ **Use the tips and strategies in this chapter to meet your time-management goals.** Keep the lists in this chapter handy as reminders of what to do and what to avoid.

Applying what you've learned . . .

Now that you have read and discussed this chapter, consider how you can apply what you have learned to your academic and personal lives. The following prompts will help you reflect on the chapter material and its relevance to you both now and in the future.

1. Review the "Time-Management Pitfalls" section in this chapter. Think of an upcoming assignment in one of your current classes and describe how you can avoid waiting until the last minute to get it done. Break down the assignment, and list each step that you will take to complete the assignment. Give yourself a due date for each step and for completing the assignment.

2. After reading about effective time-management strategies, consider the way in which you manage your own time. If you were grading your current set of time-management skills, what grade (A, B, C, or lower) would you give yourself? Why? Have you overloaded your schedule? Are you working too many hours off campus? Are you being distracted by your roommate or friends? What is your biggest challenge to becoming a more effective time manager?

Create Community

GO TO ▷ **The academic skills center:** If you need help with managing your time, studying for exams, reading textbooks, or taking notes.

GO TO ▷ **The counseling center:** If you need help with difficult emotional issues related to time management.

GO TO ▷ **Your academic adviser/counselor:** If you need help in finding another person on campus to help you with time-management issues.

GO TO ▷ **Fellow students:** If you need to commiserate with others who know what it feels like trying to find the time to do all that you need to do as a college student.

NOW . . . How do you measure up?

1. I have a better understanding of how to set academic and personal goals to guide how I prioritize my time.
   ○ Agree
   ○ Don't Know
   ○ Disagree

2. I have learned some ways to help me focus on the task at hand instead of procrastinating or getting distracted.
   ○ Agree
   ○ Don't Know
   ○ Disagree

3. I am using a daily or weekly planner, to-do lists, or other planning devices to keep track of my commitments.
   ○ Agree
   ○ Don't Know
   ○ Disagree

4. I will keep working on ways to balance my social life and my need for personal time with my academic requirements.
   ○ Agree
   ○ Don't Know
   ○ Disagree

Review the items you marked "Don't Know" or "Disagree." How do your answers here compare to your responses to the quiz you took at the start of the chapter? Which sections of this chapter left a strong impression on you? What time-management strategies have you begun to use, and are they working? What other strategies will you commit to trying?

33
Why Be an Engaged Learner?

34
Collaborative Learning Teams

36
**Is There *Really* More Than
One Way to Learn?**

41
**Know Thyself—Understanding
Emotional Intelligence**

44
How Emotions Affect Success

46
**Learning with a Learning
Disability**

Understanding How You Learn

graphixmania/Shutterstock.

Students who become genuinely engaged in their college experience have a greater chance of success than those who do not. Engagement means participating actively in your academic life, developing a passion for learning, and approaching every challenge with determination. One way to become engaged is to get to know your instructors, especially those who offer you the chance to learn actively. By developing a personal relationship with one or more instructors, you can begin to understand how their passion for learning in a particular academic area has become their life's work.

When you understand and use your preferred learning style it is easier to stay engaged. There is no one best way to learn. You may have trouble listening to a long lecture, or listening may be the way you learn best. You may love classroom discussion, or you may consider hearing other students' opinions a waste of time. Even if class discussion isn't your favorite activity, however, remember that hearing what other students think can be very useful.

Another component of college success is emotional intelligence. People who have a high level of emotional intelligence are able to control their emotions and manage their reactions to difficult or frustrating situations.

This chapter will help you engage actively with your coursework, classmates, and instructors and will ask you to complete a learning inventory to shed light on how you learn best. It will examine emotional intelligence and offer advice and resources for recognizing and treating common learning disabilities.

How do you measure up?

1. I know the benefits of studying in groups.
   - ○ Agree
   - ○ Don't Know
   - ○ Disagree

2. I understand which of my courses ask me to learn in different ways.
   - ○ Agree
   - ○ Don't Know
   - ○ Disagree

3. I understand why emotional intelligence is important to success in college and in life.
   - ○ Agree
   - ○ Don't Know
   - ○ Disagree

4. I know where I could get help if I thought I had a learning problem.
   - ○ Agree
   - ○ Don't Know
   - ○ Disagree

Review the items you marked "Don't Know" or "Disagree." Pay special attention to these topics in this chapter—you will find motivating strategies to develop in these areas.

△ **Jalen Washington**

Don't Count Your Grades Before They Hatch

Just as calculus class was ending, Professor Berman dropped the news on us: "I want every student here to participate in a study group," he said. A chorus of groans went up, but after that little moment, everyone started looking at the available times on the sign-up sheet and committing to a group. I sat at my desk and packed up my books. I aced every math course I took in high school, including precalc. So what if that was more than ten years ago? I'm good at math. Why would anyone need to show me how to study? A study group would be a waste of my time. I'm juggling school and my family, and living off campus makes my schedule less flexible than most traditional students' schedules.

In the days before the first test, I studied like a crazy man—on my own. I figured I'd get the highest grade in the class even if I had skipped a couple of classes when my kids got sick. If I'd known any of the other students, I would have asked them for notes, but I felt sure I hadn't missed much.

Fast-forward a week: When I scanned the test grades posted on Dr. Berman's door, mine was one of the lowest. And after Dr. Berman returned the test, I saw that I had gotten the first two problems right but screwed up the last three. I couldn't believe it. What else had I missed in class?

This was only the first test, so Jalen has the rest of the term to boost his grade in the course. What steps should he take? Does Professor Berman have any further responsibility to help Jalen? Why or why not?

Why Be an Engaged Learner?

No matter how good your academic skills are, you will not get the most out of college unless you become an engaged learner. Engaged students participate in learning activities both in and out of class that help them become excited and even passionate about learning. As a consequence, they learn more and gain more satisfaction from the college experience.

Although you might gain knowledge by listening to a lecture, you might not be motivated to think about what that knowledge means to you. When you are actively engaged in learning, you will learn not only the basic material in your notes and textbooks but also how to:

- work with others
- improve your critical thinking, listening, writing, and speaking skills
- function independently and teach yourself
- manage your time
- appreciate cultural differences

Engagement in learning is more than simply doing what your instructors or advisers require

you to do. As an engaged learner, you will want to become proactive by taking the initiative to go beyond what is required. For instance, you might want to do some library research to expand your understanding of a concept, make appointments to talk with faculty members about their research interests, ask someone to read a paper you have written to see whether you've stated your position clearly, or have a serious discussion with students whose personal backgrounds or values are different from yours. This active and engaged approach to learning will not only make for a richer college experience but will also prepare you to stand out in the workplace. In addition, you'll feel more comfortable socially, gain a greater appreciation for the value of education and other viewpoints, and be better able to clarify your academic major and your future career. ■

◁ **Engage in Helping**
Most colleges and universities sponsor service projects, from organizing food donations at local food banks to participating in community beautification, mentoring young people through Big Brothers Big Sisters, and serving hot food when natural disasters strike local or nearby communities. Make a difference and make some friends at the same time. © TOM MIHALEK/Reuters/Corbis.

Collaborative Learning Teams

Another strategy for engagement is to create a collaborative learning environment by joining or establishing a learning team. More than likely, you will be working with others after college, so now is a good time to learn how to collaborate. Students who engage in learning through a team approach not only learn better—they also enjoy their learning experiences more. Working in a group, you will be more likely to try new ideas and discover new knowledge by exploring different understandings instead of just memorizing facts.

Making Learning Teams Productive

Not all learning teams are equal. Sometimes teamwork fails to reach its potential because no thought was given to how the group was formed or how it should function. Use the following strategies to develop high-quality learning teams that maximize the power of peer collaboration:

- Use learning teams for more than just preparing for exams. Effective student learning teams collaborate regularly for other academic tasks besides test review sessions.

- Seek out team members who will contribute quality and diversity to the group. Look for students who are motivated, attend class regularly, are attentive and participate actively while in class, and complete assignments.

△ **Many Heads Are Better Than One**
Taking a team approach to learning not only will help you learn better; you also will have more fun learning. When you're in a group, you benefit from the companionship and you're more likely to be challenged by new techniques and ideas. © Yana Paskova/For The Washington Post via Getty Images.

- Keep the team small (four to six teammates). Small groups allow for more face-to-face interaction and eye contact and less opportunity for any one individual to shirk responsibility to the team.

- Hold individual team members personally accountable for contributing to the learning of their teammates. One way to ensure accountability is to have each member come to group meetings with specific information or answers to share with teammates. ■

TRY IT!

MAKING DECISIONS ▷ **Group Study—Give It a Chance**

Most first-year students come to college believing that studying is something they should do alone. Yet research shows and students report that studying in groups is actually more effective and, if you pay attention to the suggestions in this chapter, almost always results in more learning than studying by yourself. Make a decision to find or create at least one study group for a course that you find particularly challenging, even if you're not required to do so. Courses that many students find especially challenging include math and science courses as well as those that require a great deal of reading, such as history, sociology, and psychology. By studying with others, you not only learn more but also are virtually guaranteed to improve your grades.

Eight Great Uses for Learning Teams

1. **Note taking.** Team up with other students immediately after class to share and compare notes. Look at the level of detail in each other's notes, and adopt the best styles. Discuss places in the lecture where you got lost. Talk about confusing technical terms and symbols, and ask your instructor about concepts that are confusing to everyone in the group.

2. **Reading.** After completing reading assignments, team up with other students to compare your highlighting and margin notes.

3. **Library research.** Develop a support group for reducing "library anxiety" and for locating and sharing sources of information.

4. **Team/instructor conferences.** Schedule a time for your learning team to meet with the instructor to seek additional assistance as needed.

5. **Preparing for tests.** Divide the job of making a study outline. Team members can discuss and modify the separate outlines before a final version is created for all. Group members can quiz one another or write practice questions, or the group might create an exam and take it together.

6. **Reviewing test results.** After receiving test results, review them together. Help one another identify the sources of mistakes, and share any answers that received high scores.

7. **Teaching each other.** Split up difficult questions or problems and assign them to various members to prepare and present to the group. The best way to learn something is to explain it to someone else.

8. **Asking questions.** Never criticize a question in your study group; respond positively and express appreciation for all contributions. If you notice someone is lost, give that person an opportunity to ask a question. Above all, come to the group meeting prepared—not that you should have all the answers, but you should know the specific questions you have.

Is There *Really* More Than One Way to Learn?

You will be more likely to succeed in college if you know and use your most effective learning style. There are many models for thinking about and describing learning styles, such as the VARK Learning Styles Inventory, the Kolb Learning Styles Inventory, and the Myers-Briggs Type Indicator. The VARK Inventory investigates how learners prefer to use their senses in learning, while the Kolb Inventory focuses on abilities we need to develop in order to learn. The Myers-Briggs Type Indicator (MBTI) investigates basic personality characteristics and how they relate to human interaction and learning. In this section we present the VARK Learning Styles Inventory to help you determine your best mode of learning.

The VARK (Visual, Aural, Read/Write, and Kinesthetic) Learning Styles Inventory

Unlike learning styles theories that rely on personality or intelligence, the VARK focuses on whether learners prefer to use their visual, aural, read/write, or kinesthetic senses to learn. Visual learners prefer to learn information through charts, graphs, symbols, and other visual means. Aural learners favor hearing information. Read/write learners prefer to learn information that is displayed as words. Kinesthetic learners are most comfortable learning through experience and practice, whether simulated or real. To determine your learning style according to the VARK Inventory, respond to the following questionnaire.

> "Tell me and I forget. Teach me and I learn. Involve me and I remember."
>
> —*Benjamin Franklin*

The VARK Questionnaire (Version 7.1, 2011)

This questionnaire is designed to tell you about your preferences in working with information. Choose answers that explain your preference(s). Check the box next to those items. For each question, select *as many boxes as applies to you*. If none of the response options apply to you, leave the item blank. (You can also take the VARK online at http://www.vark-learn.com/english/page.asp?p=questionnaire.)

1. You are helping someone who wants to go to your airport, town center, or railway station. You would:
   a. go with her.
   b. tell her the directions.
   c. write down the directions as a list (without a map).
   d. draw a map or give her one.

2. You are not sure whether a word should be spelled *dependent* or *dependant*. You would:
   a. see the words in your mind and choose by the way they look.
   b. think about how each word sounds and choose one.
   c. find it in a dictionary.
   d. write both words on paper and choose one.

3. You are planning a holiday for a group. You want some feedback from the group about the plan. You would:
   a. describe some of the highlights.
   b. use a map or Web site to show them the places.
   c. give them a copy of the printed itinerary.
   d. phone, text, or e-mail them.

(continued)

4. You are going to cook a special treat for your family. You would:
   a. cook something you know without the need for instructions.
   b. ask friends for suggestions.
   c. look through a cookbook for ideas from the pictures.
   d. use a cookbook in which you know there is a good recipe.

5. A group of tourists wants to learn about the parks or wildlife reserves in your area. You would:
   a. talk about, or arrange a talk for them, about parks or wildlife reserves.
   b. show them Internet pictures, photographs, or picture books.
   c. take them to a park or wildlife reserve and walk with them.
   d. give them a book or pamphlets about the parks or wildlife reserves.

6. You are about to purchase a digital camera or mobile phone. Other than price, what would most influence your decision?
   a. trying or testing it
   b. reading the details about its features
   c. thinking that it is a modern design and looks good
   d. hearing about its features from the salesperson

7. Remember a time when you learned how to do something new. Try to avoid choosing a physical skill (e.g., riding a bike). You learned best by:
   a. watching a demonstration.
   b. listening to somebody explaining it and asking questions.
   c. diagrams and charts, e.g., visual clues.
   d. written instructions, e.g., a manual or textbook.

8. You have a problem with your knee. You would prefer that the doctor:
   a. give you an online source or written materials to read about your problem.
   b. use a plastic model of a knee to show what is wrong.
   c. describe what is wrong.
   d. show you a diagram of what is wrong.

9. You want to learn a new program, skill, or game on a computer. You would:
   a. read the written instructions that came with the program.
   b. talk with people who know about the program.
   c. use the controls or keyboard.
   d. follow the diagrams in the book that came with it.

10. You like Web sites that have:
    a. things you can click on, shift, or try.
    b. interesting design and visual features.
    c. interesting written descriptions, lists, and explanations.
    d. audio channels where you can hear music, radio programs, or interviews.

11. Other than price, what would most influence your decision to buy a new nonfiction book?
    a. thinking it looks appealing
    b. quickly reading parts of it
    c. hearing a friend talk about it and recommend it
    d. its real-life stories, experiences, and examples

12. You are using a book, CD, or Web site to learn how to take photos with your new digital camera. You would like to have:
    a. a chance to ask questions and talk about the camera and its features.
    b. clear written instructions with lists and bullet points about what to do.
    c. diagrams showing the camera and what each part does.
    d. many examples of good and poor photos and how to improve them.

13. You prefer a teacher or a presenter who uses:
    a. demonstrations, models, or practical sessions.
    b. question and answer, lecture, group discussion, or guest speakers.
    c. handouts, books, or readings.
    d. diagrams, charts, or graphs.

14. You have finished a competition or test and would like some feedback:
    a. using examples from what you have done.
    b. using a written description of your results.
    c. from somebody who talks it through with you.
    d. using graphs showing what you had achieved.

15. You are going to choose food at a restaurant or café. You would:
    a. choose something that you have had there before.
    b. listen to the waiter or ask friends to recommend choices.
    c. choose from the descriptions in the menu.
    d. look at what others are eating or look at pictures of each dish.

16. You have to make an important speech at a conference or special occasion. You would:
    a. make diagrams or use graphs to help explain things.
    b. write a few key words and practice saying your speech over and over.
    c. write out your speech and learn from reading it over several times.
    d. gather many examples and stories to make the talk real and practical.

Source: Copyright Version 7.1 (2011) is held by Neil D. Fleming, Christchurch, New Zealand. Used by permission.

Scoring the VARK

Now you will match up each of the boxes you selected with a category from the VARK using the following scoring chart. Circle the letter (V, A, R, or K) that corresponds to each of your responses (A, B, C, or D). For example, if you marked both B and C for question 3, circle both the V and the R in the third row of the scoring chart.

Count the number of each VARK letter you have circled to get your score for each VARK category.

Because you may have chosen more than one answer for each question, scoring is not simply a matter of counting. It is like four stepping stones across a stream. Enter your scores from highest to lowest on the stones in the figure below, along with their V, A, R, and K labels.

Responses to question 3

A	B	C	D
K	(V)	(R)	A

Table 3.1 ▽ Scoring Chart

Question	A category	B category	C category	D category
1	K	A	R	V
2	V	A	R	K
3	K	V	R	A
4	K	A	V	R
5	A	V	K	R
6	K	R	V	A
7	K	A	V	R
8	R	K	A	V
9	R	A	K	V
10	K	V	R	A
11	V	R	A	K
12	A	R	V	K
13	K	A	R	V
14	K	R	A	V
15	K	A	R	V
16	V	A	R	K

Total number of **V**s circled = _____

Total number of **A**s circled = _____

Total number of **R**s circled = _____

Total number of **K**s circled = _____

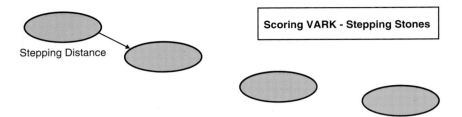

Stepping Distance

Scoring VARK - Stepping Stones

Your stepping distance comes from this table:

The total of my four VARK scores is:	My stepping distance is:
16–21	1
22–27	2
28–32	3
More than 32	4

Follow these steps to establish your preferences.

1. Your first preference is always your highest score. Check the first stone as one of your preferences.

2. Now subtract your second-highest score from your highest score. If that figure is larger than your stepping distance (see above table), you have a single preference. Otherwise check this stone as another preference and continue with step 3 below.

3. Subtract your third-highest score from your second-highest one. If that figure is larger than your stepping distance, you have a bimodal preference. If not, check your third stone as a preference and continue with step 4 below.

4. Lastly, subtract your lowest score from your third-highest one. If that figure is larger than your stepping distance, you have a trimodal preference. Otherwise, check your fourth stone as a preference, and you have all four modes as your preferences.

Note: If you are bimodal or trimodal or have checked all four modes as your preferences, you can be described as *multimodal* in your VARK preferences. ■

TRY IT!

FEELING CONNECTED ▷
Connect with VARK "Buddies"

Your first-year seminar class will help you connect with other students who have the same VARK profile as you. Once you've gotten your VARK score and determined your preferences, find a few other students who share your learning style and agree to practice some of the study strategies listed below. Challenge each other to come up with one new idea for studying that relates to your learning preference.

Using VARK Results for Success

How can knowing your VARK score help you do better in your college classes? Here are ways of using learning styles to develop your own study strategies:

- If you have a visual learning preference, underline or highlight your notes; use symbols, charts, or graphs to display your notes; use different arrangements of words on the page; and redraw your pages from memory.
- If you are an aural learner, talk with others to verify the accuracy of your lecture notes. Record your notes and listen to them, or record class lectures. Read your notes out loud; ask yourself questions and speak your answers.
- If you have a read/write learning preference, write and rewrite your notes, and read your notes silently. Organize diagrams or flowcharts into statements, and write imaginary exam questions and respond in writing.
- If you are a kinesthetic learner, you'll need to use all your senses in learning—sight, touch, taste, smell, and hearing. Supplement your notes with real-world examples; move and gesture while you are reading or speaking your notes.

TRY IT!

SETTING GOALS ▷ Developing Study Strategies That Match How You Learn

Set a goal to use the examples in "Using VARK Results for Success" to study more effectively. Read the suggestions for your learning preference, and practice each one during the next week. You might also experiment with study strategies for another learning style to tap into other strengths that you might have. For instance, even if you're an aural or read/write learner, you may find that tapping into kinesthetic strategies such as walking or gesturing helps you learn and remember. Even if you're not a visual learner as determined by the VARK, you might benefit from using a graph or mind map to help you understand concepts and details.

Know Thyself—Understanding Emotional Intelligence

Particularly in the first year of college, many students who have the ability to succeed intellectually have difficulty establishing positive relationships with others, dealing with pressure, or making wise decisions, while other students exude optimism and happiness and seem to adapt to their new environment without any trouble. The difference between the two types of students lies not in their academic talent but in their emotional intelligence (EI), or their ability to recognize and manage moods, feelings, and attitudes. A growing body of evidence shows a clear connection between students' EI and whether they stay in college.

What Is Emotional Intelligence?

Emotional intelligence is the ability to identify, use, understand, and manage emotions. You should not ignore your emotions, because the better the emotional read you have on a situation, the more appropriately you can respond to it.

There are many competing theories about EI, some of them complex. While experts vary in their definitions and models, all agree that emotions are real, can be changed for the better, and have a profound impact on whether a person is successful.

In the simplest terms, emotional intelligence consists of two general abilities:

1. *Understanding emotions* involves the capacity to monitor and label your feelings accurately (nervousness, happiness, anger, relief, and so forth) and to determine why you feel the way you do. It also involves predicting how others might feel in a given situation. Emotions contain information, and the ability to understand and think about that information plays an important role in behavior.

2. *Managing emotions* involves the ability to modify and even improve feelings. At times, you need to stay open to your feelings, learn

> Emotions are real, can be changed for the better, and have a profound impact on whether a person is successful.

from them, and use them to take appropriate action. At other times, it is better to disengage from an emotion and return to it later. Anger, for example, can lead you to act in negative or antisocial ways; used positively, however, anger can help you overcome adversity, bias, and injustice.

Identifying and using emotions can help you learn which moods are best for different situations and how to put yourself in the "right" mood. Developing an awareness of emotions allows you to use your feelings to enhance your thinking. If you are feeling sad, for instance, you might view the world in a certain way, while if you feel happy, you are likely to interpret the same events differently. Once you start paying attention to emotions, you can learn not only how to cope with life's pressures and demands but also how to harness your knowledge of the way you feel for more effective problem solving, reasoning, decision making, and creative endeavors.[1]

A number of sophisticated tools can be used to assess emotional intelligence. But even without a formal test, you can take a number of steps to get in touch with your own EI. You'll have to dig deep inside yourself and be willing to be honest about how you really think and how you really behave. This process can take time, and that's fine. Think of your EI as a work in progress.

[1]Adapted with permission from EI Skills Group, "Ability Model of Emotional Intelligence," http://www.emotionaliq. com/. © 2005–2013.

Identifying Competencies

Emotional intelligence includes many capabilities and skills that influence a person's ability to cope with life's pressures and demands. Reuven Bar-On, a professor at the University of Texas at Austin, and a world-renowned EI expert, developed a model that demonstrates how these categories of emotional intelligence directly affect general mood and lead to effective performance (see Figure 3.1).

Let's look more closely at the specific skills and competencies that Bar-On has identified as the pieces that make up a person's emotional intelligence.[2] They are similar to the pieces of a jigsaw puzzle—once you've put them all together, you will begin to see yourself and others more clearly.

Intrapersonal skills. This first category, intrapersonal skills, relates to how well you know and like yourself as well as to how effectively you can do the things you need to do to stay happy. Understanding yourself and why you think and act as you do is the glue that holds all of the EI competencies together. This category is made up of five specific competencies:

1. **Emotional self-awareness.** Knowing how and why you feel the way you do.

2. **Assertiveness.** Standing up for yourself when necessary without being too aggressive.

3. **Independence.** Making important decisions on your own without having to get everyone's opinion.

4. **Self-regard.** Liking yourself in spite of your flaws (and we all have them).

5. **Self-actualization.** Being satisfied and comfortable with your achievements.

Interpersonal skills. Recent studies have shown that people with extensive support networks are generally happier and tend to enjoy longer, healthier lives. Your ability to build relationships and get along with other people depends on the competencies that form the basis for the interpersonal skills category:

1. **Empathy.** Making an effort to understand another person's situation or point of view.

[2]Adapted from Reuven Bar-On, "The Bar-On Model of Emotional-Social Intelligence (ESI)," *Psicothema* 18, no. S1 (2006): S21, http://www.eiconsortium.org/pdf/baron_model_of_emotional_social_intelligence.pdf.

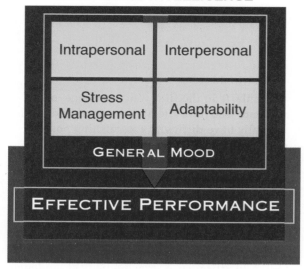

BAR-ON MODEL OF EMOTIONAL INTELLIGENCE

| Intrapersonal | Interpersonal |
| Stress Management | Adaptability |

GENERAL MOOD

EFFECTIVE PERFORMANCE

Figure 3.1 △ **Bar-On Model of Emotional Intelligence** "What Is Emotional Intelligence?" from Bar-On EQ-i Technical Manual © 1997, 1999, 2000 Multi Health Systems Inc. Toronto, Canada. Reproduced with permission from Multi-Health Systems Inc.

2. **Social responsibility.** Establishing a personal link with a group or community and cooperating with its other members in working toward shared goals.

3. **Interpersonal relationships.** Seeking out and maintaining healthy and mutually beneficial relationships, such as friendships, professional networks, family connections, mentoring relationships, and romantic partnerships.

Adaptability. Things change. Adaptability—the ability to adjust your thinking and behavior when faced with new or unexpected situations—helps you cope and ensures that you'll do well in life, no matter what the challenges. This category includes three key competencies:

1. **Reality testing.** Ensuring that your feelings are appropriate by checking them against external, objective criteria.

2. **Flexibility.** Adapting and adjusting your emotions, viewpoints, and actions as situations change.

3. **Problem solving.** Approaching challenges step by step and not giving up in the face of obstacles.

Stress management. In college, at work, and at home, now and in the future, you'll face what can seem like never-ending pressures and demands. Managing the resulting stress depends on two skills:

1. **Stress tolerance.** Recognizing the causes of stress and responding in appropriate ways; staying strong under pressure.

2. **Impulse control.** Thinking carefully about potential consequences before you act, and delaying gratification for the sake of achieving long-term goals.

General mood and effective performance. It might sound sappy, but having a positive attitude really does improve your chances of doing well. Bar-On emphasizes the importance of two emotions in particular:

1. **Optimism.** Looking on the bright side of any problem or difficulty and being confident that things will work out for the best.

2. **Happiness.** Being satisfied with yourself, with others, and with your situation in general.

It makes sense: If you feel good about yourself and manage your emotions, you can expect to get along with others and enjoy a happy, successful life. ∎

Savage Chickens   by Doug Savage

www.savagechickens.com

△ **Accentuate the Positive**
You probably know people who always find the negative in any situation. Constantly focusing on what's missing or what's not perfect will likely make you the kind of person whom others avoid. Practice looking on the bright side. © 2007 Doug Savage from www.savagechickens.com. All rights reserved.

Emotional Intelligence Questionnaire

Your daily life gives you many opportunities to take a hard look at how you handle emotions. Here are some questions that can help you begin thinking about your own EI.

1. **What do you do when you are under stress?**
   a. I tend to deal with it calmly and rationally.
   b. I get upset, but it usually blows over quickly.
   c. I get upset but keep it to myself.

2. **My friends would say that:**
   a. I play, but only after I get my work done.
   b. I am ready for fun anytime.
   c. I hardly ever go out.

3. **When something changes at the last minute:**
   a. I easily adapt.
   b. I get frustrated.
   c. I don't care, since I don't really expect things to happen according to plan.

4. **My friends would say that:**
   a. I am sensitive to their concerns.
   b. I spend too much time worrying about other people's needs.
   c. I don't like to deal with other people's petty problems.

5. **When I have a problem to solve, such as too many things being due at the end of the week:**
   a. I make a list of the tasks I must complete, come up with a plan indicating specifically what I can and cannot accomplish, and follow my plan.
   b. I am very optimistic about getting things done and just dig right in and get to work.
   c. I get a little frazzled; usually, I get a number of things done and then push aside the things that I can't do.

Review your responses. A responses indicate that you probably have a good basis for strong emotional intelligence. **B** responses indicate you may have some strengths and some challenges in your EI. **C** responses indicate that your EI could negatively affect your future success in school and in life.

How Emotions Affect Success

Emotions are strongly tied to physical and psychological well-being. For example, some studies have suggested that cancer patients who have strong EI live longer. A large study done at the University of Pennsylvania found that the best athletes do well in part because they are extremely optimistic. A number of studies link strong EI skills to college success in particular. Here are a few highlights of those studies:

- **Emotionally intelligent students get higher grades.** Researchers looked at students' grade point averages at the end of their first year of college. Students who had tested high for intrapersonal skills, stress tolerance, and adaptability when they entered in the fall did better academically than those who had lower overall EI test scores.

- **Students who can't manage their emotions struggle academically.** Some students have experienced full-blown panic attacks before tests. Others who are depressed can't concentrate on coursework. And far too many students turn to risky behaviors (drug and alcohol abuse, eating disorders, and worse) in an effort to cope. Dr. Richard Kadison, a former director of mental health services at Harvard University, has noted that "the emotional well-being of students goes hand-in-hand with their academic development. If they're not doing well emotionally, they are not going to reach their academic potential."[3]

[3]Richard Kadison and Theresa Foy DiGeronimo, *College of the Overwhelmed: The Campus Mental Health Crisis and What to Do about It* (San Francisco: Jossey-Bass, 2004), 156.

▷ **The Best Medicine**
Why do we often feel that our pets are tuned into how we are feeling and know just how to act to make us feel better? Some pets seem to understand and be aware of human emotions. What human cues do animals pick up on? What might we learn from our pets that could help us improve our own emotional intelligence? Jason van der Valk/Getty Images.

- **Students who can delay gratification tend to do better overall.** Impulse control leads to achievement. In the famous "marshmallow study" performed at Stanford University, researchers examined the long-term behaviors of individuals who, as four-year-olds, were tested to see whether they would practice delayed gratification. The children were each given one marshmallow and told that if they didn't eat it right away, they could have another. Fourteen years later, the children who had immediately eaten their marshmallow were more likely to experience significant stress, irritability, and inability to focus on goals. The children who had waited to eat their marshmallow scored an average of 210 points higher on the SAT; had better confidence, concentration, and reliability; held better-paying jobs; and reported being more satisfied with life.

- **EI skills can be enhanced in a first-year seminar.** In two separate studies, one conducted in Australia and another conducted in the United States, researchers found that college students enrolled in a first-year seminar who demonstrated good EI skills were more likely to do better in college than students who did not exhibit those behaviors.

You can do well enough to get by in college without strong EI, but you might miss out on the full range and depth of competencies and skills that can help you to succeed in your chosen field and have a fulfilling and meaningful life. ■

TRY IT!

SETTING GOALS ▷
Emotional Reactions Have Consequences

Set a goal to be aware of how your emotional reactions affect your interactions with other people. Pretend that you are your own therapist, and the next time you have an experience that generates a negative emotion such as anger, sadness, annoyance, resentment, or humiliation, pay attention to your behavior. Did you sulk in silence, cry, or lash out at another person? Or were you calm and reasonable? Take a step back and "process" what you said or did in response to your feelings. Then talk with a trusted friend or classmate about how you reacted. Ask for feedback on whether your reaction was appropriate or inappropriate. If your reaction resulted in negative consequences for yourself or others, set a goal to behave differently in the future if and when you experience a similar situation.

How to Improve Your Emotional Intelligence

Developing your EI is an important step toward getting the full benefit of a college education. Think about how you cope with emotional stress. Do you often give up because something is just too hard or because you can't figure it out? Do you take responsibility for what you do, or do you blame others if you fail? How can you communicate effectively if you are not assertive or if you are overly aggressive? If you're inflexible, how can you solve problems, get along with coworkers and family members, or learn from other people's points of view?

The good news is that you *can* improve your EI. It might not be easy—old habits are hard to change—but it can definitely be done. Here are some suggestions:

1. **Identify your strengths and weaknesses.** Take a hard look at yourself, and consider how you respond to situations. Most people have trouble evaluating their own behaviors realistically, so ask someone you trust and respect for insight.

2. **Set realistic goals.** As you identify areas of emotional intelligence that you would like to improve, be as specific as possible. Instead of deciding to be more assertive, for example, focus on a particular issue that is giving you trouble.

3. **Formulate a plan.** With a particular goal in mind, identify a series of steps you could take to achieve the goal, and define the results that would indicate success.

4. **Check your progress on a regular basis.** Continually reevaluate whether or not you have met your goals, and adjust your strategy as needed.

It's important not to try to improve everything at once. Instead, identify specific EI competencies that you can define and describe, and then set measurable goals for change. Don't expect success overnight. Remember that it took you a while to develop your specific approach to life, and changing it will take commitment and practice.

Learning with a Learning Disability

While everyone has a learning style, some people have what is characterized as a *learning disability*. Learning disabilities are usually recognized and diagnosed in grade school, but occasionally students successfully compensate for a learning problem and reach college without ever having been properly diagnosed or assisted.

Learning disabilities can affect people's ability to interpret what they see or hear or to link information across different parts of the brain. These limitations can show up as specific difficulties with spoken or written language, coordination, self-control, or attention. Such difficulties can impede learning to read, write, or do math. Because the term *learning disability* covers a broad range of possible causes, symptoms, treatments, and outcomes, diagnosing a learning disability or pinpointing its causes is difficult. The types of learning disabilities that most commonly affect college students are attention disorders and disorders that affect the development of academic skills, including reading, writing, and mathematics.

Attention Disorders

Attention disorders are common in children, adolescents, and adults. Some students who have attention disorders appear to daydream excessively, and once you get their attention, they can be easily distracted. Individuals with attention deficit disorder (ADD) or attention deficit hyperactivity disorder (ADHD) often have trouble organizing tasks or completing their work. They don't seem to listen to or follow directions, and their work might be messy or appear careless. Although ADD and ADHD are not strictly classified as learning disabilities, they can seriously interfere with academic performance, leading some educators to group them with other learning disabilities.[4]

[4]Adapted and reprinted from the public domain source by Sharyn Neuwirth, *Learning Disabilities* (Darby, PA: National Institute of Mental Health, 1993), 9–10.

If you have trouble paying attention or getting organized, you won't really know whether you have ADD or ADHD until you are evaluated. Check out resources on campus or in the community. After you have been evaluated, follow the advice you get, which may mean taking medication. If you receive a prescription for medication, be sure to take it according to the physician's directions. You can also improve your focus through your own behavioral choices, whether or not you have an attention disorder. The Web site for the National Institute of Mental Health (NIMH) offers the following suggestions for adults with attention disorders:

> Adults with ADD or ADHD can learn how to organize their lives by using "props," such as a large calendar posted where it will be seen in the morning, datebooks, lists, and reminder notes. They can have a special place for keys, bills, and the paperwork of everyday life. Tasks can be organized into sections so that completion of each part can give a sense of accomplishment. Above all, adults who have ADD or ADHD should learn as much as they can about their disorder.

Cognitive Learning Disabilities

Other learning disabilities are related to cognitive skills. Dyslexia, for example, is a common developmental reading disorder. Though a person can have problems with any of the tasks involved in reading, scientists have found that a significant number of people with dyslexia share an inability to distinguish or separate the sounds in spoken words. For instance, dyslexic individuals sometimes have difficulty assigning the appropriate sounds to individual letters or to letters that have been combined to form words. Reading is more than just recognizing words, however. If the brain is unable to form images or relate new ideas to ideas stored in memory, the reader can't understand or remember the new concepts. So other types of

reading disabilities can appear when the focus of reading shifts from word identification to comprehension.[5]

Writing involves several brain areas and functions as well. The brain networks for vocabulary, grammar, hand movement, and memory must all be in good working order. A developmental writing disorder might result from problems in any of these areas. Someone who can't distinguish the sequence of sounds in a word will often have problems with spelling. People with a writing disability, particularly an expressive language disorder (the inability to express oneself using accurate language or sentence structure), are often unable to compose complete, grammatical sentences.[6]

A student with a developmental arithmetic disorder will have difficulty recognizing numbers and symbols, memorizing facts such as multiplication tables, aligning numbers, and

TRY IT!

FEELING CONNECTED ▷
Prepare for a Learning Disability to Touch Your Life

Consider whether you or someone close to you might have a learning or attention disorder. What you discover may be helpful in the future. Remember that learning disabilities are not related to basic intelligence, so there should be no stigma attached to identifying resources and seeking help. Find out whether your college or university has a special office to diagnose and treat learning disabilities. If so, visit this office or your campus library to learn how you can help yourself or someone else overcome a learning disability and succeed in college and in life.

[5] Ibid., 7., [6] Ibid., 7–8.

Between 15 and 20 percent of Americans have a learning disability.

understanding abstract concepts such as place value and fractions.[7]

The following questions may help you determine whether you or someone you know should be screened for a possible learning disability:

- Do you perform poorly on tests even when you feel that you have studied and are capable of performing better?

- Do you have trouble spelling words?

[7] Ibid., 8.

- Do you work harder than your classmates at basic reading and writing?

- Do your instructors point out inconsistencies in your classroom performance, such as answering questions correctly in class but incorrectly on a written test?

- Do you have a really short attention span, or do your family members or instructors say that you do things without thinking?

Although responding yes to any of these questions does not mean that you have a disability, the resources of your campus learning center or the office for student disability services can help you address any potential problems and devise ways to learn more effectively. Anyone who is diagnosed with a learning disability is in good company. According to national data, between 15 and 20 percent of Americans have a learning disability. ■

A Learning Disability = Learning Difference

Having a learning disability is not a sign that you are stupid. In fact, some of the most intelligent individuals in human history have had a learning disability—Benjamin Franklin, George Washington, Alexander Graham Bell, and Woodrow Wilson. Well-known and successful people today who have diagnosed learning disabilities include the TV anchor Anderson Cooper; pop stars Jewel and Justin Timberlake; actors Tom Cruise, Keira Knightley, and Orlando Bloom; Paul Orfalea, the founder of the Kinko's copy shop chain; Gareth Cook, a Pulitzer Prize–winning science writer; and Gavin Christopher Newsom, lieutenant governor of California. Each of these individuals has a story to tell about living with and overcoming his or her particular learning disability.

Chapter Review

Steps to Success:
Understanding How You Learn

○ **Take a learning styles inventory, either in this chapter or at your campus learning or counseling center(s).** See whether the results might at least partly explain your level of performance in each class you are taking this term.

○ **Learn about and accept your unique learning preferences.** Especially make note of your strengths in terms of those things you learn well and easily. See whether those skills could be applied to other learning situations.

○ **Use your learning style to develop study strategies that work best for you.** You can walk, talk, read, listen, or even dance while you are learning.

○ **If you need help with making the best use of your learning style, visit your learning center.** Consider taking some courses in the social and behavioral sciences that would help you better understand how humans learn.

○ **Using the questionnaire in this chapter, assess your emotional intelligence.** Note areas in which your EI is strong and areas that need improvement.

○ **Be aware of how your emotions affect the way you react to difficult or frustrating situations.** Use your awareness ahead of time to try to control your negative reactions.

○ **If you aren't satisfied with your emotional reactions, make an appointment at the campus counseling center to discuss your feelings and get help.** Counselors can help you monitor and understand your emotional responses in a confidential setting.

○ **If you think you might have a learning disability, go to your campus learning center and ask for a diagnostic assessment so that you can develop successful coping strategies.** Make sure to ask for a personal interpretation and follow-up counseling or tutoring.

Applying what you've learned . . .

Now that you have read and discussed this chapter, consider how you can apply what you have learned to your academic and personal lives. The following prompts will help you reflect on the chapter material and its relevance to you both now and in the future.

1. Managing your emotions is an important skill in college. What relationships or situations tend to incite a negative emotional reaction from you? Think about when your reactions are appropriate and when they are inappropriate. Get some feedback on your behavior from a trusted friend.

2. It is important to understand various learning styles and how your own style(s) of learning can affect your experience in the classroom. Considering your learning style(s), what kinds of teaching and learning methods do you think will work best for you? What teaching and learning methods will be especially challenging?

Create Community

GO TO ▷ The learning assistance/support center: If you need help with deciding which learning strategies will work best for you. Almost every campus has one or more of these centers that offer help, like tutoring, for students in all subjects at all levels.

GO TO ▷ The counseling center: If you need help managing stress, a fairly common issue among new college students.

GO TO ▷ An approachable instructor: If you need help with your academic work.

GO TO ▷ Your academic adviser or counselor: If you need help in a particular course, especially if the style of instruction or life circumstances are keeping you from earning higher grades.

GO ONLINE TO ▷ LD Pride (http://www.ldpride.net/learningstyles.MI.htm): If you want general information about learning styles and learning disabilities and an interactive diagnostic tool to determine your learning style. This site was developed in 1998 by Liz Bogod, an adult with learning disabilities.

GO ONLINE TO ▷ The National Center for Learning Disabilities (http://www.ncld. org): To access a variety of resources for diagnosing and understanding learning disabilities.

GO TO ▷ Your first-year seminar instructor: If you want to find out more about learning styles and learning disabilities. You also may have professors in the areas of education and psychology who have a strong interest in the processes of learning.

GO TO ▷ The library: If you want help locating additional resources, such as: Kathleen G. Nadeau, *Survival Guide for College Students with ADHD or LD* (Washington, DC: Magination Press, 2006); and Patricia O. Quinn, MD, ed., *ADD and the College Student: A Guide for High School and College Students with Attention Deficit Disorder* (Washington, DC: Magination Press, 2001).

NOW . . . How do you measure up?

1. I understand the benefits of studying in groups.
   - ○ Agree
   - ○ Don't Know
   - ○ Disagree

2. I can identify the different ways in which the classes that I am taking ask me to learn.
   - ○ Agree
   - ○ Don't Know
   - ○ Disagree

3. I can appreciate how emotional intelligence is important to success in college and in life.
   - ○ Agree
   - ○ Don't Know
   - ○ Disagree

4. I can recognize the signs of common learning disabilities, and I know where to get help with a learning problem I might have.
   - ○ Agree
   - ○ Don't Know
   - ○ Disagree

Review the items you marked "Don't Know" or "Disagree." How do your answers here compare to your responses to the quiz you took at the start of the chapter? Which sections of this chapter left a strong impression on you? What topics left you wanting to learn more? Remember that your campus has resources for finding answers to every question you might have. Take advantage of all your college or university has to offer.

53
Preparing for Class

54
Pay Attention! Listening, Participating, and Note Taking

57
Approaches to Note Taking

63
Keep It Fresh by Reviewing Your Notes

Getting the Most Out of Class

In every college class you take, you will need to master two skills to earn high grades: listening and note taking. It all begins with listening. If you are thinking about what happened the night before or your plans later in the day, you won't be able to listen effectively. If you are too sleepy or if you're distracted by people around you, your attention to the main purpose of class will suffer. Successful listening in college classes is about "being in the moment" and focusing on the lecture or discussion related to the topic of the day. By taking an active role in your classes—genuinely participating by asking questions, contributing to discussions, and providing answers—you will listen better and take more meaningful notes. Your experience with note taking before coming to college may be limited. High schools and other educational or work settings sometimes require note taking, but more often they do not. Some students even find it difficult to listen and take notes at the same time. If this is a problem

for you, don't give up. With practice and experience, you'll be able to both listen and write down what's most important. The reward for your efforts will be greater understanding of course material, a feeling of empowerment that comes from offering your perspectives in class discussions, and improvement in your ability to find new possibilities, understand abstract ideas, organize those ideas, and recall the material once the class is over.

You can then connect your understanding of what went on in class with your understanding of the reading assignments. This increased capacity to analyze and understand complex material will result in better academic performance while you are in college and will also be valued by a wide range of employers.

This chapter provides valuable suggestions for becoming a skilled listener, note taker, and class participant. Decide which techniques work best for you. Practice them regularly until they become part of your study routine.

How do you measure up?

1. I do a good job in identifying key points of lectures and discussions and in writing them down in my notes.

   ○ Agree
   ○ Don't Know
   ○ Disagree

2. When I don't understand something, I know how important it is to ask questions in class—even in large classes.

   ○ Agree
   ○ Don't Know
   ○ Disagree

3. In math or science courses students should write down everything the instructor puts on the board or screen.

   ○ Agree
   ○ Don't Know
   ○ Disagree

4. I know that one of the most effective ways to learn is to join study groups for each of my classes.

   ○ Agree
   ○ Don't Know
   ○ Disagree

Review the items you marked "Don't Know" or "Disagree." Pay special attention to these topics in this chapter—you will find motivating strategies to develop in these areas.

Tongue-Tied

△ **Amy Gailliard**

© Matelly/cultura/Corbis.

"So, Amy, why do you think Harper Lee chose to give *To Kill a Mockingbird* a child narrator?" my professor asked me at our second literature class. Minutes earlier I'd been tapping my pencil on my notebook, feeling happy as we discussed my favorite book. Suddenly I was grasping for something to say.

"Er," I managed. Thirty-two 20-something-year-old faces were looking at me. I felt my face go beet red. They don't want to hear from the "old lady" in the class, twice their age.

"Anyone else?" he asked, looking around. "Speak up."

"Scout has an innocent perspective," said the girl sitting next to me.

"Exactly," said Professor Kelso. "And why is that such an effective device here?"

Because the difference between what the reader sees happening in the book and what Scout perceives generates a lot of irony, I thought to myself. Because we see her learn something important. Because her childlike tone disguises the serious purpose of the plot.

"Because we see her start to understand how her world works—in good and bad ways," said a student across the room.

The professor crossed his arms and nodded. "Good job, Aziz. That's a point toward your class participation grade." Then he caught a glance at my stricken face. "Amy, did you have something to add?"

"Uh, well . . . I, um," I said. Yep, it looked like being back in college was going to be rough.

How is Amy's reticence about speaking in front of her younger classmates affecting her performance in college? What kind of preparation before class would have helped Amy? Flip through the chapter. What other suggestions can you find that would have helped her speak up?

Preparing for Class

Imagine you're a track star. Would you come to a meet without having trained—a lot? Of course not. Think of each class as an important event, like a track meet. To do your best, you'll need to prepare ahead of time, just like any athlete would. A great way to prepare is to follow the active learning steps listed below. Doing so before you hit the classroom will get you in shape and help make the time you spend in class much more valuable.

1. **Pay attention to your course syllabus.** A syllabus is not something you ignore or discard. It is an important, formal statement of course expectations, requirements, and procedures.

2. **Do the assigned reading.** Unless you do the assigned reading before class, you may not be able to follow the lecture. When you have done the reading, you will find that the lecture means more to you and class participation is a lot easier.

3. **Use additional materials provided by the instructor.** Many professors post lecture outlines or notes online. If you download and print these materials, they can create an organizational structure for note taking.

4. **Warm up for class.** Before class begins, preview by reviewing chapter introductions and summaries as well as your notes.

5. **Get organized.** Decide whether a three-ring binder, a spiral notebook, a digital device, or some combination of the three will work best for you. You might also want to create a folder for each course. If you use a laptop or tablet, create a Documents folder for each class, and carefully label the notes for each class meeting. ■

TRY IT!

SETTING GOALS ▷
Do All of Your Assigned Reading before Class

It's easy to think that doing the assigned reading is something you could skip or postpone until after class or just before the exam. However, that's putting the cart before the horse. Instructors assign reading prior to class for a reason: They want you to have a good understanding of the material *before* they expand on it during the lecture. They also want you to participate knowledgeably in class discussions—something you can't do unless you have done the reading. Material presented in textbooks or other sources will often give you the basics—a foundation that instructors will assume you've been exposed to before they give you their views and interpretations. Set a goal to do all assigned reading before you go to class; if you don't quite finish, complete your reading assignment as soon as possible after class.

◁ **Prepare Better by Working Together**
A great way to prepare for class is to discuss readings, lectures, and other course materials with your classmates. Some of them are sure to know the material, and they may understand concepts that you find challenging. At the same time, explaining concepts to your classmates will help you solidify your own understanding. © Peter Muller/Corbis.

Pay Attention! Listening, Participating, and Note Taking

Think about your conversations with friends and family members. When you listen carefully to what the other person says, you can communicate effectively. But if you "tune out," you won't have much to contribute, and you might get caught off guard if asked a direct question. The same is true in class—there is a give-and-take between students and the instructor, especially in classes where the instructor emphasizes interactive discussion, calls on students by name, shows students signs of approval and interest, and avoids criticizing anyone for an incorrect answer.

Listening carefully in class—really paying attention—is one of the most important skills you can develop. If you don't listen, you won't know what your instructor cares about, or what he or she has identified as the most important concepts—concepts that are likely to show up on tests. And of course, paying attention will help you remember and understand what you have heard, and it naturally will make you more likely to participate in a class, especially when you are prepared.

> Listening carefully in class— really paying attention—is one of the most important skills you can develop.

△ **Listen Up**
Develop your listening skills by practicing the eight steps to becoming a critical listener. Making use of these suggestions and reviewing your notes after class will help the information stick. © Hero Images/Corbis.

Listening Critically

When you explored your learning style in the preceding chapter, "Understanding How You Learn," was aural learning, which is learning by listening, one of your learning preferences? About one-third of us prefer to learn by listening. The other two-thirds do not. If you are taking classes in which instructors lecture all or part of the time, then aural (auditory) learning is a skill you will need to develop to be academically successful, whether or not learning by listening is your preference. Critical listening involves examining how we listen and evaluating what is said so that we can form our own ideas and opinions.

Step by Step to Becoming a Critical Listener

Here are some suggestions for being a critical listener:

1. **Be ready for the message.** Prepare yourself to hear, listen, and receive the message. If you have done the assigned reading, you will know the details in the text, so you can focus your notes on key concepts during the lecture.

2. **Listen for the main concepts and central ideas, not just facts and figures.** Facts will be easier to remember when you can place them in the context of a broader theme.

3. **Listen for new ideas.** Even if you know a lot about a topic, you can still learn something new.

4. **Repeat mentally.** Think about what you hear and restate it silently in your own words. If you don't understand a concept, ask for clarification.

5. **Decide whether what you have heard is not important, somewhat important, or very important.** If a point in the lecture is not important, let it go. If it is very important, highlight or underline the point in your notes. If it is somewhat important, relate it to a very important topic.

6. **Keep an open mind.** Your classes will expose you to new ideas and different perspectives. But instructors want you to think for yourself, and they do not expect you to agree with everything they or your classmates say.

7. **Listen to the entire message.** Concentrate on the big picture, but also pay attention to specific details and examples that can assist you in understanding and retaining the information.

8. **Sort, organize, and categorize.** When you listen, try to match what you are hearing with what you already know. Take an active role in deciding how best to recall what you are learning.

Step by Step to Becoming an Active Class Participant

In all your classes, try using the following techniques to ramp up your participation:

1. **Sit as close to the front as possible.** If students are seated by name and your name begins with a letter that comes toward the end of the alphabet, request to be moved up front.

2. **Keep your eyes on the instructor.** Sitting close to the front of the classroom will make this easier for you to do.

3. **Focus on the lecture.** Do not let yourself be distracted by other students.

4. **Raise your hand when you don't understand something.** But don't overdo it—the instructor and your peers will tire of too many questions that disrupt the class.

TRY IT!

FEELING CONNECTED ▷ Work Up the Nerve

Participating in class not only helps you learn but also shows your instructor that you're interested and engaged, and it will help you to connect to what is happening in each class and to become an active part of the learning experience. Like anything else, raising your hand for the first time might make you anxious. But after that first time, you'll likely find that contributing to class raises your interest and enjoyment. Think about the number of times during the past week you have raised your hand in class to ask a question. Do you ask questions frequently, or is it something you avoid? Make a list of the reasons you either do or don't ask questions in class. Would asking more questions help you earn better grades? How does participating in class make you feel about being there?

5. **Speak up in class.** It becomes easier every time you do so.

6. **Never feel that you're asking a "stupid" question.** You have a right to ask for an explanation.

7. **When the instructor calls on you to answer a question, don't bluff.** If you know the answer, give it. If not, just say so.

8. **If you've recently read a book or an article that is relevant to the class, bring it in.** You can provide additional information that was not covered in class.

Listening and note-taking skills are especially important in college because your instructors are likely to introduce material in class that your texts don't cover.

Taking Notes

Listening and note taking go hand-in-hand. Some students find it difficult to take notes while they are listening. As you gain experience, you will improve your ability to do these things simultaneously. If you find your notes are missing lots of important details, you may want to record the lecture (with the instructor's permission), but continue to take notes regardless. Listening to the recording will actually improve your auditory learning abilities.

Listening and note-taking skills are especially important in college because your instructors are likely to introduce material in class that your texts don't cover. This is one way that college is very different from most high schools. College and university professors have spent entire careers developing their own ideas that might add to—or even differ from—what you read in your textbooks. Be aware that an instructor often thinks that what is discussed in class is more important than what the text says. Chances are very good that your instructors will include much of the material they introduce in class on weekly quizzes and major exams.

While you are listening and taking notes, also be sure to participate in class discussion when you have something important to say or a question to ask. The instructor is always the best place to start for answers. You will tend to remember what you have said or answers to questions you have asked more easily than what you have only heard. If you have questions about your notes, you might choose to approach the instructor after class or go over your notes with a classmate.

Learning how to balance these three aspects of being in class will help you get the most out of each class meeting. ■

Approaches to Note Taking

Taking notes in college classes isn't optional. You must do it in order to make the best use of your class time, but first you have to decide on a system.

Cornell Format

In the Cornell format, you create a "recall" column on each page of your notebook by drawing a vertical line a few inches from the left border (see Figure 4.1). As you take notes during the lecture—whether writing down ideas, making lists, or using an outline or paragraph format—write only in the wider column on the right; leave the recall column blank. Then, as soon after class as feasible, sift through your notes and write down the main ideas and important details in the recall column. Many students have found the recall column to be an important study device for tests and exams.

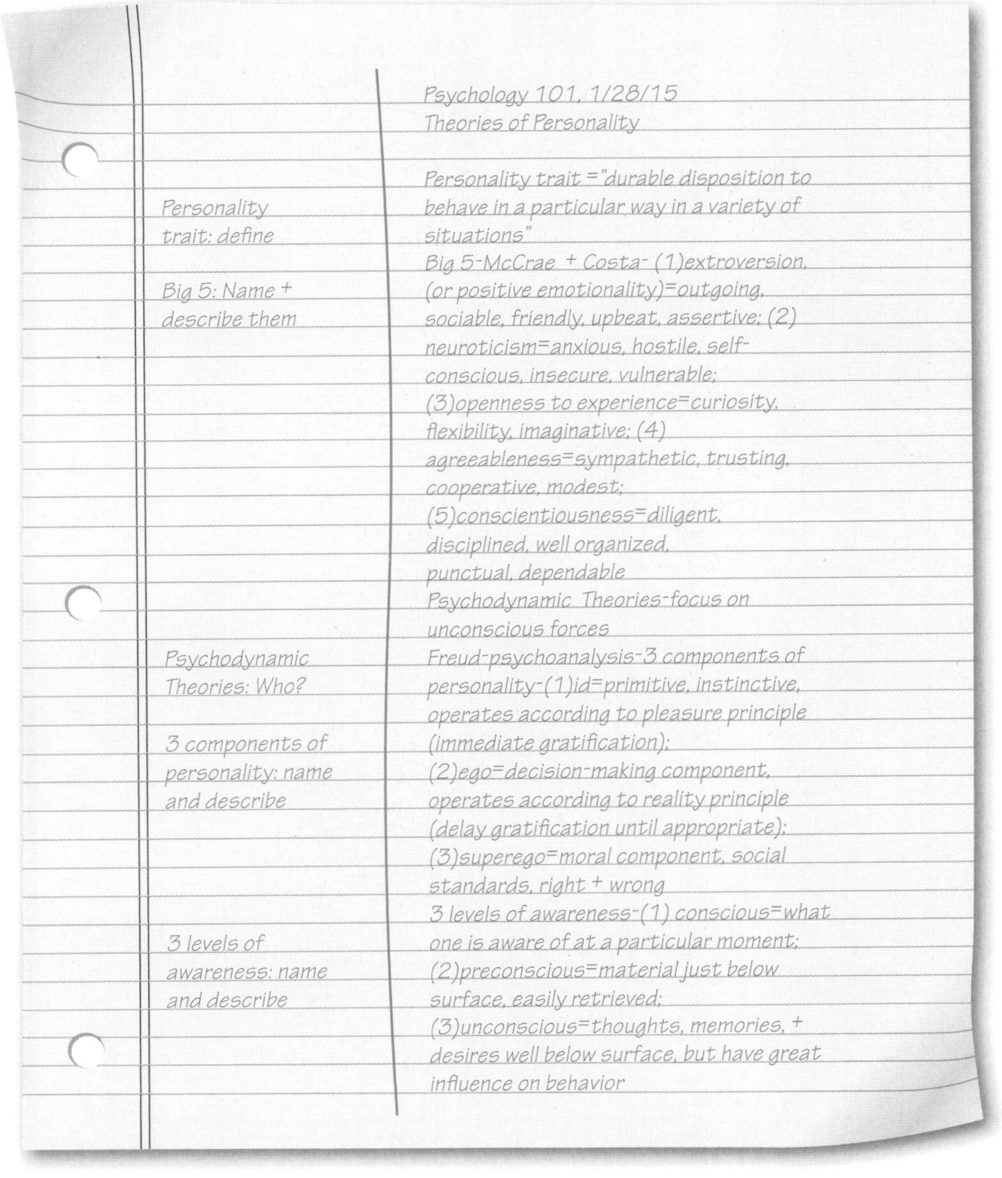

Figure 4.1 ◁ Note Taking in the Cornell Format

> Psychology 101, 1/28/15
> Theories of Personality
>
> | |
> |---|
> | *Personality trait: define* — Personality trait ="durable disposition to behave in a particular way in a variety of situations" |
> | *Big 5: Name + describe them* — Big 5-McCrae + Costa- (1)extroversion, (or positive emotionality)=outgoing, sociable, friendly, upbeat, assertive; (2) neuroticism=anxious, hostile, self-conscious, insecure, vulnerable; (3)openness to experience=curiosity, flexibility, imaginative; (4) agreeableness=sympathetic, trusting, cooperative, modest; (5)conscientiousness=diligent, disciplined, well organized, punctual, dependable |

Psychodynamic Theories-focus on unconscious forces

Psychodynamic Theories: Who? — Freud-psychoanalysis-3 components of personality-(1)id=primitive, instinctive, operates according to pleasure principle (immediate gratification);

3 components of personality: name and describe — (2)ego=decision-making component, operates according to reality principle (delay gratification until appropriate); (3)superego=moral component, social standards, right + wrong

3 levels of awareness: name and describe — 3 levels of awareness-(1) conscious=what one is aware of at a particular moment; (2)preconscious=material just below surface, easily retrieved; (3)unconscious=thoughts, memories, + desires well below surface, but have great influence on behavior

Outline Format

You probably already know what a formal outline looks like, with key ideas represented by Roman numerals and other ideas relating to each key idea represented in order by uppercase letters, numbers, and lowercase letters (see Figure 4.2). If you use this approach, try to determine how the instructor is outlining the lecture or presentation, and re-create that outline in your notes.

Figure 4.2 ▽ **Note Taking in the Outline Format**

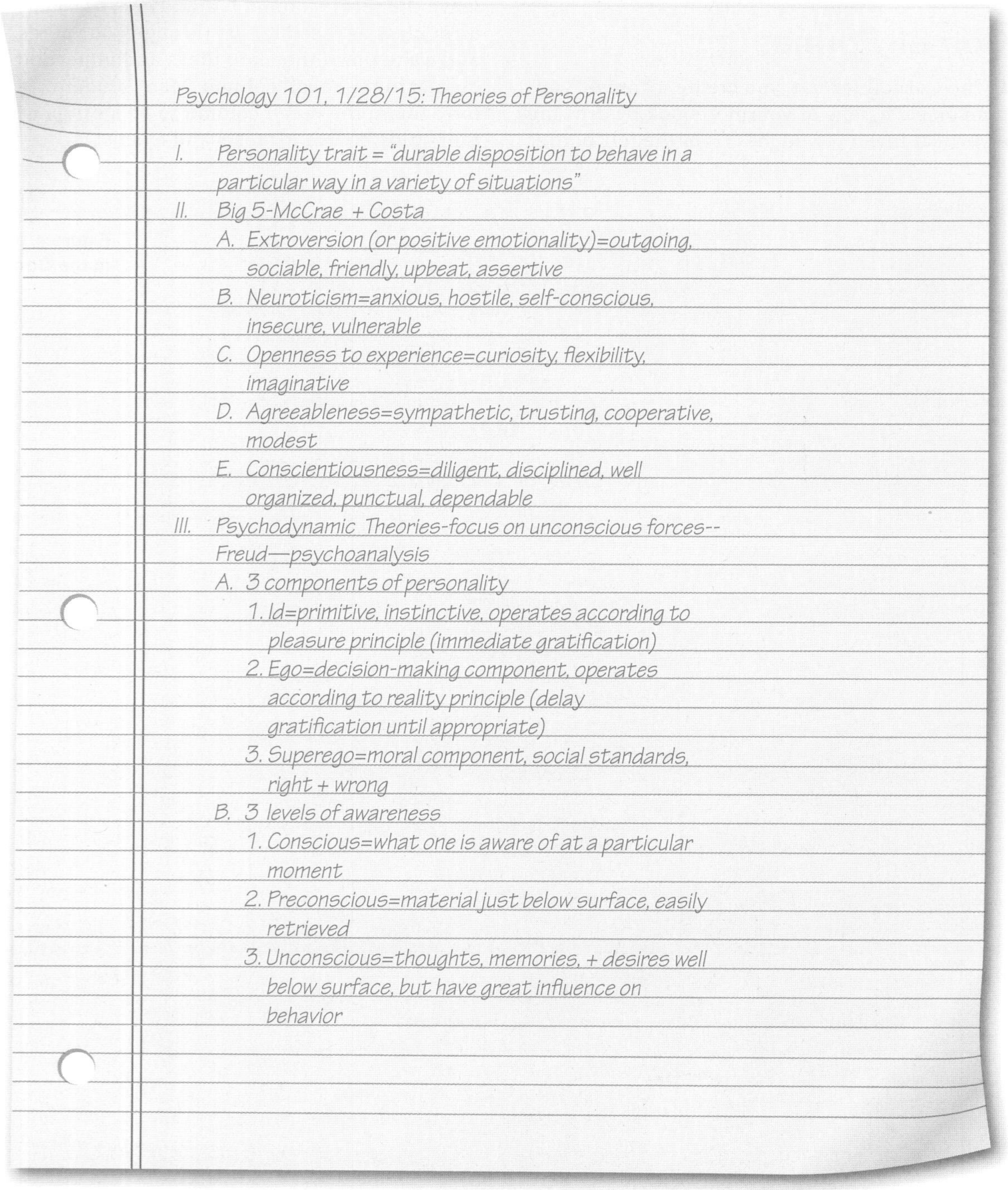

Psychology 101, 1/28/15: Theories of Personality

I.   Personality trait = "durable disposition to behave in a particular way in a variety of situations"

II. Big 5-McCrae + Costa
   A. Extroversion (or positive emotionality)=outgoing, sociable, friendly, upbeat, assertive
   B. Neuroticism=anxious, hostile, self-conscious, insecure, vulnerable
   C. Openness to experience=curiosity, flexibility, imaginative
   D. Agreeableness=sympathetic, trusting, cooperative, modest
   E. Conscientiousness=diligent, disciplined, well organized, punctual, dependable

III. Psychodynamic Theories-focus on unconscious forces-- Freud—psychoanalysis
   A. 3 components of personality
      1. Id=primitive, instinctive, operates according to pleasure principle (immediate gratification)
      2. Ego=decision-making component, operates according to reality principle (delay gratification until appropriate)
      3. Superego=moral component, social standards, right + wrong
   B. 3 levels of awareness
      1. Conscious=what one is aware of at a particular moment
      2. Preconscious=material just below surface, easily retrieved
      3. Unconscious=thoughts, memories, + desires well below surface, but have great influence on behavior

Paragraph Format

The paragraph format involves writing detailed paragraphs, with each paragraph containing a summary of a particular topic (see Figure 4.3). You might decide to write summary paragraphs when you are taking notes on what you are reading. This method might not work as well for class notes, however, because it's difficult to summarize a topic until your instructor has covered it completely.

Figure 4.3 ▽ Note Taking in the Paragraph Format

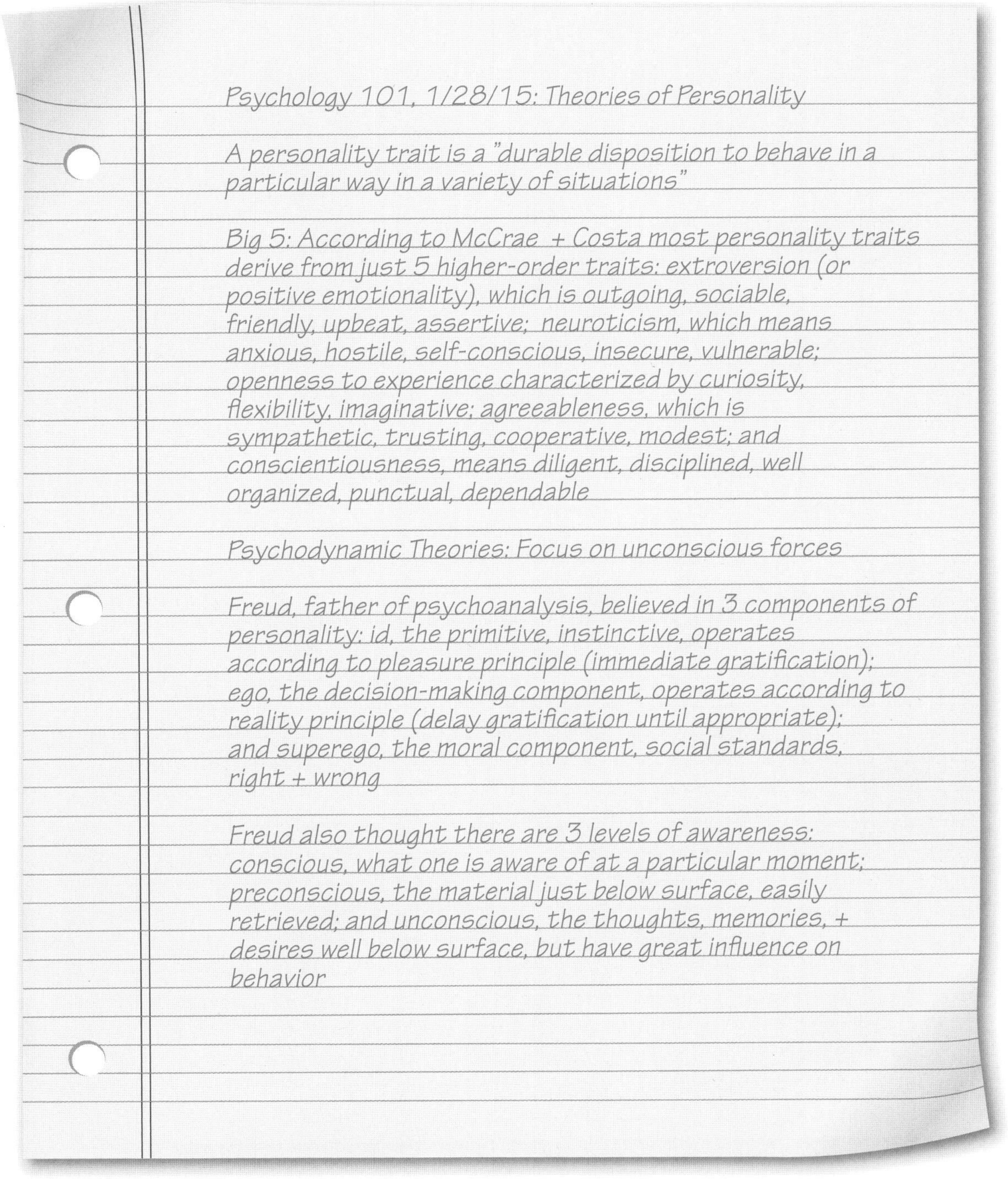

Psychology 101, 1/28/15: Theories of Personality

A personality trait is a "durable disposition to behave in a particular way in a variety of situations"

Big 5: According to McCrae + Costa most personality traits derive from just 5 higher-order traits: extroversion (or positive emotionality), which is outgoing, sociable, friendly, upbeat, assertive; neuroticism, which means anxious, hostile, self-conscious, insecure, vulnerable; openness to experience characterized by curiosity, flexibility, imaginative; agreeableness, which is sympathetic, trusting, cooperative, modest; and conscientiousness, means diligent, disciplined, well organized, punctual, dependable

Psychodynamic Theories: Focus on unconscious forces

Freud, father of psychoanalysis, believed in 3 components of personality: id, the primitive, instinctive, operates according to pleasure principle (immediate gratification); ego, the decision-making component, operates according to reality principle (delay gratification until appropriate); and superego, the moral component, social standards, right + wrong

Freud also thought there are 3 levels of awareness: conscious, what one is aware of at a particular moment; preconscious, the material just below surface, easily retrieved; and unconscious, the thoughts, memories, + desires well below surface, but have great influence on behavior

List Format

The list format can be effective when taking notes on terms and definitions, sequences, or facts (see Figure 4.4). It's easy to use lists in combination with the Cornell format, with key terms on the left and their definitions and explanations on the right.

Figure 4.4 ▽ Note Taking in the List Format

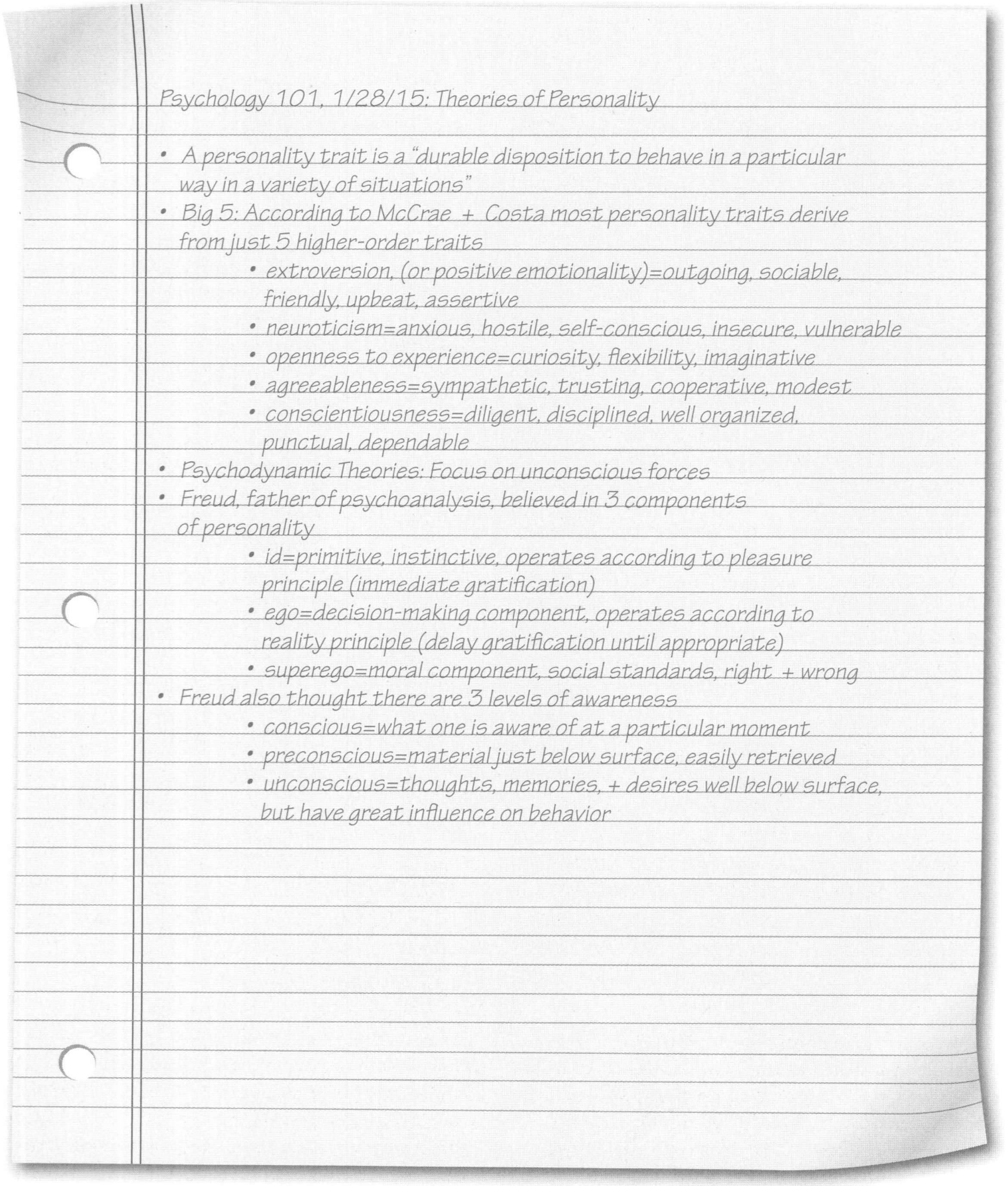

Psychology 101, 1/28/15: Theories of Personality

- *A personality trait is a "durable disposition to behave in a particular way in a variety of situations"*
- *Big 5: According to McCrae + Costa most personality traits derive from just 5 higher-order traits*
    - *extroversion, (or positive emotionality)=outgoing, sociable, friendly, upbeat, assertive*
    - *neuroticism=anxious, hostile, self-conscious, insecure, vulnerable*
    - *openness to experience=curiosity, flexibility, imaginative*
    - *agreeableness=sympathetic, trusting, cooperative, modest*
    - *conscientiousness=diligent, disciplined, well organized, punctual, dependable*
- *Psychodynamic Theories: Focus on unconscious forces*
- *Freud, father of psychoanalysis, believed in 3 components of personality*
    - *id=primitive, instinctive, operates according to pleasure principle (immediate gratification)*
    - *ego=decision-making component, operates according to reality principle (delay gratification until appropriate)*
    - *superego=moral component, social standards, right + wrong*
- *Freud also thought there are 3 levels of awareness*
    - *conscious=what one is aware of at a particular moment*
    - *preconscious=material just below surface, easily retrieved*
    - *unconscious=thoughts, memories, + desires well below surface, but have great influence on behavior*

Taking Notes in Class

Once you've decided on an approach to note taking, you'll need to actually use it in class. To do so effectively, try these techniques:

1. **Identify the main ideas.** Well-organized lectures always contain key points. The first principle of effective note taking is to write down the main ideas around which the lecture is built. Some instructors announce the purpose of a lecture or offer an outline, thus providing the class with the skeleton of main ideas, followed by the details. Others develop overhead transparencies or PowerPoint presentations and may make these materials available on a class Web site before the lecture.

2. **Don't try to write down everything.** Attempting to record every word from a class lecture or discussion will distract you from an essential activity: thinking. If you're an active listener, you will ultimately have shorter but more useful notes.

3. **Don't be thrown by a disorganized lecturer.** When a lecturer is disorganized, it's your job to organize what he or she says into general and specific frameworks. When the order is not apparent, indicate the gaps in your notes. After the lecture, consult your reading material, your study team, or a classmate to fill in these gaps, or visit the instructor during office hours with your questions.

4. **Prepare to use your notes as a study tool.** As soon after class as feasible, preferably within an hour or two, sift through your notes and create a recall column to identify the main ideas and important details for tests and examinations. In anticipation of using your notes later, treat your notes as part of an exam preparation system.

Make Adjustments for Different Classes

As you become comfortable with the different systems for note taking, you will learn to adjust your approach depending on the kind of class. Nonlecture courses pose special challenges because they tend to be less organized and more free-flowing. Be ready to adapt your note-taking methods to match the situation. Group discussion has become a popular way to teach in college because it involves active learning. On your campus you may also have Supplemental Instruction (SI) classes that provide further opportunity to discuss the information presented in lectures. Take advantage of this option if it's available, and keep a record of what's happening in such classes.

Students who participate in Supplemental Instruction predictably earn higher grade point averages than students who do not. But it doesn't work to attend only a few SI sessions. You have to attend regularly in order to reap the benefits. At some colleges, Supplemental Instruction isn't optional—it's required for certain courses, especially those in which students tend to struggle. Generally these courses are a "gateway" to premed, science, engineering, and math majors. But even if SI isn't required, be sure to take advantage of this valuable option, and keep a written record of what is happening in SI classes.

Assume you are taking notes in a problem-solving group assignment. You would begin your notes by asking yourself, "What is the problem?" and writing the problem down. As the discussion progresses, you would list the solutions offered. These solutions would be your main ideas. The important details might include the positive and negative aspects of each view or solution. The important thing to remember when taking notes in nonlecture courses is that you need to record the information presented by your classmates as well as by the instructor and to consider all reasonable ideas, even though they may differ from your own.

How to organize the notes you take in a class discussion depends on the purpose or form of the discussion. It usually makes good sense to begin with the list of issues or topics that the discussion leader announces. Another approach is to list the questions that the participants raise for discussion. If the discussion is an exploration of the reasons for and against a particular argument, it's reasonable to divide your notes into columns or sections for pros and cons. When conflicting views arise in the discussion, record the different perspectives and the rationales behind them. ■

Strategies for Note Taking in Quantitative Courses

Taking notes in math and science courses can be different from taking notes in other types of classes, where it may not be a good idea to try to write down every word the instructor says. In a quantitative course, quote the instructor's words as precisely as possible. Technical terms often have exact meanings and cannot be paraphrased.

Quantitative courses such as mathematics, chemistry, and physics often build on each other from term to term and from year to year. When you take notes in these courses, you are likely to need to refer to them in future terms. For example, when taking organic chemistry, you may need to go back to notes taken in earlier chemistry courses. This review process can be particularly important when time has passed since your last course, such as after a summer break. Here are some ideas for getting organized:

1. **Create separate binders for each course.** Keep your notes and supplementary materials (such as instructors' handouts) for each course in a separate three-ring binder labeled with the course number and name.

2. **Download materials from your instructor *before* class.** Your instructor may post a broad range of materials on a class Web site, such as notes, outlines, diagrams, charts, graphs, and other visual explanations. Be sure to download these materials before class and to bring them with you. You can save yourself considerable time and distraction during the lecture if you do not have to copy complicated graphs and diagrams while the instructor is talking.

3. **Take notes only on the front of each piece of loose-leaf paper**. Later, you can use the back of each sheet to add further details, annotations, corrections, comments, questions, and a summary of each lecture. Alternatively, once you've placed what have now become the left-hand pages in the binder, you can use them the same way that you would use the recall column in the Cornell format, noting key ideas to be used for testing yourself when preparing for exams.

4. **Listen carefully to other students' questions and the instructor's answers**. Take notes on the discussion and during question-and-answer periods.

5. **Use asterisks, exclamation points, question marks, or symbols of your own** to highlight important points or questions in your notes.

6. **Consider taking your notes in pencil or erasable pen, even if you prefer to type your notes.** In science and math classes it can be hard to create diagrams and equations onscreen.

7. **Write down any equations, formulas, diagrams, charts, graphs, and definitions that the instructor puts on the board or screen**, and expect that you'll need to erase and make changes. You want to keep your notes as neat as possible.

8. **Use standard symbols, abbreviations, and scientific notation.**

9. **Write down all worked problems and examples, step by step.** These often provide the format for exam questions. Actively try to solve each problem yourself as it is solved at the front of the class. Be sure that you can follow the logic and understand the sequence of steps.

10. **Organize your notes in your binder chronologically.** Then create separate tabbed sections for homework, lab assignments, returned tests, and other materials.

11. **Label and store handouts immediately.** If the instructor distributes handouts in class, label them and place them in your binder either immediately before or immediately after the notes for that day.

12. **Refer to the textbook after class.** The text may contain diagrams and other visual representations that are more accurate than those you are able to draw while taking notes in class.

13. **Keep your binders for math and science courses until you graduate** (or even longer if there is any chance that you will attend graduate school in the future). They will serve as beneficial review materials for later classes in math and science sequences and for preparing for standardized tests such as the Graduate Record Exam (GRE) or the Medical College Admission Test (MCAT).

Keep It Fresh by Reviewing Your Notes

Most forgetting of information takes place within the first twenty-four hours of encountering it, a phenomenon known as "the forgetting curve." If you do not review your notes almost immediately after class, it can be difficult to retrieve the material later. In two weeks, you will have forgotten up to 70 percent of the material or information! Don't let the forgetting curve take its toll on you. As soon after class as possible, review your notes and fill in the details you still remember but missed writing down. If you are an aural learner, you might want to repeat your notes out loud.

For interactive learners, the best way to learn something might be to teach it to someone else. You will understand something better and remember it longer if you try to explain it. Explaining material to someone else helps you discover your own reactions and uncover gaps in your comprehension. (Asking and answering questions in class can also provide you with the feedback you need to make certain your understanding is accurate.) Now you're ready to embed the major points from your notes in your memory. Use the following three important steps for remembering the key points from the lecture.

1. **Write down the main ideas.** For 5 or 10 minutes, quickly review your notes and select key words or phrases that will act as labels or tags for main ideas and key information in your notes.

2. **Recite your ideas out loud.** Recite a brief version of what you understand from the class. If you don't have a few minutes after class when you can concentrate on reviewing your notes, find some other time during that same day to review what you have written. You might also want to ask your instructor to glance at your notes to determine whether you have identified the major ideas.

3. **Review your notes from the previous class just before the next class session.** As you sit in the classroom waiting for the lecture to begin, use the time to quickly review your notes from the previous class session. As discussed above, this is an effective way to prepare for class. This review will put you in tune with the lecture that is about to begin and prompt you to ask questions about material from the previous lecture that might not have been clear to you.

Stay Put ◁ As the room empties out at the end of class, stay put and review your notes, if your schedule allows it. You can steer clear of the forgetting curve by looking over your notes from what was just covered and filling in the gaps. You can also prepare for your next class before you get on your way. © Whisson/Jordan /Corbis.

Class Notes and Homework

Good class notes can help you complete homework assignments, too. Follow these steps.

1. **Take 10 minutes to review your class notes.** Skim the notes and put a question mark next to anything you do not understand at first reading. Draw stars next to topics that are especially important. The Try It on this page is devoted to this helpful tip.

2. **Do a warm-up for your homework.** Before starting the assignment, look through your notes again. Use a separate sheet of paper to rework examples, problems, or exercises. If there is related assigned material in the textbook, review it. Go back to the text examples. Cover the solutions and attempt to answer each question or complete each problem.

3. **Do assigned problems and answer assigned questions.** When you start your homework, read each question or problem and ask: What am I supposed to find or find out? What is essential and what is extraneous? Read each problem several times and restate it in your own words. Work the problem without referring to your notes or the text.

4. **Don't give up.** When you encounter a problem or question that you cannot readily handle, move on only after a reasonable effort. After you have reached the end of the assignment, return to the items that stumped you. Try once more, and then take a break. You may need to mull over a particularly difficult problem for several days.

5. **Complete your work.** When you finish an assignment, consider what you learned from the exercise. Think about how the problems and questions were different from one another, which strategies you used to solve them, and what form the answers took. Review any material you have not mastered.

Most forgetting of information takes place within the first twenty-four hours of encountering it.

Ask the professor, a classmate, your study group, someone in the campus learning center, or a tutor to help you with difficult problems and questions. ■

TRY IT!

MANAGING TIME ▷ **Review Your Notes before Class**

Depending on the amount of time between class sessions—two days, a weekend, or longer—you might find that it's hard to remember exactly what happened in the previous class. That's why good class notes are so important. Before class, take 10 or 15 minutes to read over your notes from the previous class, and draw stars next to topics that you remember were especially important. Put a question mark next to anything you wrote down but don't completely understand. This review will get you ready for the lecture that is about to begin and remind you to ask questions about material from the previous lecture that isn't clear to you. If you find yourself confused about something the instructor said, you can be sure that other classmates are confused as well. Speaking up to clarify any confusing points or misunderstandings you might have is a great way for you to participate in class.

What if you have three classes in a row and no time for studying between them? Recall and recite as soon after class as possible. Review the most recent class first. Never delay recall and recitation longer than one day; if you do, it will take you longer to review, select main ideas, and recite. With practice, you can quickly complete the review of your main ideas from your notes, perhaps between classes, during lunch, or while riding the bus.

Chapter Review

Steps to Success: Getting the Most Out of Class

○ **Prepare for class before class; it is one of the simplest and most important things you can do.** Read your notes from the previous class and do the assigned readings.

○ **Practice the behaviors of effective learning during class.** These behaviors include listening attentively, taking notes, and contributing to class discussion.

○ **As you review your notes before each class, make a list of any questions you have and ask both your instructor and fellow students for help.** Other students will appreciate your asking these questions. Don't wait until just before the exam to try to find answers to your questions.

○ **Identify the different types of note taking covered in this chapter and decide which one(s) might work best for you.** We recommend the Cornell method; however, any method can work as long as you use it consistently. Compare your notes with those of another good student to make sure that you are covering the most important points.

Applying what you've learned . . .

Now that you have read and discussed this chapter, consider how you can apply what you have learned to your academic and personal lives. The following prompts will help you reflect on the material and its relevance to you both now and in the future.

1. How would you rate your current level of participation in the classes you are taking this term? Do you speak up, contribute to discussion, and ask questions, or do you daydream or sit silently? Do your instructors encourage you to participate, or do they seem to intentionally discourage your involvement? Research finds that students learn more when they contribute to class discussions and feel comfortable asking and responding to questions. Think about how your own level of participation—whether it's high or low—relates to learning and enjoyment in the classes you're currently taking.

2. Review the content on note-taking systems in this chapter. How would you describe your current method of taking notes? Are you organized or disorganized? How is your current method of taking notes similar to or different from the methods suggested in "Approaches to Note Taking"? Do your notes help you study for exams? If not, what suggestions from this chapter might help you become a better note taker?

Create Community

GO TO ▷ The learning assistance center: If you need help with developing strategies for learning and good study skills. Students at all levels use campus learning centers to improve in the skills discussed in this chapter.

GO TO ▷ Fellow college students: If you need help finding a tutor or joining a study group. Often the best help you can get is from your fellow students—look for the most serious, purposeful, and directed students.

GO ONLINE TO ▷ This article: If you want some tips on overcoming a fear of public speaking: http://voices.yahoo.com/10-tips-college-students-fear-public-8422175.html.

NOW . . . How do you measure up?

1. I do a good job in identifying key points of lectures and discussions and in writing them down in my notes.
   - ○ Agree
   - ○ Don't Know
   - ○ Disagree

2. When I don't understand something, I know how important it is to ask questions in class— even in large classes.
   - ○ Agree
   - ○ Don't Know
   - ○ Disagree

3. In math or science courses students should write down everything the instructor puts on the board or screen.
   - ○ Agree
   - ○ Don't Know
   - ○ Disagree

4. I know that one of the most effective ways to learn is to join study groups for each of my classes.
   - ○ Agree
   - ○ Don't Know
   - ○ Disagree

How do your answers here compare to your responses to the quiz you took at the start of the chapter? Which sections of this chapter left a strong impression on you? What listening and note-taking strategies have you begun to use, and are they working? What other strategies will you commit to trying?

69
Four-Step Plan for Active Reading

75
Different Courses—Different Kinds of Textbooks

79
Improving Your Reading

Reading for Success

Why is reading a college textbook more challenging than reading a high school text or reading for pleasure? The answer is that college textbooks are loaded with terms, concepts, and complex information that you are expected to learn on your own in a short time. The amount of material you will be expected to read, especially for courses like English literature, history, psychology, and sociology, may come as a surprise. To accomplish this, you will find it helpful and worthwhile to learn and use the active reading strategies in this chapter, which together form a textbook reading plan that will help you get the most out of your college reading.

How much reading did you do in high school? Many college students tell us that they did very little reading — only what they were required to do. Today, many readers opt for online sources, which tend to be shorter and

often use more informal language. But whatever your previous reading habits might have been, college will require a higher level of focus and attention. Some students may be able to read quickly but find that their comprehension level is low. While you're in college, you will find that occasionally you need to reread a particularly difficult set of pages more than once so that you really understand the concepts. Depending on how much reading you did before coming to college—reading for pleasure, reading for classes, reading for work—you might find that reading is your favorite way to learn, or it may be your least favorite. Even if it *isn't* your favorite thing to do, however, reading is absolutely essential to doing well in college and in life. Any professional career that you might choose — such as medicine, engineering, law, accounting, or teaching — will require you to do lots of reading.

How do you measure up?

1. It's important to skim or "preview" a textbook chapter before beginning to read.
   - ○ Agree
   - ○ Don't Know
   - ○ Disagree

2. It's not a good idea to underline, highlight, or annotate the text when reading a page or section for the very first time.
   - ○ Agree
   - ○ Don't Know
   - ○ Disagree

3. Taking notes on textbook readings helps keep up with key ideas without having to read the material over and over.
   - ○ Agree
   - ○ Don't Know
   - ○ Disagree

4. When reading a textbook with lots of new words, it's a good idea to have a dictionary close by to check word meanings.
   - ○ Agree
   - ○ Don't Know
   - ○ Disagree

Review the items you marked "Don't Know" or "Disagree." Pay special attention to these topics in this chapter—you will find motivating strategies to develop in these areas. A follow-up quiz at the end of the chapter will prompt you to consider what you have learned.

You Can't Put a Price on Knowledge

△ **Titus Indra**

Santhosh Kumar/Shutterstock.

The day after I registered for classes and got my list of assigned textbooks, I looked up the books on the campus online bookstore. My biology textbook alone was $200. I figured borrowing the textbook from a classmate or from the library would be OK. I could even photocopy a few sections if necessary, or I could order an old edition online. We'd probably cover most chapters in class anyway.

That was the plan, but because we had a ton of assigned reading, nobody wanted to share a book. Most of my classmates were premed and studied nonstop. My lab partner said that I could borrow his book on *Saturday nights* if I returned it by 8 a.m. each Sunday. The 400-page beast was as thick as a toaster, and photocopying was a pain.

I realized three things: (1) the lone library copy would never be available; (2) old editions were marked up and lacked important updates; and (3) a huge part of learning in college involves teaching yourself. I went to see my professor during her office hours. She suggested I buy an e-book version from the publisher's Web site, which saved me some money. It felt good to have the book on my iPad so I could stay on pace with the syllabus.

Titus demonstrated poor judgment at the start, but he showed initiative in meeting with his biology instructor to figure out a solution that worked for him before he fell too far behind. Why is it so important to keep up with your outside reading assignments in college?

Four-Step Plan for Active Reading

A textbook reading plan can pay off by increasing your focus and concentration, promoting greater understanding of what you read, and preparing you to study for tests and exams. The plan you'll learn in this section is based on four main steps: previewing, reading and marking, reading with concentration, and reviewing.

Step 1: Previewing

When you read actively, you use strategies that help you stay focused. The first strategy, previewing, will give you an idea or overview of what is to come in the chapter. By previewing, you get the big picture—you see what you are about to read, and you can begin to consider how it's connected to what you already know and to the material the instructor is covering in class. Begin your preview by reading the title of the chapter. Next, skim the learning objectives (if they appear at the beginning of the chapter) and the introductory paragraphs, and then scan the list of key terms and read the summary at the end of the chapter (if the chapter includes either of these features). Skim the chapter headings and subheadings. Finally, look for any study exercises at the end of the chapter.

As part of your preview, check the number of pages in the chapter. Estimate how many pages you can reasonably expect to cover in your first 50-minute study period. You may require more or less time to read different types of textbooks. For example, depending on your interests and previous knowledge, you may be able to read a psychology text more quickly than a foreign language text that presents a whole new system of words and meanings.

As you preview the text, look for connections between the text material and the related lecture material. Call to mind the terms and concepts that you remember from the lecture. Use these strategies to warm up. Ask yourself: Why am I reading this? What do I need to learn? You'll find that if you have previewed a chapter, you will be able to read it more quickly and with greater comprehension.

When you read actively, you use strategies that help you stay focused.

◁ **Be Prepared**
Go through the textbook before class and see what you think the main points might be. Later you'll be able to compare your thoughts on the main points with what your instructor emphasized. Was there any overlap, and if so, where? What did you miss?

Map It!

Mapping a chapter as you preview it provides a visual guide for how different chapter ideas fit together. Because about 75 percent of students identify themselves as visual learners, mapping is an excellent learning tool.

To map a chapter while you are previewing, draw either a wheel structure or a branching structure (see Figure 5.1). In the wheel structure, place the central idea of the chapter in the circle. You should find the central idea in the chapter introduction; it may also be apparent in the chapter title. For example, the central idea of this chapter is "reading successfully." Place secondary ideas on the spokes radiating from the circle, and draw offshoots of those ideas on the lines attached to the spokes. In the branching structure, put the main idea (most likely the chapter title) at the top, followed by supporting ideas on the second tier, and so forth. If you prefer a more step-by-step visual image, make an outline of the headings and subheadings of the chapter (see Figure 5.2).

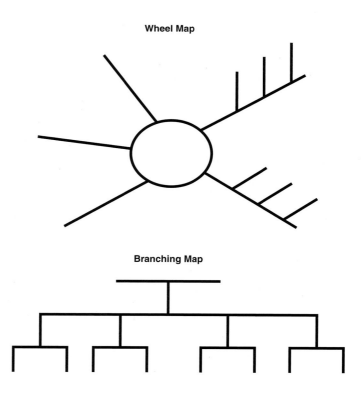

Wheel Map

Branching Map

I. Active Reading

    A. Previewing: Get lay of the land, skim
        1. Mapping
        2. Outlining or listing
    B. Reading and marking textbooks: Read and think
        BEFORE marking
        1. Underlining
        2. Highlighting
        3. Annotating (margin notes)
    C. Reading with concentration
        1. Focus! Find proper location, turn off phone, set aside
           blocks of time with breaks, set study goals
        2. Monitor comprehension
    D. Reviewing: Review each week

Figure 5.1 △ Wheel and Branching Maps

Figure 5.2 ◁ Sample Outline

Figure 5.2 shows how a student might have outlined the first section of this chapter.

Step 2: Reading and Marking

Marking your textbooks is another active reading strategy that will help you concentrate on the material as you read. Marking means underlining, highlighting, or using margin notes or annotations. Figure 5.3 provides an example of many of these methods. No matter which method you prefer, remember these important guidelines:

1. **Read and think before you mark.** Finish reading a section before you decide which are the most important ideas and concepts. When you read a text for the first time, everything can seem important. After you complete a section, reflect on it to identify the key ideas. Ask yourself: What are the most important ideas? What will I see on the test? This step can help you avoid marking

---

Figure 5.3 ▽ Examples of Reading and Marking

Using a combination of highlighting and margin notes, the reader has made the content of this page easy to review. Without reading the text, note the highlighted words and phrases and the margin notes, and see how much information you can gather from them. Then read the text itself. Does the markup serve as a study aid? Does it cover the essential points? Would you have marked this page any differently? Why or why not?

Source: "The Stress of Adapting to a New Culture." Adapted from *Psychology*, 6th ed., p. 534, by D. H. Hockenbury and S. E. Hockenbury. © 2013 by Worth Publishers. Used with permission.

CULTURE AND HUMAN BEHAVIOR

The Stress of Adapting to a New Culture

differences affecting cultural stress

Refugees, immigrants, and even international students are often unprepared for the dramatically different values, language, food, customs, and climate that await them in their new land. The process of changing one's values and customs as a result of contact with another culture is referred to as *acculturation*. **Acculturative stress** is the stress that results from the pressure of adapting to a new culture (Sam & Berry, 2010).

acceptance of new culture reduces stress

also speaking new language, education, & social support

Many factors can influence the degree of acculturative stress that a person experiences. For example, when the new society accepts ethnic and cultural diversity, acculturative stress is reduced (Mana & others, 2009). The transition is also eased when the person has some familiarity with the new language and customs, advanced education, and social support from friends, family members, and cultural associations (Schwartz & others, 2010). Acculturative stress is also lower if the new culture is similar to the culture of origin.

how attitudes affect stress

Cross-cultural psychologist John Berry (2003, 2006) has found that a person's attitudes are important in determining how much acculturative stress is experienced (Sam & Berry, 2010). When people encounter a new cultural environment, they are faced with two questions: (1) Should I seek positive relations with the dominant society? (2) Is my original cultural identity of value to me, and should I try to maintain it?

4 patterns of acculturation

The answers produce one of four possible patterns of acculturation: integration, assimilation, separation, or marginalization (see the diagram). Each pattern represents a different way of coping with the stress of adapting to a new culture (Berry, 1994, 2003). 1 *Integrated* individuals continue to value their original cultural customs but also seek to become part of the dominant society. They embrace a *bicultural* identity (Hunyh & others, 2011). Biculturalism is associated with higher self-esteem and lower levels of depression, anxiety, and stress, suggesting that the bicultural identity may be the most adaptive acculturation pattern (Schwartz & others, 2010). The successfully integrated individual's level of acculturative stress will be low (Lee, 2010). 2 *Assimilated* individuals give up their old cultural identity and try to become part of the new society. They adopt the customs and social values of the new environment, and abandon their original cultural traditions.

possible rejection by both cultures

Assimilation usually involves a moderate level of stress, partly because it involves a psychological loss—one's previous cultural identity. People who follow this pattern also face the possibility of being rejected either by members of the majority culture or by members of their original culture (Schwartz & others, 2010). The

Acculturative Stress Acculturative stress can be reduced when immigrants learn the language and customs of their newly adopted home. Here, two friends, one from China, one from Cuba, help each other in an English class in Miami, Florida.

process of learning new behaviors and suppressing old behaviors can also be moderately stressful.

3 Individuals who follow the pattern of *separation* maintain their cultural identity and avoid contact with the new culture. They may refuse to learn the new language, live in a neighborhood that is primarily populated by others of the same ethnic background, and socialize only with members of their own ethnic group.

In some cases, separation is not voluntary, but is due to the dominant society's unwillingness to accept the new immigrants. Thus, it can be the result of discrimination. Whether voluntary or involuntary, the level of acculturative stress associated with separation tends to be high.

4 Finally, the *marginalized* person lacks cultural and psychological contact with *both* his traditional cultural group and the culture of his new society. By taking the path of marginalization, he lost the important features of his traditional culture but has not replaced them with a new cultural identity.

Although rare, the path of marginalization is associated with the greatest degree of acculturative stress. Marginalized individuals are stuck in an unresolved conflict between their traditional culture and the new society, and may feel as if they don't really belong anywhere. Fortunately, only a small percentage of immigrants fall into this category (Schwartz & others, 2010).

*separation may be self-imposed or discriminating

higher stress with separation

*marginalized = higher level of stress

	Question 1: Should I seek positive relations with the dominant society?	
	Yes	**No**
Question 2: Is my original cultural identity of value to me, and should I try to maintain it? **Yes**	Integration	Separation
No	Assimilation	Marginalization

Patterns of Adapting to a New Culture
According to cross-cultural psychologist John Berry, there are four basic patterns of adapting to a new culture (Sam & Berry, 2010). Which pattern is followed depends on how the person responds to the two key questions shown.

too much material. On a practical note, if you find that you have made mistakes in how you have highlighted, or if another student has already highlighted your textbook, select a different color highlighter to use.

2. **Take notes while you read and mark.** Think about it: If you rely on marking alone, you will have to read all the pages again. But if you take notes while you preview in addition to making a map, an outline, a list, or flash cards (see Figure 5.4), you are actively learning and also creating tools you can use to review, whether on your own or with a friend or study group.

3. **Avoid developing bad habits with marking.** Highlights and underlines are intended to pull your eye only to important terms and facts. For some, highlighting or underlining is actually a form of procrastination. If you are reading through the material but aren't planning to learn it until sometime later, you might be giving yourself a false sense of security and thus doing yourself more harm than good. And don't highlight or underline nearly everything you read; you won't be able to identify important concepts quickly if they're lost in a sea of color or underlines. Ask yourself whether your highlighting or underlining is helping you be more active in your learning process. If not, you might want to try a different

technique, such as making margin notes or annotations. When you force yourself to put something in your own words while taking notes, you not only are predicting exam questions but also are evaluating whether you can answer them.

Step 3: Reading with Concentration

Instructors cannot provide all you need to know about an academic topic only by lecturing. Learning in any class will also depend on your doing the assigned textbook reading. Reading a college textbook, especially if the material is completely unfamiliar or highly technical, is a challenge for most new college students, but using tested strategies such as those outlined here will make you a more effective reader.

Focus, Focus, Focus. Like many students, you may have trouble concentrating or understanding the content when reading textbooks. Many factors may affect your ability to concentrate and to understand texts: the time of day, your energy level, your interest in the material, and your study location.

Consider the following suggestions, and decide which would be most helpful in improving your reading ability.

- Find a quiet study location. If you are on campus, the library is your best option. Set your mobile phone to mute with vibrate off, and store it where you can't see it. If you are reading an electronic document, download the information and disconnect from the network to reduce online distractions.

- Read in blocks of time, with short breaks in between. Reading in small blocks throughout the day instead of cramming in all your reading at the end of the day should help you understand and retain the material more easily.

- Set goals for your study period, such as "I will read twenty pages of my psychology text in the next 50 minutes." Reward yourself with a 10-minute break after each 50-minute study period.

- If you're having trouble concentrating or staying awake, take a quick walk around the library or down the hall. Stretch and take

---

TRY IT!

SETTING GOALS ▷
Practice Marking a Chapter

You probably have reading assignments for every class. Have you been marking your assigned chapters to identify the most important points? If so, have you been following the suggestions in the list above? If marking chapters is not something you do when you study, set a goal for this week to mark every chapter you are assigned to read. You can underline, use margin notes, or use a light-colored highlighter—one that you can see through to read the text. Try using a different method in each chapter to see which approach works best for you.

some deep breaths and think positively about your study goals. Then resume studying.

- Jot study questions in the margins, take notes, or recite key ideas. Reread confusing parts of the text, and make a note to ask your instructor for clarification.

- Focus on the important portions of the text. Pay particular attention to the first and last sentences of paragraphs and to words in italics or in bold print.

- Use the glossary in the text or a dictionary to define unfamiliar terms.

Monitor Your Comprehension. An important aspect of textbook reading is monitoring your comprehension. As you read, ask yourself whether you understand the material, and check your understanding with a study partner. If you don't understand it, stop and reread the material. Look up words that you don't know. Try to clarify the main points and their relationship to one another.

After you have read the first section of the chapter and marked or taken notes on the key ideas, proceed to each subsequent section until you have finished the chapter. After you have completed each section—and before you move on to the next section—ask yourself again: What are the key ideas? What will I see on the test? At the end of each section, try to guess what information the author will present in the

TRY IT!

FEELING CONNECTED ▷

Two (or More) Are Better Than One

One way to get immediate feedback on your comprehension of your reading is to work with a study partner or study group. The give-and-take that you will experience will improve your learning and your motivation. Another way that study group members can work together is to divide up a chapter for previewing and studying and then get together later to teach the material to one another.

following section. Effective reading should lead you from one section to the next, with each new section adding to your understanding.

Ask yourself: What are the key ideas? What will I see on the test?

Get the Most Out of Your Textbook

It's important to know how to get the most out of your textbook. As you begin reading, you can learn more about the textbook and its author(s) by reading the frontmatter of the book, which usually includes a preface, an introduction, and an "About the Author" section. The preface explains why the book was written, how it is organized, what material is covered, and how to use the features in each chapter to their fullest extent.

Some textbooks include lists of key terms as well as questions at the end of each chapter that you can use as a study guide or as a quick check of your understanding of the chapter's main points. Take time to read and respond to these questions, whether or not your instructor requires you to do so. You might be able to order a study guide from the publisher's Web site or obtain access to a companion Web site at which online quizzing is available for free or for purchase. Usually information about these study aids can be found on the back cover of your textbook or in the preface.

Because some textbooks offer "test banks" to aid instructors in creating quizzes and tests, your instructors may draw their exams directly from the text. On the other hand, they may consider the textbook to be supplementary to their lectures. When in doubt, ask for a clarification of what will be covered on tests and what types of questions will be used.

Step 4: Reviewing

The final step in effective textbook reading is reviewing. Many students expect the improbable—that they will read through the text material once and be able to remember the ideas at exam time, which may be four, six, or even twelve weeks later. Realistically, you will need to include regular reviews in your study process. Here is where your notes, study questions, annotations, flash cards, visual maps, or outlines will be most useful. See Figure 5.4 for an example of how to prepare flash cards. Your study goal should be to review the material from each chapter every week.

Consider ways to use your many senses to review. Recite aloud. Tick off each item in a list on each of your fingertips. Post diagrams, maps, or outlines around your living space so that you will see them often and will likely be able to visualize them while taking the test. ■

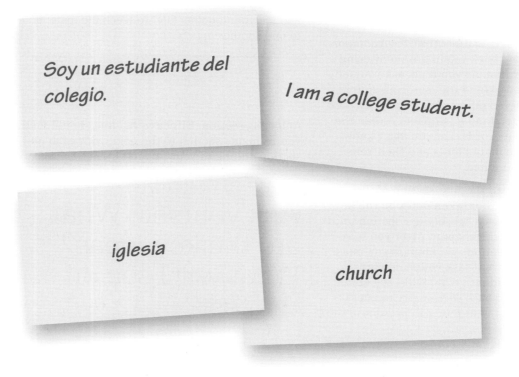

Soy un estudiante del colegio.

I am a college student.

iglesia

church

Figure 5.4 △ Examples of Flash Cards

Different Courses— Different Kinds of Textbooks

While textbooks in the major disciplines, or areas of academic study, differ in their organization and style of writing, you can depend on the four-step active reading plan to help you navigate all of them. Some textbooks may be easier to understand than others, but don't give up if the reading level is challenging.

Different instructors use textbooks in different ways. Some instructors expect you to read the textbook carefully, while others are much more concerned that you understand broad concepts that come primarily from their lectures. Ask your instructors what the tests will cover and what types of questions will be used.

Finally, not all textbooks are written in the same way. Some are better designed and better written than others. If your textbook seems disorganized or hard to understand, let your instructor know your opinion; if other students likely feel the same way, your instructor might spend some class time explaining the text. He or she can also meet with you during office hours to help you with the material, and you might visit the learning center for help as well.

Because college textbooks are not all the same, you will need to learn and use different reading strategies depending on the material in the text.

Reading Math Textbooks

Let's start with math textbooks, which are filled with sample problems, graphs, and figures that you will need to understand to grasp the content and the classroom presentations. Math textbooks are also likely to have fewer long blocks of text and more practice exercises than other textbooks. As you read, also pay special attention to the definitions—learning the meaning of each term in a new topic is the first step toward complete understanding.

Math texts usually have symbols, derivations of formulas, and proofs of theorems. You must understand and be able to apply the formulas and theorems, but unless your course has an especially theoretical emphasis, you are less likely to be responsible for all the proofs. So if you get lost in the proof of a theorem, go on to the next item in the section.

◁ **Getting the Most out of Your Textbooks**
Math and science texts are filled with graphs and figures that you will need to understand to grasp the content and the classroom presentations. If you have trouble reading and understanding any of your textbooks, get help from your instructor or your learning center.

When you come to a sample problem, pick up pencil and paper and work through it. Then look at the solution and think through the problem on your own. You'll spend the most time completing the exercises that follow each text section of the math book.

To be successful in any math or science course, you must keep up with all assignments. Always do your homework on time, whether or not your instructor collects it. After you complete an assignment, skim through the other exercises even if they weren't assigned. Just reading the unassigned problems will deepen your understanding of the topic and its scope. Finally, talk yourself through the assignment. As you do, focus on understanding the problem and its solution, not just on memorization.

Reading Science Textbooks

Science textbooks resemble math textbooks in many ways. Your approach to a particular science textbook will depend somewhat on whether you are studying a math-based science such as physics or a text-based science such as biology or zoology. First, you need to familiarize yourself with the overall format of the book. Review the table of contents, the glossary of terms, and the appendices. The appendices will include lists of physical constants, unit conversions, and various charts and tables.

As you begin an assigned section in a science text, skim the material quickly to get a general idea of the topic. Begin to absorb the new vocabulary and technical symbols. Then skim the end-of-chapter problems so you'll know what to look

TRY IT!

MAKING DECISIONS ▷ **Weighing the Pros and Cons of Tablets and E-readers**

The most popular digital e-readers include versions of the iPad, Kindle, Nook, and Kobo Touch. Some e-readers are basic, no-frills models designed to replicate the experience of reading a traditional ink-on-paper book. Others offer color touch screens, Web browsers, video and music playback, and thousands of free and for-purchase apps. Reading on a digital reader or tablet differs from—and can even be better than—reading printed books. Consider some of these pros and cons:

Pros of Reading on a Digital Device	Cons of Reading on a Digital Device
Digital devices are portable and can hold thousands of books.	Digital devices are expensive.
They save trees, and they have no shipping costs and a low carbon footprint.	They can break if you drop them.
They let you buy books online from any location, so you can start reading within minutes.	It's harder to flip through the pages of an e-book than those of a printed book.
You can type notes and highlight passages. You can also print out pages simply by hooking the device up to your printer.	You've never tried reading a textbook on a digital device, and you doubt it would be for you.
Many of the books you can access are free: You can download books from the public library.	You don't understand how you'd mark while you read.
Some devices link directly to a built-in dictionary; just highlight a word, and the device will look it up. Others will also link to reference Web sites like Google or Wikipedia when a wi-fi or 3G connection is available.	

If you haven't yet explored reading in the digital world, consider whether now is the time to try it.

for as you do a second and more detailed reading of the chapter. State a specific goal—for example: "I'm going to distinguish between mitosis and meiosis," or "Tonight I'll focus on the topics in this chapter that were stressed in class."

You may decide to underline or highlight in a subject such as anatomy, which involves a lot of memorization of terms. Be restrained in your use of a highlighter; highlighting should pull your eye only to important terms and facts.

In most sciences, outlining the text chapters is the best strategy. You can usually identify main topics, subtopics, and specific terms under each subtopic by the size of the type. Headings printed in larger type will introduce major sections; smaller type is used for subtopics within these sections. To save time when you are outlining, don't write full sentences, but include clear explanations of new technical terms and symbols. Pay special attention to topics that were covered in the lecture class or in the lab. If you aren't sure whether your outlines contain too much or too little detail, compare them with those of a classmate or the members of your study group.

Reading Social Science and Humanities Textbooks

Many of the suggestions that apply to reading science textbooks also apply to reading in the social sciences (sociology, psychology, anthropology, economics, political science, and history). Social science texts are filled with terms that are unique to a particular field of study. They also describe research and theory building and have references to many primary sources. In addition, your social science texts may describe differences in opinions or perspectives. In fact, your reading can become more interesting if you seek out different opinions about a common issue by looking at resources in your campus library or on the Internet.

Textbooks in the humanities (philosophy, religion, literature, music, and art) provide facts, examples, opinions, and original material such as stories and essays. You will often be asked to react to your reading by identifying central themes or characters.

The Value of Primary Source Material

While textbooks cover a lot of material in a fairly limited space, they can't tell you everything you want to know about a topic, and they may omit things that would make your reading more interesting. If you find yourself fascinated by a particular topic, go to the primary sources—the original research or documents used in writing the text. You'll usually find these sources cited in footnotes or endnotes at the end of each chapter or at the end of the book.

These primary sources may be journal articles from a literary or scientific journal such as the *Journal of the American Medical Association*; research papers or dissertations (the major research papers that students write to earn a doctoral degree);

recent laws enacted by the U.S. Congress or the Supreme Court; personal letters from soldiers on the front line of major wars; diaries belonging to U.S. presidents such as George Washington, John Quincy Adams, Thomas Jefferson, or Harry Truman; or the inaugural addresses of presidents or governors. Reading primary source material gives you the real scoop that you won't always find in your textbooks.

Many primary sources were originally written for other instructors or researchers. Therefore they often use language and refer to concepts you may never have heard before. If you are reading a journal article that describes a theory or research

study, one technique for easier understanding is to read the article from the end to the beginning. Read the conclusion or "discussion" section, and then go back to see how the experiment was done. In almost all scholarly journals, each article is introduced by an abstract, a paragraph-length summary of the methods and major findings described in the article. Reading an abstract is sort of like reading a CliffsNotes study guide—you'll get the gist of a research article before you dive in. As you're reading research articles, always ask yourself: So what? Was the research important to what we know about the topic, or was it a waste of time and money, in your opinion?

Some professors believe that the way courses and majors are structured artificially divides human knowledge and experience. Those with this view may argue that subjects such as history, political science, and philosophy are closely linked and that studying each subject separately results in only partial understanding. These instructors will stress the connections between courses and encourage you to think in an interdisciplinary manner. You might be asked to consider how the book you're reading, the music you're studying, or a particular painting reflects the political atmosphere or prevailing culture of the period. ■

TRY IT!

MANAGING TIME ▷ Planning Out Your Reading Assignments

Create a simple table with four columns and with horizontal lines for all of your reading assignments for this week. Following the example provided, use the first column to list each reading assignment. In the second column, rate each assignment on a scale of 1 to 5 according to how easy (1) or difficult (5) you think the reading will be. Estimate how many hours each assignment will take and enter that estimate in the third column. (Remember that a difficult reading will take longer.) Use the fourth column to keep track of how much time you actually spend reading.

Estimated reading time this week:

Assignment	Difficulty (1–5)	Estimated time	Actual time
History (Ch. 1)	4	1.5 hrs	2.0 hrs
Psychology (Chs. 2 & 3)	4	1.5 hrs	4.0 hrs
Math (Ch. 3)	5	2.0 hrs	2.5 hrs
Speech (Ch. 2)	2	1.0 hr	1.25 hrs
College Success (Ch. 5)	2	1.0 hr	1.0 hr

Total actual reading time: 10.75 hours

Thoughts: *I used all 4 steps of active reading. My reading took me a bit longer, but I can tell that I learned much more.*
I also feel like I knew how to use my textbooks better after reading this chapter from my college success book.

Estimated reading time this week:

Assignment	Difficulty (1–5)	Estimated time	Actual time

Total actual reading time:

Thoughts:

At the end of the week, go back and analyze the table. Did you spend more time or less time reading than you predicted? How accurate were your predictions about the difficulty levels of the readings?

Improving Your Reading

With effort, you can improve your reading dramatically. Remember to be flexible. How you read should depend on the material. Evaluate the relative importance and difficulty of the assigned reading, and then adjust your reading style and the time you allot. Connect one important idea to another by asking yourself: Why am I reading this? Where does this fit in? Reading textbooks and other assignments with good understanding and recall takes planning.

Developing Your Vocabulary

When reading books and articles for your college classes, you will inevitably encounter lots of unfamiliar words. Some terminology will be specific to a particular academic field, but other terms can be used in a variety of settings and contexts. Increasing your ability to use language is something you'll do throughout your life, not only while you're in college but also after you begin your career.

If words are such a basic and essential component of our knowledge, what is the best way to learn them? As you do your assigned reading, follow the basic vocabulary-building strategies outlined here:

- **Pay attention to key terms in bold type.** Often these key terms are defined in the text margin, repeated at the end of the chapter, and then compiled in a glossary at the back of the book. These features are there to help students master the content.

- **Notice and write down unfamiliar words.** Consider making flash cards or lists of new words you want to remember.

- **Consider the context.** When you encounter a challenging or unfamiliar term, see if you can predict its meaning by using the surrounding words.

- **Analyze terms to uncover meaning.** If context by itself is not enough, try analyzing the term to discover its root, or base part, or other meaningful parts of the word. For example, *emissary* has a root that means "to emit" or "to send forth," so we can guess that an emissary is

△ **Word Power**
Understanding the meaning of words is a key aspect of reading and understanding your texts. Take hints from contestants at the Scripps National Spelling Bee—take your time, think about context, consider a word's root, and use each term in your writing and speaking.
MCT via Getty Images.

someone sent forth with a message. Similarly, note prefixes and suffixes. For example, *anti-* means "against" and *pro-* means "for." Use the glossary in the text, a print dictionary, or the Merriam-Webster Online Dictionary (http://www.merriam-webster.com/netdict.htm) to locate the definition. If a word has more than one definition, search for the meaning that fits the usage you are looking for.

- **Take every opportunity to use new terms in your writing and speaking.** If you use a new word a few times, you'll soon know it. In addition, studying new terms on flash cards or study sheets can be handy at exam time.

- **Consult a thesaurus.** A thesaurus is like a dictionary except that it groups words that mean more or less the same thing. If you think there may be a better word to convey

△ **A Marathon, Not a Sprint**

If you fall behind in your reading, you won't be alone—eventually almost every student does. Remember that your studies are more like a marathon than a sprint, so you should plan to make up lost ground slowly but steadily: Do your assigned readings, study with others, get help, and *do not give up!* Jerome Prevost/TempSport/Corbis.

your meaning, a thesaurus will help you discover the right word to express what you want to say. Your campus bookstore will have plenty of thesauruses to choose from. Online dictionaries often have access to a hyperlinked thesaurus, and word processing programs generally include a limited thesaurus to help you check out similar words.

- **Play word games.** Doing so will increase the words that you know. If you never played Scrabble when you were growing up, you'll find that it's fun, even for adults. Try playing the popular app Words with Friends. Or you might download a crossword puzzle app or pick up some puzzle books. By working crossword puzzles, you'll become familiar with lots of new words, some of which you may never have heard before.

- **Review word lists.** You may want to start building your vocabulary, especially if you're planning to go to graduate or professional school; an expansive vocabulary will help you perform well in interviews and on high-stakes exams like the Scholastic Aptitude Test (SAT) or the Graduate Record Exam (GRE). The word lists at Majortests.com (http://www.majortests.com/word-lists) can be very helpful; see how many of the words on the lists you already know, and identify words you need to add to your working vocabulary.

What to Do When You Fall Behind in Your Reading

Occasionally, life might get in the way of doing your assigned readings on time. You may get sick or have to take care of a sick family member for a couple of days, you may have to work extra hours, or you may have a personal problem that prevents you from concentrating on your courses for a short time. Unfortunately, some students procrastinate and think that they can always catch up. That is a myth. The less you read and do your assignments, the harder you'll have to work to make up for the lost time. Try to follow the schedule of assigned readings for each course, but if you fall behind, don't panic. Here are some suggestions for getting back on track:

- **Plan to do the assigned readings as scheduled.** Add one or two hours a day to your study time so you can go back and read the parts that you missed. In particular, take advantage of every spare moment to read; for example, read during your lunch hour at work, or while you are waiting for public transportation or at the doctor's office.

- **Join a study group.** If each member of your study group reads a section of the assigned

If you fall behind, don't panic.

chapter and shares and discusses his or her notes, summary, or outline with the group, you can all cover the content more quickly.

- **Ask for help.** Visit your campus learning center to work with a tutor who can help you with difficult concepts in the textbook.

- **Talk to your instructor.** If you have a valid reason for falling behind, such as sickness or a personal problem, ask for extra time to make up your assignments. Most instructors are willing to make a one-time exception to help students catch up.

- **Do not give up.** You may have to work harder for a short period of time, but you will soon get caught up. ■

If English Is Not Your First Language

Learning English is difficult when it is not your first language. You'll notice that words are often spelled differently from the way they sound and that the language is full of idioms—phrases that are peculiar and cannot be understood from the meanings of the individual words. If you are learning English and are having trouble reading your texts, don't give up. Reading the material slowly and more than once can help you improve your comprehension. Make sure that you have two good dictionaries—one in English and one that links English with your primary language—and look up every word that you don't know. Be sure to practice thinking, writing, and speaking in English, and take advantage of your campus's helping services. Your campus may have ESL (English as a second language) tutoring and workshops. Ask your adviser or your first-year seminar instructor to help you locate those services.

Chapter Review

Steps to Success:
Reading for Success

○ **Practice the four steps of active reading: previewing, marking, reading with concentration, and reviewing.** If you practice these steps, you will understand and retain more of what you read.

○ **Take your course textbooks seriously.** They contain essential information that you'll be expected to learn and understand. Never try to "get by" without the text.

○ **Remember that not all textbooks are the same.** They vary by subject area and style of writing. Some may be easier to comprehend than others, but don't give up if the reading level is challenging.

○ **Learn and practice the techniques suggested in this chapter for reading and understanding texts on different subjects.** Which texts come easiest for you? Which are the hardest? Why?

○ **In addition to the textbook, read all assigned supplemental materials.** You should also try to find additional materials to take your reading beyond just what is required. The more you read, the more you will understand, and the better your performance will be.

○ **As you read, take notes on the material.** Indicate in your notes the specific ideas you need help in understanding.

○ **Get help with difficult material before much time goes by.** College courses use sequential material that builds on previous material. You will need to master the material as you go along.

○ **Discuss difficult readings in study groups.** Explain to one another what you do and don't understand.

○ **Find out what kind of assistance your campus offers to increase reading comprehension and speed.** Check out your learning and counseling centers for free workshops. Even faculty and staff sometimes take advantage of these services. Most everyone wants to improve his or her reading speed and comprehension.

○ **Use reading as a means to build your vocabulary.** Learning new words is a critical learning skill and outcome of college. The more words you know, the more you'll understand.

Applying what you've learned . . .

Now that you have read and discussed this chapter, consider how you can apply what you have learned to your academic and personal lives. The following prompts will help you reflect on the chapter material and its relevance to you both now and in the future.

1. Choose a reading assignment for one of your upcoming classes. After previewing the material, begin reading until you reach a major heading or until you have read at least a page or two. Now stop and write down what you remember from the material, and then go back and review what you just read. Were you able to remember all of the main ideas?

2. It's easy to say that there is not enough time in the day to get everything done, especially a long reading assignment. However, your future depends on how well you do in college. Challenge yourself not to use that excuse. How can you modify your daily activities to make time for reading?

Create Community

GO TO ▷ **The learning assistance center:** If you need help with your reading. Most campuses have a learning center, and reading assistance is among its specialties. The best students, good students who want to be the best students, and students with academic difficulties all use learning centers. Services are offered by both full-time professionals and highly skilled student tutors.

GO TO ▷ **Fellow college students:** If you need help understanding your reading assignments. Often the best help is closest to you. Keep an eye out in your classes, residence hall, and campus groups for the best students—those who appear to be the most serious, purposeful, and directed. Hire a tutor. Join a study group. If you do these things, you are much more likely to be successful.

GO ONLINE TO ▷ **Southwestern College (http://www2.swccd.edu/~asc/lrnglinks/ txtrdg.html):** If you need more help in reading your textbooks. The Web site of the Academic Success Center includes a page entitled "Effective Textbook Reading Skills" that offers a wealth of helpful resources and links.

GO ONLINE TO ▷ **Niagara University's Office for Academic Support (http://www .niagara.edu/general-study-skills):** If you want to view "21 Tips for Better Textbook Reading."

NOW . . . How do you measure up?

1. It's important to skim or "preview" a textbook chapter before beginning to read.

   ○ Agree
   ○ Don't Know
   ○ Disagree

2. It's not a good idea to underline, highlight, or annotate the text when reading a page or section for the very first time.

   ○ Agree
   ○ Don't Know
   ○ Disagree

3. Taking notes on textbook readings helps keep up with key ideas without having to read the material over and over.

   ○ Agree
   ○ Don't Know
   ○ Disagree

4. When reading a textbook with lots of new words, it's a good idea to have a dictionary close by to check word meanings.

   ○ Agree
   ○ Don't Know
   ○ Disagree

How do your answers here compare to your responses to the quiz you took at the start of the chapter? Which sections of this chapter left a strong impression on you? What strategies for reading college textbooks have you started to use? Are they working? What other strategies will you commit to trying?

87
Preparing for Tests

91
Study to Make It Stick

95
Taking Tests and Exams

99
Academic Honesty and Misconduct

Taking Exams & Tests

In this chapter you will find advice for preparing academically for tests and exams, as well as advice for preparing physically and emotionally. This chapter also discusses what kind of collaboration is acceptable and reminds you why the guidelines for academic honesty and integrity are so important in college and beyond.

Does the thought of your first college test or exam fill you with anxiety? Many students who have had particular problems with certain subjects such as math or science or with certain kinds of tests will feel that they are doomed to repeat old problems in college. Nothing could be further from the truth. You were admitted to this college because of your potential to do well, but good grades on tests and exams don't happen by magic. It is your responsibility to attend all classes, take good notes, do all assigned readings, and seek help when you need it. Helping services available on campus will include tutoring, Supplemental Instruction, the learning center, and special help from your instructor with test-preparation sessions or one-to-one assistance. If you prepare and seek help when you have trouble, you should do well.

Most college instructors will expect you to be responsible for your own learning. They'll provide good information but won't give you specific instructions about how to study and prepare for tests and major projects. Although some study strategies, such as not waiting until the last minute to prepare for an exam or a project, will apply to all courses, the usefulness of other strategies will vary according to the subject matter. This chapter will help you determine the most effective study strategies for different courses.

How do you measure up?

1. To do well on exams, students should maintain good eating, sleeping, and exercise habits, especially before the exam date.
   - ○ Agree
   - ○ Don't know
   - ○ Disagree

2. In order to prevent last-minute cramming, it's important to begin studying for an exam at least a week in advance.
   - ○ Agree
   - ○ Don't know
   - ○ Disagree

3. Doing well on essay exam questions requires reading each question carefully and responding with complete and precise answers.
   - ○ Agree
   - ○ Don't know
   - ○ Disagree

4. I understand clearly how cheating is defined in each of my classes.
   - ○ Agree
   - ○ Don't know
   - ○ Disagree

Review the items you marked "Don't know" or "Disagree." Pay special attention to these topics in this chapter—you will find motivating strategies to develop in these areas. A follow-up quiz at the end of the chapter will prompt you to consider what you have learned.

Just Say No

△ **Emily Vonn**

racron/Shutterstock.

I took a college success course in my first year of college and learned how to prepare well for tests and how to manage my time so that I can get my projects and papers finished before they are due. Classmates sometimes ask to copy my notes, and a few have wanted to copy a term paper I wrote in the past for a course they're taking now. I'm glad to compare notes with other students—our instructors encourage us to share our notes to learn from each other—but I'm uncomfortable just handing out my notes to be copied. And agreeing to let another student copy a major paper that I wrote would definitely be over the line. I actually think the instructors would remember my papers because I routinely run my topics by them and ask them to suggest sources of information. Even if the instructor didn't recognize the paper as mine, I don't think that giving someone my work is fair to me, nor is it doing that person any favors. The first couple of times a student asked to copy one of my papers, I felt slightly flattered but also a little guilty for refusing. I guess I was afraid of being thought of as a goody-two-shoes. But our campus honor code is clear that this is plagiarism; I decided it was worth it to just say no.

Emily has made the most of the test-taking and time-management strategies that she learned in her college success course, and she has also applied what she learned about maintaining academic integrity. Can you relate to Emily's experience of being asked for her papers and notes? Or can you relate more to the students who asked Emily for favors?

Preparing for Tests

In your first months of college, you will notice that students have different ways of preparing for tests. Some keep up with their assignments so that when test day comes, they need only to review what they have already studied. Others wait until the last minute and try to cram their test preparation into one night. Needless to say, cramming rarely results in good test grades.

You actually began preparing for tests and examinations on the first day of the term. Your note taking, assigned reading, and homework are all part of your preparation; keeping up with all of this work during each term will contribute to good test performance.

Work with Instructors, Peers, and Tutors

Preparing for tests does not have to be a lonely pursuit. In fact, it shouldn't be. Enlisting the help of *human* resources—people—will help you succeed.

Start with your instructor. Well in advance of test day, you need to get information. Before each exam, talk to your instructor to find out the types of questions you'll have to answer, the time you will have to complete them, and the content to be covered. Ask how the exam will be graded and whether all questions will have the same point value. Keep in mind, though, that most instructors dislike being asked, "Is this going to be on the test?" They believe that everything that goes on in class is important enough for you to learn, whether or not you'll actually be tested on it.

Use the information that you get from your instructor to design an exam plan. It is very important to check the exam dates on your syllabus, as in Figure 6.1. Then you can create a schedule that will give you time to review effectively for the exam instead of waiting until the night before to review. Develop a to-do list of the major steps you need to take to be ready. Be sure you have read and learned all the material by one week before the exam. Try to attend all test or exam review sessions offered by your instructor.

You actually began preparing for tests and examinations on the first day of the term.

Join a study group. Your instructor may allow class time for the formation of study groups. If not, ask your instructor, adviser, or campus tutoring or learning center to help you identify other interested students, and then decide on guidelines for the group. Study groups can meet throughout the term, or they can just review for midterms or final exams. Group members should complete their assignments before the group meets and should prepare study questions or points of discussion ahead of time.

△ **Strength in Numbers**
Study groups can meet anytime, but studying and reviewing with others in your class can be most helpful just before and just after a test or an exam. © Bedford/St. Martin's.

Figure 6.1 ▷ **Exam Schedule from Sample Course Syllabus**

History 111, US History to 1865
Fall 2015

Examinations
Note: In this course, most of your exams will be on Fridays, except for the Wednesday before Thanksgiving. This is to give you a full week to study for the exam and permit me to grade them over the weekend and return the exams to you on Monday. I believe in using a variety of types of measurements. In addition to those scheduled below, I reserve the right to give you unannounced quizzes on daily reading assignments. Also, current events are fair game on any exam! Midterm and final exams will be cumulative (on all material since beginning of the course). Other exams cover all classroom material and all readings covered since the prior exam. The schedule is as follows:

Friday, 9/11: Objective type

Friday, 9/25: Essay type

Friday, 10/2: Midterm: essay and objective

Friday, 11/6: Objective

Wednesday, 11/25: Essay

Friday, 12/18: Final exam: essay and objective

Numerous research studies have shown that joining a study group is one of the most effective strategies for preparing for exams. You can hear other group members' views of your instructor's goals, objectives, and emphasis; have partners quiz you on facts and concepts; and gain the enthusiasm and friendship of others, which will help build and sustain your motivation.

Get a tutor. Tutoring is not just for students who are struggling. Often the best students seek tutorial assistance. Most campus tutoring centers offer their services for free. Ask your academic adviser or counselor or the campus learning center about arranging for tutoring. Learning centers often employ student tutors who have done well in the same courses you are taking. Many learning centers also have computer tutorials that can help you refresh basic skills. And think about eventually becoming a tutor yourself; tutoring other students will greatly deepen your own learning.

FEELING CONNECTED ▷ **Tutoring and Study Groups**

Believe it or not, one of the best ways to feel connected with other students is by participating in tutoring or in a study group. You can probably locate options for tutoring on your institution's Web site, or you can visit the campus learning center to find out about tutoring for a course that is difficult for you. Remember also that you can seek tutoring help for classes in which you are doing well in order to stretch your muscles, so to speak. Whether or not you need one-on-one help, you'll benefit from joining a study group. Research proves that students learn more studying in a group than they do studying alone, and so we reinforce this idea often in this book. Study groups can also be about more than academic work. As a plus, you might find that you and some of your "study buddies" develop strong friendships that last throughout your college experience.

Prepare for Math and Science Exams

More than in other academic areas, your grades in math and science courses will be determined by your scores on major exams. To pass a math or science course, you must perform well on timed tests. Here are some strategies you can use to prepare fully:

Ask about test rules and procedures. Are calculators allowed? Are formula sheets permitted? If not, will any formulas be provided? Will you be required to give definitions? Derive formulas? State and/or prove theorems?

Work as many problems as you can before the test. Practicing with sample problems is the best way to prepare for a problem-solving test.

Practice understanding the precise meaning and requirements of problems. Failure to read problems carefully and to interpret and answer what is asked is the most common mistake made by students taking science and math exams.

Prepare in advance to avoid other common mistakes. Errors with parentheses (failing to use them when they are needed, failing to distribute a multiplier) and mistakes with negative signs are common in math-based courses. Pay attention to these details in class so that you don't fall into the typical traps when you are taking an exam.

Your grades in math and science courses will be determined by your scores on major exams.

△ **Inhale . . . Exhale . . .**
Before each test or exam, allow several minutes for some positive self-talk and a few deep breaths. © Bedford/St. Martin's.

SETTING GOALS ▷

Be at Your Best for the Next Test

Doing your best on tests and exams takes more than hours of study. You must also be physically and emotionally ready. Set a goal to stay in good physical shape during this term and especially before midterms and final exams. That means paying attention to the suggestions in this chapter as well as those in Chapter 12, Staying Healthy, such as making sure that you get regular exercise and enough rest and that you have a nutritious diet. If you take care of yourself, you'll find that all of the hard work you've put into studying really pays off.

Study from your outline. In a subject such as anatomy, which requires memorizing technical terms and understanding the relationships among systems, focus your preparation on your study outline.

Prepare Physically and Emotionally

Academic preparation—the studying you do to get ready for a test—is important, but physical and emotional preparation will also play a role in your success.

Here are some tips for physical preparation:

Maintain a regular sleep routine. To do well on exams, you need to be alert so that you can think clearly, and you are more likely to be alert when you are well rested. Last-minute, late-night cramming is not an effective study strategy.

Follow a regular exercise program. Walking, running, swimming, and other aerobic activities are effective stress reducers. They provide positive and much-needed breaks from intense studying and may help you think more clearly.

Eat right. Avoid drinking too many caffeinated drinks and eating too much junk food. Be sure to eat breakfast before a morning exam. Ask the instructor if you can bring a bottle of water with you to exams.

Here are some tips for emotional preparation:

Know the material. Study by testing yourself or by quizzing others in a study group so that you will be sure you really know the material. If you allow adequate time to review, on exam day you will enter the classroom confident that you are prepared.

Practice relaxing. If you experience an upset stomach, sweaty palms, a racing heart, or other unpleasant physical symptoms of test anxiety before an exam, see your counseling center about relaxation techniques. Practice them regularly.

Use positive self-talk. Instead of telling yourself, "I never do well on math tests," or "I'll never be able to learn all the information for my history essay exam," make positive statements such as "I have attended all the lectures, done my homework, and passed the quizzes. Now I'm ready to pass the test." ∎

Study to Make It Stick

The benefits of having a good memory are obvious. In college, your memory will help you retain information and ace tests. After college, the ability to recall names, procedures, presentations, and appointments will save you energy and time and will prevent a lot of embarrassment. Learning how to exercise the "memory muscle" is just as important as using the tools and activities that can enhance memory.

Help Your Memory Help You

For many college courses, remembering concepts and ideas can be much more important than recalling details and facts. One of your primary tasks as a student is to figure out whether the instructor wants you to concentrate on the big-picture concepts and ideas, the smaller individual facts and details, or both types of information. To embed important ideas in your mind as you review your notes and books, ask yourself these questions:

1. What is the essence of the idea?

2. Why does the idea make sense? What is the logic behind it?

3. How does this idea connect to other ideas in the material?

4. What are some possible arguments against the idea?

"Is this the memory seminar?"

△ **An Elephant (Almost) Never Forgets**
While elephants apparently do have pretty good memories, they're like the rest of us in that they sometimes forget. Work to develop your memory by using the specific strategies in this chapter. One of the most important strategies you can use is to think about the big-picture context behind bits and pieces of information. Shannon Burns.

The human mind has discovered ingenious ways to remember information. Here are some tips that you may find useful as you're trying to sort out the causes of World War I or remember the steps in a chemistry problem.

1. **Pay attention.** This is perhaps the most basic and the most important suggestion. If you are sitting in class thinking about everything except what the instructor is saying, your memory doesn't have a chance. If you are reading and you find that your mind is wandering, you're wasting your study time. Force yourself to focus, and pay attention to what you are hearing and reading.

2. **"Overlearn" the material.** Once you think you understand the material you're studying, go over it again to make sure that you'll retain it for a long time. Test yourself or ask someone else to test you. Recite what you're trying to remember aloud and in your own words.

3. **Use the Internet.** If you're having trouble remembering what you have learned, Google a key word and try to find interesting details that will engage you in learning more about the subject. Many first-year courses cover such a large amount of material that you'll overlook the more interesting information unless you seek it out and explore it for yourself. As your interest increases, so will your memory.

4. **Get the big picture.** Whenever you begin a course, review the syllabus, talk with someone who has already taken the course, and look briefly at all of the reading assignments. Having the big picture in mind will help you understand and remember the details of what you're learning. For example, the big picture for a first-year college success class is to give students the knowledge and strategies to be successful in college.

5. **Look for connections between your life and the content of your courses.** Finding connections between course material and your daily life can help you remember what you're learning. For example, if you're taking a sociology class and studying marriage and the family, think about how your own family experiences relate to those described in your readings or in the lectures.

6. **Get organized.** If your desk and computer are organized, you won't waste time trying to remember where you put a particular document or what name you gave a file. And as you rewrite your notes, ordering them in a way that makes sense to you (for example, by topic or by date) will help you learn and remember them.

7. **Manage stress.** We don't know how much worry or stress causes us to forget, but most people agree that stress can be a distraction. Healthful, stress-reducing activities such as meditating, exercising, and getting enough sleep are especially important.

Review Sheets, Mind Maps, and Flash Cards

To prepare for an exam covering large amounts of material, you need to condense the volume of notes and text pages into manageable study units. Review your materials with these questions in mind: Is this one of the key ideas in the chapter or unit? Will it be on the test? You may prefer to highlight, underline, or annotate the most important ideas, or you may create outlines, lists, or visual maps containing the key ideas.

Use your notes to develop review sheets. Make lists of key terms and ideas that you need to remember. Also, do not underestimate the value of using a recall column from your lecture notes to test yourself or others on information presented in class. A recall column is a narrow space on the left side of your notebook paper that you can use to rewrite the ideas from the lecture that you most want to remember. A mind map is essentially a review sheet with a visual element (see Figure 6.2). Its word and visual patterns provide you with graphic clues to jog your memory. Because the mind map approach is visual, it helps many students recall information easily.

In addition to using review sheets and mind maps, you may want to create flash cards. An advantage of flash cards is that you can keep them in an outside pocket of your backpack and pull them out anywhere to study. Apps such as Flashcardlet and Chegg Flashcards enable

Figure 6.2 ▽ **Sample Mind Map**

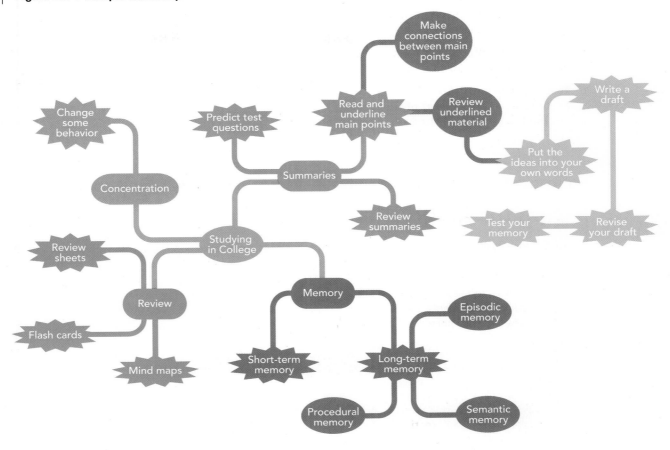

you to create flash cards on your electronic devices. Flash cards can help you make good use of time that might otherwise be wasted, such as time spent riding the bus or waiting for a friend. Flash cards are excellent tools for improving your vocabulary, especially if you are learning English as a second language.

Summaries

Writing summaries of course topics can help you prepare to be tested, especially in essay and short-answer exams. By condensing the main ideas into a concise summary, you store information in your long-term memory so that you can retrieve it when answering an essay question. Here's how to create a good summary in preparation for taking a test:

1. **Read the assigned material, your class notes, and your instructor's PowerPoint slides.** Underline or mark main ideas as you go, make explanatory notes or comments about the material, or make an outline on a separate sheet of paper. Predict test questions based on your active reading.

2. **Make connections between main points and key supporting details.** Reread to identify each main point and the supporting evidence. Create an outline in the process.

3. **Review underlined material.** Put those ideas into your own words and in a logical order.

4. **Write your ideas in a draft.** In the first sentence, state the purpose of your summary.

Follow this statement with each main point and its supporting ideas. See how much of the draft you can develop from memory without relying on your notes.

5. **Review your draft.** Read it over, adding missing details or other information.

6. **Test your memory.** Put your draft away and try to repeat the contents of the summary out loud to yourself, or to a study partner who can let you know whether you have forgotten anything.

7. **Schedule time to review your summary and double-check your memory shortly before the test.** You might want to do this with a partner, but some students prefer to review alone. Some instructors might be willing to help you in this process and give you feedback on your summaries. ■

Tips for Nailing Your Test Prep

- Pay close attention to what your instructors emphasize in class. Take good notes, and learn the material well before each exam. Unless they tell you otherwise, instructors are quite likely to stress in-class material on exams.
- Review assigned readings before class and again after class, and note any material covered in both the reading assignments and class. You will likely see this material again—on your test.
- As you reread your notes, look for repeated ideas, themes, and facts. These are likely to appear on your test.
- Think through and say aloud the key concepts and terminology of the course. The more your brain uses these ideas and words, the more likely you are to remember them.

Taking Tests and Exams

Throughout your college career, you will take tests in many different formats, in many subject areas, and with many different types of questions. Some test-taking tips, however, apply to nearly all test situations.

Write your name on the test. Unless you're directed not to, write your name on the test and on the answer sheet.

Analyze, ask, and stay calm. Read all the directions so that you understand what to do. Ask the instructor or exam monitor for clarification if anything confuses you. Be confident. Don't panic.

Use your time wisely. Quickly survey the entire test, and decide how much time you will spend on each section. Be aware of the point values of different sections of the test.

Answer the easy questions first. Expect that you'll be puzzled by some questions. Make a note to come back to them later. If different sections consist of different types of questions (such as multiple-choice, short-answer, and essay), complete the types you are most comfortable with first. Be sure to leave enough time for any essays.

If you feel yourself starting to panic or go blank, stop whatever you are doing. Take a long, deep breath and slowly exhale. Remind yourself that you know the material and can do well on this test. Then take another deep breath. If necessary, go to another section of the test and come back later to the item that triggered your anxiety.

If you finish early, don't leave. Stay and check your work for errors. Reread the directions one last time. If you are using a Scantron answer sheet, make sure that all your answers are filled in accurately and completely.

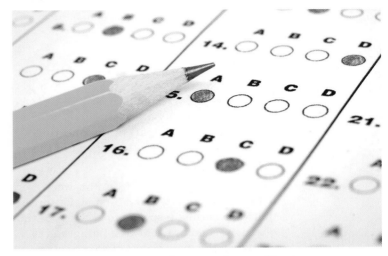

Figure 6.3 △ Example of a Scantron Answer Sheet
Each time you fill in a bubble on a Scantron answer sheet, make sure that the question number on the answer sheet corresponds to the number of the question on the test. And make sure that all bubbles are filled in accurately and completely. Vixit/Shutterstock.

Be Ready for Every Kind of Pitch

Just like a batter in baseball has to be ready for any pitch—fastball, curve, slider, changeup—on test day you have to be ready for whatever may be coming your way. Some test-taking tips depend on the type of exam you are taking or the type of test questions that you have to answer within the exam. Different types of exam questions call for different strategies.

Essay Questions Essay exams include questions that require students to write a few paragraphs in response. Some college instructors have a strong preference for essay exams, for a simple reason: They promote critical thinking, whereas other types of exams tend to be exercises in memorization. To succeed on essay exams, follow these guidelines:

1. **Budget your exam time.** Quickly survey the entire exam, and note the questions that are easiest for you to answer, along with their

point values. Take a moment to weigh their values, estimate the approximate time you should allot to each question, and write the time beside each item number. Be sure you understand whether you must answer every question or choose among the questions provided.

2. **Actively read the whole question.** Many well-prepared students write a good answer to a question that was not asked—when that happens, they may lose points or even fail the exam. Many other students write a good answer to only part of the question—they also may lose points or even fail the exam.

3. **Develop a brief outline of your answer before you begin to write.** First make sure that your outline responds to all parts of the question. Then use your first paragraph to introduce the main points, and use subsequent paragraphs to describe each point in more depth. If you begin to lose your concentration, you will be glad to have the outline to help you regain your focus. If you find that you are running out of time and cannot complete an essay question, at least provide an outline of key ideas. Instructors usually assign points based on your coverage of the main topics from the material. Thus you will usually earn more points by responding to all parts of the question briefly than by addressing just one aspect of the question in detail.

4. **Write concise, organized answers.** Some students answer essay questions by quickly writing down everything they know on the topic. Long answers are not necessarily good answers. Answers that are too general, unfocused, or disorganized may not earn high scores.

5. **Know the key task words in essay questions.** The following key task words appear frequently on essay tests: *analyze, compare, contrast, criticize/critique, define, describe, discuss, evaluate, explain, interpret, justify, narrate, outline, prove, review, summarize,* and *trace.* Take time to learn them so that you can answer essay questions accurately and precisely.

Multiple-Choice Questions. Multiple-choice questions provide any number of possible answers, often between three and five; the answer choices are usually numbered (1, 2, 3, 4, . . .) or lettered (a, b, c, d, . . .), and the test-taker is supposed to select the correct or best answer for each question. Preparing for multiple-choice tests requires you to actively review all of the course material. Reciting from flash cards, summary sheets, mind maps, or the recall column in your lecture notes is a good way to review.

Take advantage of the many cues that multiple-choice questions include. Note terms in the question such as *not, except,* and *but* so that the answer you choose fits the question. Also, read each answer choice carefully; be suspicious of choices that use words such as *always, never,* and *only.* These choices are often (but not always) incorrect. Often the correct answer is the option that is the most comprehensive.

In some multiple-choice questions, the first part of the question is an incomplete sentence (called the stem), and each answer choice completes the sentence. In these questions, any answer choices that do not use correct grammar are usually incorrect. For example, in Figure 6.3, "Margaret Mead was an" is the stem. Which of the four options is grammatically wrong and can be ruled out?

To avoid becoming confused by answer choices that sound alike, predict the answer to each question before reading the options. Then choose the answer that best matches your prediction. If a question totally confuses you,

TRY IT!

MANAGING TIME ▷
Time Flies—Even When You're Taking an Essay Test

Have you ever taken an essay test or exam and the instructor called "time" before you had finished all your answers? Don't let this happen to you. Remember that writing long responses to the first few questions can be a costly error, because doing so takes up precious time that you may need to answer the questions at the end of the exam. Divide the total time by the number of questions, wear a watch to monitor your time as you move through the exam, and remember to give yourself enough time at the end for a quick review.

Figure 6.3 ◁ Example of a
Multiple-Choice Question

Name *Jack Brown* Date *9/18/15*

Examination 1

1. Margaret Mead was an
   a. psychologist
   b. anthropologist
   c. environmental scientist
   d. astronomer

place a check mark in the margin and come back to it later. Sometimes a question later in the exam will provide a clue for the one you are unsure about. If you have absolutely no idea, look for an answer that at least has some pieces of information. If there is no penalty for guessing, fill in an answer for every question, even if it is sometimes just a guess. If there is a penalty for guessing, don't just choose an answer at random; leaving an answer blank might be a wiser choice. Finally, if you have time at the end, always go back and double-check that you chose the right answer for the right question, especially if you are using a Scantron form.

Fill-in-the-Blank Questions. Fill-in-the-blank questions consist of a phrase, sentence, or paragraph with a blank space indicating where the student should provide the missing word or words. In many ways, preparing for fill-in-the-blank questions is similar to getting ready for multiple-choice items, but fill-in-the-blank questions can be harder because you do not have a choice of possible answers right in front of you. Not all fill-in-the-blank questions are constructed the same way. Sometimes the answer consists of a single word, while at other times the instructor is looking for a phrase. In the latter case, there may be a series of blanks to give you a clue about the number of words in the answer, or there may be just one long blank. If you are unsure, ask the instructor whether the answer is supposed to be one word or more than one word.

△ **Ace the Test**
No matter what type of test you are taking, read each question carefully so that you have the best chance of selecting the right answer. And remember that when you take a machine-scored test, one of the simplest and most important steps you can take is to make sure the question numbers correspond to your answer sheet numbers. fStop/Alamy.

True/False Questions. True/false questions ask students to determine whether a statement is accurate or not. For the statement to be true, every detail in the statement must be true. As in multiple-choice tests, statements containing words such as *always, never,* and *only* tend to be false, whereas less definite terms such as *often* or *frequently* suggest that the statement may be true. Read through the entire exam to see if information in one question will help you answer another. Do not second-guess what you know or doubt your answers just because a sequence of questions appears to be all true or all false.

Matching Questions. Matching questions are set up with terms in one column and descriptions in the other, and you must make the proper pairings. Before matching any items, review all of the terms and descriptions. Match those terms you are sure of first. As you do so, cross out both the term and its description, and then use the process of elimination to assist you in matching the remaining items. ■

Fear Not the Online Test

Many students take online tests in traditional, hybrid, and online courses. Don't let these tests trip you up. Avoid rookie mistakes by using these strategies:

1. **Don't wait until the last minute to study.** Whether the online test is part of a self-paced online course or a face-to-face course, start a study group (either in person or online) as far in advance as possible.
2. **Get organized.** An open-book quiz can take longer than a normal test if you're not sure where to locate the information you need. Having a solid grasp of the material going in is key; your notes and books should be for occasional reference only.
3. **Resist the temptation to surf the Web for answers.** The answer you pick might not be what your instructor is looking for. It's much better to check your notes to see what you were taught in class.
4. **If your instructor doesn't forbid collaboration on tests,** open up an instant message window with a fellow student. Take the test together, and take it early.
5. **Don't get distracted.** When you're taking a cyberexam, it's easy to fall prey to real-life diversions like Facebook, iTunes, or a sudden urge to rearrange your closet. Whatever you do, take the test seriously. Go somewhere quiet where you can concentrate—not Starbucks. A quiet, remote spot in the library is ideal. You might try wearing noise-canceling headphones!
6. **While taking the test, budget your time.** Keep an eye on the clock so that you'll be sure to finish the entire test.
7. **Tackle easy questions first.** Once you get the easy questions out of the way, you can revisit the harder ones.
8. **Find out in advance if there's a penalty for wrong answers.** If bluffing is allowed, be sure to fill in an answer for every question.
9. **Beware: There's always the risk of losing your Internet connection midtest.** To be on the safe side, type all of your answers and essays into a Word document. Then leave time at the end to cut and paste them into the test itself.
10. **Did you finish early?** Take a few minutes to obsessively check your answers and spelling. (That's good advice for traditional tests, too.)

Academic Honesty and Misconduct

Imagine what our world would be like if researchers reported fraudulent results that were then used to develop new machines or medical treatments or to build bridges, airplanes, or subway systems. Integrity is a cornerstone of higher education, and activities that compromise that integrity damage everyone: your country, your community, your college or university, your classmates, and yourself.

Cheating

Institutions vary widely in how they define broad terms such as *lying* or *cheating*. One university defines cheating as "intentionally using or attempting to use unauthorized materials, information, notes, study aids, or other devices . . . [including] unauthorized communication of information during an academic exercise." This would apply to looking over a classmate's shoulder for an answer, using a calculator when it is not authorized, obtaining or discussing an exam (or individual questions from an exam) without permission, copying someone else's lab notes, purchasing a term paper over the Internet, watching the movie version of a book instead of reading it, and duplicating computer files.

△ **Stop! Thief!**
When students are seated close to each other while taking a test, they may be tempted to let their eyes wander to someone else's answers. Don't let this happen to you. Cheating is the same as stealing. Also, don't offer to share your work or make it easy for other students to copy your work. Reduce temptation by covering your answer sheet. © Bedford/St. Martin's.

Plagiarism

Plagiarism, or taking another person's ideas or work and presenting them as your own, is especially intolerable in an academic culture. Just as taking someone else's property constitutes physical theft, taking credit for someone else's ideas constitutes intellectual theft. On most tests, you don't have to credit specific sources. In written reports and papers, however, you must give credit any time you use (a) another person's actual words; (b) another person's ideas or theories, even if you don't quote the person directly; or (c) information that is not considered common knowledge.

Many schools prohibit certain activities in addition to lying, cheating, unauthorized assistance, and plagiarism. Some examples of prohibited behaviors are intentionally inventing information or results, earning credit more than once for the same piece of academic work without permission, giving your work or exam answers to another student to copy during the actual exam or before that exam is given to another section, giving or selling a paper you have written to another student, and bribing someone in exchange for any kind of academic advantage. Most schools also prohibit helping or attempting to help another student commit a dishonest act.

TRY IT!

MAKING DECISIONS ▷
Ignorance Is No Excuse

Make a decision to learn about the rules of academic honesty for each of your classes by asking questions in class or by setting up appointments with your instructors during their office hours. Some rules will be the same for all classes; others will depend on how the course is taught or how students are expected to study. Pleading ignorance of the rules is not a good strategy. Having all of the information at hand each term will allow you to make good decisions with regard to maintaining your academic integrity.

Consequences of Cheating and Plagiarism

Although some students may seem to be getting away with cheating or plagiarizing, such behaviors can have severe and life-changing consequences. In recent years college students have been suspended or expelled for cheating on examinations or plagiarizing major papers, and some college graduates have even had their degrees revoked. Writers and journalists such as Jayson Blair, formerly of the *New York Times,* and Stephen Glass, formerly of the *New Republic,* have lost their jobs and their journalistic careers after their plagiarism was discovered. Even college presidents have occasionally been guilty of using the words of others in writing and speaking. Such discoveries can result not only in embarrassment and shame but also in lawsuits and criminal actions.

Because plagiarism can be a problem on college campuses, faculty members are now using electronic systems such as http://www.turnitin.com to identify passages in student papers that have been plagiarized. Many instructors routinely check their students' papers to make sure that the writing is original. So even though the temptation to cheat or plagiarize might be strong, the chance of possibly getting a better grade isn't worth misrepresenting yourself or your knowledge and suffering the potential consequences.

Reducing the Likelihood of Academic Dishonesty

To avoid becoming intentionally or unintentionally involved in academic misconduct, consider the reasons why it could happen:

- **Ignorance.** In a survey at the University of South Carolina, 20 percent of students incorrectly thought that buying a term paper wasn't cheating. Forty percent thought that using a test file (a collection of actual tests from previous terms) was fair behavior. Sixty percent thought that it was acceptable to get answers from someone who had taken the exam earlier in the same or a prior term. What do you think?

- **Cultural and campus differences.** In other countries and on some U.S. campuses, students are encouraged to review past exams as practice exercises. Some student government associations maintain test files for student use. Make sure you know the policy on your campus.

- **A belief that grades are all that matter.** This might reflect our society's competitive atmosphere. It also might be the result of pressure from parents, peers, or teachers. In truth, grades mean nothing if you have cheated to earn them. Even if your grades help you get a job, what you have actually learned is what will help you keep the job and be promoted. If you haven't learned what you need to know, you won't be ready to work in your chosen field.

- **Lack of preparation or inability of students to manage their time and activities.** If your lack of preparation is a time-management problem, be honest with yourself and unlearn old habits of procrastination. If you've done your best and still need extra time, ask an instructor to extend a deadline so that a project can be done well. ■

Guidelines for Academic Honesty

Take these steps to reduce the likelihood of problems:

1. **Set clear boundaries.** Refuse if another student asks you to help him or her cheat. Tell the student that you both would risk failing the assignment, failing the course, or worse. During tests, keep your answers covered and put away all materials, including your cell phone. Instructors may become suspicious when they see students checking their cell phones during an exam. During class or outside class, resist showing another student your homework or a major paper you have written, unless your judgment says that doing so presents a good opportunity for student collaboration and you can ensure that your work doesn't leave your sight. Turning someone down can be hard because so many of us are instinctively polite and helpful, but assure yourself that saying no is the right thing to do.

2. **Seek help.** Find out where you can obtain assistance with study skills, time management, and test taking. If your methods are in good shape but the content of the course is too difficult, consult your instructor, join a study group, or visit your campus learning center or tutorial service. As a last resort, consider withdrawing from the course.

3. **Seek advice.** Your college will have a deadline for dropping a course without penalty. But before withdrawing, be sure to talk with your academic adviser or counselor.

4. **Reexamine goals.** Rather than giving in to unfair pressure from family members or friends to achieve impossibly high standards, stick to your own goals. If you are being pressured to enter a career that does not interest you, sit down with a counseling or career services professional to explore alternatives.

Chapter Review

Steps to Success:
Taking Exams & Tests

○ **Start preparing for test taking the very first day of the course.** Classes early in the term are the most important ones *not* to miss.

○ **Learn as much as you can about the type of tests you will be taking.** You will study differently for an essay exam than you will for a multiple-choice test.

○ **Prepare yourself physically through proper sleep, diet, and exercise.** These behaviors are as important as studying the actual material. You may not control what is on the exams, but you can control your physical readiness to do your best.

○ **Prepare yourself emotionally by being relaxed and confident.** Confidence comes from the knowledge that you are well prepared and know the material.

○ **Seek help from your counseling center if you experience severe test anxiety.** Professionals can help you deal with this problem.

○ **Develop a systematic plan of preparation for every test.** Be specific about when you are going to study, how long you'll study, and what material you will cover.

○ **Join a study group and participate conscientiously and regularly.** Students who join study groups perform better on tests. Studying with a group is a habit you should practice.

○ **Never cheat or plagiarize.** Experience the satisfaction that comes from learning and doing your own work and from knowing that you don't have to worry about getting caught or using material that may be incorrect.

○ **Learn what constitutes cheating and plagiarism on your campus so that you don't inadvertently do either.** If you are not clear about your institution's policies, ask your instructors or the professionals in your campus learning center or writing center.

Applying what you've learned . . .

Now that you have read and discussed this chapter, consider how you can apply what you have learned to your academic and personal lives. The following prompts will help you reflect on the chapter material and its relevance to you both now and in the future.

1. Identify your next test or exam. What class is it for? When is it scheduled (the morning, afternoon, or evening)? What type of test will it be (problem-solving, multiple-choice, open book, etc.)? List the specific strategies described in this chapter that will help you prepare for and take this test.

2. Do you know how your institution or your different instructors define cheating or plagiarism? Look up the definitions of these terms in your institution's student handbook, and read about the penalties for students who are dishonest. Then check your syllabi for class-specific guidelines. If you still have questions about what behaviors are or are not acceptable in a particular class, check with your instructor.

Create Community

GO TO ▷ The learning center: If you need help solving your academic problems. The best students, good students who want to be the best students, and students with academic difficulties all use learning centers and tutoring services. These services are offered by both full-time professionals and highly skilled student tutors.

GO TO ▷ Your college's counseling services center: If you need help dealing with test anxiety. College and university counseling centers offer a wide array of services, often including workshops and individual or group counseling.

GO TO ▷ Fellow college students: If you need help staying on track academically. Seek the help of classmates who are serious, purposeful, and directed. Or you can secure a tutor or join a study group.

GO ONLINE TO ▷ The Academic Center for Excellence, University of Illinois at Chicago (http://www.uic.edu/depts/ace/strategies.shtml): If you need help studying and preparing for exams. This Web site provides a list of tips to help you prepare for exams.

GO ONLINE TO ▷ The Learning Centre at the University of New South Wales in Sydney, Australia (http://student.unsw.edu.au/exam-preparation): If you need help studying and preparing for exams. This site's tips and recommendations include the popular SQ3R reading comprehension method.

NOW . . . How do you measure up?

1. To do well on exams, students should maintain good eating, sleeping, and exercise habits, especially before the exam date.
   - ○ Agree
   - ○ Don't know
   - ○ Disagree

2. In order to prevent last-minute cramming, it's important to begin studying for an exam at least a week in advance.
   - ○ Agree
   - ○ Don't know
   - ○ Disagree

3. Doing well on essay exam questions requires reading each question carefully and responding with complete and precise answers.
   - ○ Agree
   - ○ Don't know
   - ○ Disagree

4. I understand clearly how cheating is defined in each of my classes.
   - ○ Agree
   - ○ Don't know
   - ○ Disagree

How do your answers here compare to your responses to the quiz you took at the start of the chapter? Which sections of this chapter left a strong impression on you? What strategies for taking exams and tests have you started to use? Are they working? What other strategies will you commit to trying?

WonderfulPixel/Shutterstock.

07

107
Becoming a Critical Thinker

110
Faulty Reasoning: Logical Fallacies

112
Bloom's Taxonomy

114
Critical Thinking in College and in Life

Thinking Critically

One of the main purposes of a college education is to empower you to become a good critical thinker. Becoming a critical thinker does not mean that you will become more argumentative and "critical" but that you will be able to evaluate information by using logical and rational processes. In our nation and world, there are many authorities, including politicians, religious leaders, media pundits, and marketers, who want others to accept what they say as "the truth." But before you accept any viewpoint, you should consider it through the lens of critical thinking. You will often find that there isn't just one right answer to a particular question; the best answer may depend on the particular context or situation. Thinking critically may cause you to challenge some of your own viewpoints. As you develop your critical-thinking skills, you will become

more cautious about accepting the opinions of others before weighing the evidence and deciding for yourself.

Some of your courses will require more critical thinking than others. For instance, learning in the social and behavioral sciences requires you to evaluate different theories and opinions. But even mathematicians and accountants disagree about the best way to work a problem or find the right answer. So be on the lookout for critical-thinking opportunities, even in courses that seem less open to debate.

This chapter will provide you with valuable strategies for critical thinking. It will also help you understand why critical thinking is one of the most important and desirable skills for succeeding in college and the workplace and for living in a democracy.

How do you measure up?

1. Even when people are irritating, it's important to try to listen to what they have to say.
   ○ Agree
   ○ Don't Know
   ○ Disagree

2. There can be more than one right answer to almost any question.
   ○ Agree
   ○ Don't Know
   ○ Disagree

3. It's important not to allow emotions to get in the way of making the right decision.
   ○ Agree
   ○ Don't Know
   ○ Disagree

4. Good critical thinkers listen to all sides of an argument before taking a position.
   ○ Agree
   ○ Don't Know
   ○ Disagree

Review the items you marked "Don't know" or "Disagree." Pay special attention to these topics in this chapter—you will find motivating strategies to develop in these areas.

Seeing Things in New Ways

△ **Tamara Jacobs**

bikeriderlondon/Shutterstock.

For a week before our first college debate team meeting, I had nightmares about being thrown in the deep end with some horrendous topic, like whether terrorism can be justified. When the day arrived, our team adviser, Mr. Randall, gave us a subject I could really work with: capital punishment. Even better, he put me in the "pro" camp. I mean, how can you argue against executing violent murderers?

"Be sure to set aside your opinions on the subject and use your critical-thinking skills," Mr. Randall said. "Remember: you'll be arguing only one side of the issue. But you'll need to understand both sides if you want to outthink your opponent."

Fast-forward to the next debate meeting: "So I'd been studying both sides of the issue," I told Mr. Randall. "It turns out that it's more expensive to put people to death in the United States than it is to keep them locked up. Also, many studies show that the death penalty doesn't prevent murders from happening. What's worse, a lot of people who've been put to death turned out to be innocent. . . . So now I don't know what to think."

"Don't worry, Tamara," said Mr. Randall. "That just means that your mind is working—and that's a good thing. It sounds like it's going to be a great debate."

Can you think of a time when learning more about an issue caused you to question your prior opinions? Did you, like Tamara, feel confused about "what to think"?

Becoming a Critical Thinker

In essence, critical thinking is a search for truth. In college and in life, you'll be confronted by a mass of information and ideas. Much of what you read and hear will seem suspect, and a lot of it will be contradictory. (If you have ever rolled your eyes at an online pop-up ad, talked back to a television commercial, or doubted a politician's campaign promises, then you know all of this already.) How do you decide what to believe?

On the Web site for the Foundation for Critical Thinking, Richard Paul and Linda Elder offer this definition: "Critical thinking is that mode of thinking—about any subject, content, or problem—in which the thinker improves the quality of his or her thinking by skillfully . . . imposing intellectual standards upon [his or her thoughts]."[1] Paul and Elder believe that much of our thinking, left to itself, is biased, distorted, partial, uninformed, or downright prejudiced.

Paul and Elder also caution that shoddy thinking is costly. How so? You probably know people who simply follow authority. They do not question, are not curious, and do not challenge people or groups who claim special knowledge or insight. These people do not usually think for themselves but rely on others to think for them. They might indulge in wishful, hopeful, and emotional thinking. As you might have noticed, such people tend not to have much control over their circumstances or to possess any real power in business or society.

Paul and Elder remind us that there may be more than one right answer to any given question. The task is to determine which of the "truths" you read or hear are the most plausible and then draw on them to develop ideas of your own. Difficult problems practically demand that you weigh options and think through consequences before you can reach an informed decision. Critical thinking also involves improving the way you think about a subject, statement, or idea. To do that, you'll need to ask questions, consider several different points of view, and draw your own conclusions.

[1]http://www.criticalthinking.org/pages/defining-critical-thinking/410.

There may be more than one right answer to any given question.

Ask Questions

The first step to thinking critically is to engage your curiosity. When you come across an idea or a "fact" that strikes you as interesting, confusing, or suspicious, ask yourself first what it means. Do you fully understand what is being said, or do you need to pause and think to make sense of the idea? Do you agree with the statement? Why or why not? Can the material be interpreted in more than one way?

Don't stop there. Ask whether you can trust the person or institution making a particular claim, and ask whether enough evidence has been provided to back up the assertion (more on this later). Finally, ask yourself about the implications and consequences of accepting something

△ **Comparison Shopping**
Use your critical-thinking abilities to exercise healthy skepticism in your life. Shopping is a great opportunity to practice. What questions do you need to ask to find out whether a deal is really a deal? What examples from your own life can you think of? Randy Glasbergen.

Set a goal to draw your own conclusions based on evidence rather than to blindly follow others. For instance, if you're out with friends who are trying e-cigarettes, and they are trying to persuade you that e-cigarettes aren't dangerous like conventional cigarettes are, should you believe them? Develop an attitude of healthy skepticism. That doesn't mean you have to be rude or combative. Instead, you can request more time to ask questions, do research, or think carefully about a decision before following the crowd. It never works to blame others when you blindly follow them over a cliff.

as truth. Will you have to change your perspective or give up a long-held belief? Will it require you to do something differently? Will you need to investigate the issue further? Do you anticipate having to try to bring other people around to a new way of thinking?

Consider Multiple Points of View

Once you start asking questions, you will typically discover a slew of possible answers competing for your attention. Don't be too quick to latch on to an answer and move on. To be a critical thinker, you need to be fair and open-minded, even if you don't agree with certain ideas at first. Give each idea a fair hearing, because your goal is to find the truth or the best action, not to confirm what you already believe.

Often, you will recognize the existence of competing points of view on your own, perhaps because they're held by people you know personally. You might discover them in what you read, watch, or listen to for pleasure. College reading assignments might deliberately expose you to conflicting arguments and theories about a subject, or you might encounter differences of opinion as you do research for a project.

The more ideas you entertain, the more sophisticated your thinking will become. Ultimately, you will discover not only that it is okay to change your mind, but also that a willingness to do so is the mark of a reasonable, educated person.

Draw Conclusions

Once you have considered different points of view, it's up to you to reach your own conclusions, to craft a new idea based on what you've learned, or to make a decision about what you'll do with the information you have. This process isn't necessarily a matter of figuring out the best idea. Depending on the goals of the activity, the "right" idea might simply be the one that you think is the most fun or the most practical, or it might be a new idea of your own creation.

Drawing conclusions involves looking at the outcome of your inquiry in a more demanding, critical way. If you are looking for solutions to a problem, which ones seem most promising after you have conducted an exhaustive search for materials? If you have found new evidence, what does that new evidence show? Do your original beliefs hold up? Do they need to be modified? Which notions should be abandoned? Most important, consider what you would need to do or say to persuade someone else that your ideas are valid. Thoughtful conclusions are not very useful if you can't share them with others. ■

Decide whether you will join a study group. Make a list of the ways that you think you could benefit from joining a study group. Make another list of the reasons you might decide *not* to join one. Compare your lists with those of a few classmates. What insights into the arguments for or against joining a study group did you gain? If you have decided to join a study group, how will you proceed?

Collaboration and Critical Thinking

Researchers who study critical thinking in elementary school, high school, and college find that critical thinking and collaboration go hand in hand. Students at all levels are more likely to exercise their critical-thinking abilities when they are confronted by the experiences and opinions of others than when they are not. Having more than one student involved in the learning process generates a greater number of ideas than just one person can generate. People think more clearly when they talk as well as listen (which is a very good reason to participate actively in your classes). Creative brainstorming and group discussion encourage original thought. These habits also teach participants to consider alternative points of view carefully and to express and defend their own ideas clearly. As a group negotiates ideas and learns to agree on the most reliable thoughts, it moves closer to a surer solution.

Collaboration occurs not only face-to-face but also over the Internet. Christopher D. Sessums, creator of an award-winning blog, writes the following: "Web logs offer several key features that I believe can support a constructive, collaborative, reflective environment. For one, it's convenient. The medium supports self-expression and 'voice.' Collaboration and connectivity can be conducted efficiently, especially in terms of participants' time or place. . . . Publishing your thoughts online forces you to concretize your thoughts."

"Collaborative Web logs," Sessums concludes, "promote the idea of learners as creators of knowledge, not merely consumers of information."[2] The same is true of online discussion groups, wikis (which allow users to add, update, and otherwise improve material that others have posted), and, of course, face-to-face collaboration.

Whether in person or through electronic communication, teamwork improves your ability to think critically. As you leave college and enter the working world, you will find that collaboration—not only with people in your work setting but also with others around the globe—is essential to almost any career you may pursue.

[2]Christopher Sessums, *Eduspaces*. Web. 9 Nov. 2005. <http://eduspaces .net/csessums/weblog/archive/2005/11>.

Faulty Reasoning: Logical Fallacies

Good critical thinkers want to avoid nonsense, find the truth, and discover the best action. They reject a reliance on intuition alone and prefer that actions be backed up by sound reasons. Instead of being defensive or emotional, critical thinkers always try to be logical.

PENGUINS ARE BLACK AND WHITE. SOME OLD TV SHOWS ARE BLACK AND WHITE. THEREFORE, SOME PENGUINS ARE OLD TV SHOWS.

GLASBERGEN

Logic: another thing that penguins aren't very good at.

Copyright 1997 by Randy Glasbergen.

www.glasbergen.com

△ **Logic That Just Doesn't Fly**
This cartoon presents an obvious example of faulty reasoning. Some conversations or arguments tend to include reasoning like this. Can you think of a similarly illogical leap that someone used in an argument with you? Did you use critical thinking to counter it? Or did your emotions get the best of you? Randy Glasbergen.

Although logical reasoning is essential to solving any problem, whether simple or complex, you need to go one step further to make sure that an argument hasn't been compromised by faulty reasoning. Here are some of the most common missteps people make in their use of logic:

- **Attacking the person.** Arguing against other people's positions or attacking their arguments is perfectly acceptable. Going after their personalities, however, is not okay. Any argument that resorts to personal attack ("Why should we believe a cheater?") is unworthy of consideration.

- **Begging.** "Please, officer, don't give me a ticket! If you do, I'll lose my license, and I have five little children to feed and won't be able to feed them if I can't drive my truck." None of the driver's statements offer any evidence, in any legal sense, as to why she shouldn't be given a ticket. Pleading *might* work, if the officer is feeling generous, but an appeal to facts and reason would be more effective: "I fed the meter, but it didn't register the coins. Since the machine is broken, I'm sure you'll agree that I don't deserve a ticket."

- **Appealing to false authority.** Citing authorities, such as experts in a field or the opinions of qualified researchers, can offer valuable support for an argument. But a claim based on the authority of someone whose expertise is questionable relies on the appearance of authority rather than on real evidence. We see examples of false authority all the time in advertising: Sports stars who are not doctors, dieticians, or nutritionists urge us to eat a certain brand of food; famous actors and

TRY IT!

FEELING CONNECTED ▷ True Confessions

Have you ever resorted to "attacking the person" instead of the argument, been unduly influenced by the opinion of a famous person, or practiced "slippery slope" thinking? These are examples of logical fallacies that almost every-one has engaged in at one time or another. Discuss with your class-mates the temptation to use these illogical ways of thinking. Share examples of when you were guilty of doing so and how you felt at the time versus how you feel now as you look back on those experiences. Come up with strategies for countering logical fallacies when they are used against you.

△ **What's for Breakfast?**
Do you believe everything you read? Outlandish claims are out there. Use your critical-thinking abilities to practice healthy skepticism about what you see in print and online that seems far-fetched. Use credible sources to check it out. Can you think of examples of claims that seemed too good to be true? Roz Chast/The New Yorker Collection/www.cartoonbank.com.

singers who are not dermatologists extol the medical benefits of a pricey remedy for acne.

- **Jumping on a bandwagon.** Sometimes we are more likely to believe something if a lot of other people believe it. Even the most widely accepted truths, however, can turn out to be wrong. There was a time when nearly everyone believed that the world was flat—until someone came up with evidence to the contrary.

- **Assuming that something is true because it hasn't been proven false.** If you go to a bookstore or look online, you'll find dozens of books detailing close encounters with flying saucers and extraterrestrial beings. These books describe the people who had such encounters as beyond reproach in their integrity and sanity. Because critics could not disprove the claims of the witnesses, the events are said to have actually occurred. Even in science, few things are ever proved completely false, but evidence can be discredited.

- **Falling victim to false cause.** Frequently, we make the assumption that just because one event followed another, the first event must have caused the second. This reasoning is the basis for many superstitions. The ancient Chinese once believed that they could make the sun reappear after an eclipse by striking a large gong, because they knew that on a previous occasion the sun had reappeared after a large gong had been struck. Most effects, however, are usually the result of a complex web of causes. Don't be satisfied with easy before-and-after claims; they are rarely correct.

- **Making hasty generalizations.** If someone selected a green marble from a barrel containing a hundred marbles, you wouldn't assume that the next marble drawn from the barrel would also be green. After all, you know nothing about the colors of the ninety-nine marbles still in the barrel. However, if you were given fifty draws from the barrel, and each draw produced a green marble after the barrel had been shaken thoroughly, you would be more willing to conclude that the next marble drawn would be green, too. Reaching a conclusion based on the opinion of one source is like figuring that all the marbles in the barrel are green after pulling out only one marble.

- **Slippery slope.** "If we allow tuition to increase, the next thing we know it will be $20,000 a term." Such an argument is an example of "slippery slope" thinking.

Fallacies like these can slip into even the most careful reasoning. One false claim can derail an entire argument, so be on the lookout for weak logic in what you read and write. Never forget that accurate reasoning is a key factor in succeeding in college and in life. ■

TRY IT!

MAKING DECISIONS ▷ **I Can't Believe I Fell for That!**

Have you ever purchased something because of a pop-up or TV ad that turned out to be a hoax? Maybe it was a weight-loss plan, or a way to become buff in six weeks. What about the ad that lured you and made you believe the false promises? Make a decision to research a product before you spend money on it. Share a weight-loss or bodybuilding ad with a fitness expert on campus and ask what he or she thinks of it. Investigate nutrition claims made by food manufacturers. Decide to avoid buying impulsively and to "do your homework" in checking out advertising claims.

Bloom's Taxonomy

Benjamin Bloom, a professor of education at the University of Chicago during the second half of the twentieth century, worked with a group of other researchers to design a system of classifying goals for the learning process. His efforts to develop this system were based on his work as university examiner. In this role he designed tests that would determine whether a student at the university should receive a bachelor's degree. This system is known as Bloom's taxonomy, and it is now used at all levels of education to define and describe the process that students use to understand and think critically about what they are learning.

Bloom's Six Levels of Learning

Bloom identified six levels of learning, as represented in Figure 7.1. The higher the level, the more critical thinking it requires.

Bloom's Taxonomy and Your First Year of College

As you progress through your first year of college, you will recognize material you've learned before and will practice your skills

Figure 7.1 ▽ **The Six Levels of Learning of Bloom's Taxonomy**

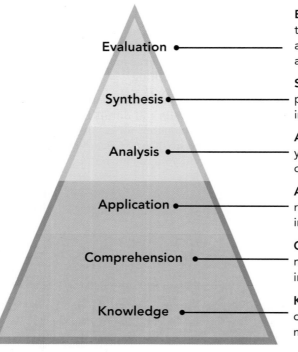

Evaluation, Bloom's highest level, is defined as using your ability to judge the value of ideas and information you are learning according to internal or external standards. Evaluation includes appraising, arguing, defending, and supporting.

Synthesis is defined as bringing ideas together to form a new plan, proposal, or concept. Synthesis includes collecting, organizing, creating, and composing.

Analysis is defined as breaking down material into its parts so that you can understand its structure. Analysis includes categorizing, comparing, contrasting, and questioning.

Application is defined as using what you have learned, such as rules and methods, in new situations. Application includes choosing, illustrating, practicing, and interpreting.

Comprehension is defined as understanding the meaning of material. Comprehension includes classifying, describing, explaining, and translating.

Knowledge, the bottom level, is defined as remembering previously learned material. Knowledge includes arranging, defining, memorizing, and recognizing.

of defining and remembering. But you'll soon find that Bloom's bottom level isn't going to get you very far. To remember new information, you'll need to understand it clearly enough so that you can describe the concepts to someone else (level 2). Many of your classes will require you to apply what you learn to new situations (level 3), and you'll also need to use levels 4 and 5 to analyze (break apart) and synthesize (bring together) new concepts. Finally, you'll reach level 6 as you begin trusting your own judgments in evaluating what you are learning. As you progress through your first year, be aware of how you use each of these levels to build your critical-thinking skills. ■

Figure 7.2 ▽ Rate Your Critical-Thinking Skills

Now that you have read about critical thinking, it would be beneficial to rate yourself as a critical thinker.

Circle the number that best fits you in each of the situations described below.

Situations	Never				Sometimes					Always
In class, I ask lots of questions when I don't understand.	1	2	3	4	5	6	7	8	9	10
If I don't agree with what the group decides is the correct answer, I challenge the group opinion.	1	2	3	4	5	6	7	8	9	10
I believe there are many solutions to a problem.	1	2	3	4	5	6	7	8	9	10
I admire those people in history who challenged what was believed at the time, such as "the earth is flat."	1	2	3	4	5	6	7	8	9	10
I make an effort to listen to both sides of an argument before deciding which way I will go.	1	2	3	4	5	6	7	8	9	10
I ask lots of people's opinions about a political candidate before making up my mind.	1	2	3	4	5	6	7	8	9	10
I am not afraid to change my belief system if I learn something new.	1	2	3	4	5	6	7	8	9	10
Authority figures do not intimidate me.	1	2	3	4	5	6	7	8	9	10

The more 7–10 scores you have circled, the more likely it is that you use your critical-thinking skills often. The lower scores indicate that you may not be using critical-thinking skills very often or use them only during certain activities, such as an educational class.

Critical Thinking in College and in Life

Being a college graduate and a citizen will lead to many future opportunities to think critically about matters that affect the quality of life for you and your family. Answers are often not clear-cut but rather can be loaded with ambiguity and contention. Taking a position on behalf of you and your family will require careful, critical thinking.

For instance, what should be done about the growing problem of childhood and adult obesity? Should we tackle this problem as a society because reducing the rates of obesity would benefit society as a whole? How could you approach this public health crisis in your community?

Let's assume that you and a few neighbors decide to petition the local school board to place on its next agenda a discussion of whether to ban soft drinks in the public schools. In response to your request, the board grants you permission to speak at its next meeting. Your team collaborates to identify the questions that you need to explore:

1. What is the current obesity rate of adults in this community?

2. What is the current obesity rate of school-age children in this community, and how does it compare with the rate twenty years ago?

3. What health interventions do schools currently have in place to offset the potential for obesity?

△ **Thirsty?**
Companies that sell sugary drinks know that students of all ages are a prime market. Considering the current obesity rates of children and adults, do you think that school vending machines should be limited to healthy options? Or does the end justify the means when profits from vending machines are used to raise funds for schools? Bloomberg via Getty Images.

4. When were soft-drink machines placed in the schools?

5. How much profit does each school realize from the sale of such beverages?

6. How do the schools use these profits?

7. Have there been any studies of the student population in this community correlating obesity levels with other health problems, such as diabetes?

You collect data using resources at your town library, and in your search for evidence to support your position, you discover that, according to the local health department, obesity rates for adults and children in your community exceed the national average and have gone up dramatically in the past twenty years. The rate of diabetes among young adults is also increasing every year.

You also learn that soft-drink machines first appeared in schools in your district fifteen years ago. Other than regular physical education classes, the schools don't have programs in place to encourage healthy eating. Schools receive money from the soft-drink companies, but you cannot get a clear answer about how much money they receive or how it is being used.

The data about the health of the community and the schoolchildren is powerful. You carefully cite all your sources, and your team believes that it is ready to make its case. You assume that the school board will make an immediate decision to remove soft-drink machines from school grounds based on what you have discovered. You cannot imagine another side to this issue, and you wonder how anyone could possibly object to removing from schools a substance that, in your view, clearly harms children.

However, much to your surprise, your position meets stiff opposition during the board meeting. You are shocked to hear arguments such as the following:

1. Students don't have to buy these drinks. Nobody makes them do it.

2. Students will be unhappy if their soft drinks are taken away, and that will negatively affect their academic performance.

3. The United States is all about freedom of choice. It is morally wrong for any agency of government to interfere with someone's freedom of choice, no matter the person's age.

4. If we allow the school board to tell children what they can and cannot drink, pretty soon it will be telling children what to think or not to think.

5. This proposed restriction interferes with what is best for our country and therefore our children: protection of the free enterprise system.

6. This proposed policy will lead to significant revenue loss for our schools, which will result in higher taxes to make up the shortfall.

7. There is no evidence that the consumption of soft drinks actually causes obesity. Other sugary foods might be the problem.

8. If students aren't able to purchase these drinks in school, they will just sneak them in from home.

Challenge Assumptions

To some extent, it's unavoidable to have beliefs based on gut feelings or blind acceptance of something we've heard or read. However, some assumptions should be examined more thoughtfully, especially if they will influence an important decision or serve as the foundation for an argument. What are the assumptions behind the opposition's arguments? What assumptions lay behind the arguments *you* have made?

How could you and your neighbors use critical thinking to strengthen your own arguments and respond to those of the opposition? What factual bases support the assumptions and arguments on both sides? Are there exaggerations on both sides? Do you detect the use of any logical fallacies on either side? How can you evaluate the facts? If your goal is to ban soft drinks from schools in your community and to address the issue at hand—childhood obesity—what additional evidence do you need to gather, and what steps should you take next?

Thinking Critically about Arguments

What does the word *argument* mean to you? If you're like most people, the first image it conjures up might be an ugly fight you had with a friend, a yelling match you witnessed on the street, or a heated disagreement between family members. True, such unpleasant confrontations are arguments, but the word also refers to a calm, reasoned effort to persuade someone of the value of an idea.

When you think of it this way, you'll quickly recognize that arguments are central to academic study, work, and life in general. Scholarly articles, business memos, and requests for spending money all have something in common: The effective ones make a general claim, provide reasons to support it, and back up those reasons with evidence. That's what argument is.

As we have already seen, it's important to consider multiple points of view, or arguments, in tackling new ideas and complex questions. Arguments are not all equally valid, however. Good critical thinking involves thinking creatively about the assumptions that might have been left out and scrutinizing the quality of the evidence that is used to support a claim. Whether examining an argument or communicating one, a good critical thinker is careful to ensure that ideas are presented in an understandable, logical way.

As this scenario suggests, well-meaning people will often disagree. It's important to listen to both sides of an argument before making up your mind. If you hang on to the guidelines in this chapter, we can't promise that your classes will be easier or that you'll solve community problems, but you'll be better equipped to handle them. You have the skills to use critical thinking to figure things out instead of depending purely on how you feel or what you've heard. As you listen to a lecture, debate, or political argument about what is in the public's best interest, try to predict where it is heading and why. Ask yourself whether you have enough information to justify your own position.

Examine the Evidence

Another important part of thinking critically is checking that the evidence supporting an argument—whether someone else's or your own—is of the highest possible quality. To do that, simply ask a few questions about the argument as you consider it:

- What general idea am I being asked to accept?
- Are good and sufficient reasons given to support the overall claim?
- Are those reasons backed up with evidence in the form of facts, statistics, and quotations?
- Does the evidence support the conclusions?
- Is the argument based on logical reasoning, or does it appeal mainly to the emotions?
- Do I recognize any questionable assumptions?
- Can I think of any counterarguments? What facts can I muster as proof?
- What do I know about the person or organization making the argument?

If you have evaluated the evidence used in support of a claim and are still not certain of its quality, it's best to keep looking for evidence. Drawing on questionable evidence for an argument has a tendency to backfire. In most cases, a little persistence will help you find something better. ■

Chapter Review

Steps to Success: Thinking Critically

○ **Understand what *critical thinking* means.** If you are not clear about this term, discuss it with another student, the instructor of this course, or a staff member in the learning center.

○ **Find ways to express your imagination and curiosity, and practice asking questions.** If you have the impulse to raise a question, don't stifle yourself. College is for self-expression and exploration.

○ **Challenge your own and others' assumptions that are not supported by evidence.** To help you better understand the position an individual may be taking, practice asking for additional information in a calm, polite manner that is not rejecting.

○ **During class lectures, presentations, and discussions, practice thinking about the subjects being discussed from multiple points of view.** Start with the view that you would most naturally take toward the matter at hand. Then force yourself to imagine what questions might be raised by someone who doesn't see the issue the same way you do.

○ **Draw your own conclusions and explain to others what evidence you considered that led you to these positions.** Don't assume that anyone automatically understands why you reached your conclusions.

○ **Join study groups or class project teams and work as a team member with other students.** When you are a member of a team, volunteer for roles that stretch you. That is how you will really experience significant gains in learning and development.

○ **Learn to identify false claims in commercials and political arguments.** Then look for the same faulty reasoning in people's comments you hear each day.

○ **Practice critical thinking not only in your academic work but also in your everyday interactions with friends and family.** Your environment both in and out of college will give you lots of opportunities to become a better critical thinker.

Applying what you've learned . . .

Now that you have read and discussed this chapter, consider how you can apply what you have learned to your academic and personal lives. The following prompts will help you reflect on the chapter material and its relevance to you both now and in the future.

1. After reading this chapter, think of professions (for example, medicine, engineering, and marketing) in which problem solving and "thinking outside the box" are necessary. Choose one and describe why you think critical thinking is a necessary and valuable skill for that career.

2. In your opinion, is it harder to think critically than to base your arguments on how you feel about a topic? Why or why not? What are the advantages of finding answers based on your feelings? Based on critical thinking? How might you use both approaches in seeking answers?

Create Community

GO TO ▷ **Your course catalog and investigate some logic courses:** If you need help developing your critical-thinking skills. For instance, check out your philosophy department's introduction to logic course. This course may be the single best one to take for learning critical-thinking skills.

GO TO ▷ **The English department:** If you need help in formulating logical arguments. Investigate courses that will help you develop the ability to formulate logical arguments and to avoid such pitfalls as logical fallacies.

GO TO ▷ **Your student activities office or the speech or drama department:** If you need help practicing your debating skills. Find out if your campus has a debate club/ society or a debate team.

GO TO ▷ **Your library and ask for help identifying works of literature such as *Twelve Angry* Men by Reginald Rose (New York: Penguin Classics, 2006):** If you need help figuring out about how critical thinking applies to life situations. This work is a reprinting of the original teleplay, which was written in 1954 and made into a film in 1958 (the film is available on DVD). The stirring courtroom drama pits twelve jurors against one another as they argue the outcome of a murder trial in which the defendant is a teenage boy. Although critical thinking is needed to arrive at the truth, all but one juror employ every noncritical argument in the book to convince themselves of the defendant's guilt until the analysis of the lone holdout produces remarkable changes in the other jurors' attitudes.

GO TO ▷ **These online sources:** If you need more help with critical thinking. Check the following Web site for a critical review of *The Encyclopedia of Stupidity:* http://metapsychology.mentalhelp.net/poc/view_doc.php?type=book&id=2558. Also check out the ICYouSee Guide to Critical Thinking about What You See on the Web: http://www.icyousee.org/think/think.html.

NOW . . . How do you measure up?

1. Even when people are irritating, it's important to try to listen to what they have to say.

   ○ Agree
   ○ Don't Know
   ○ Disagree

2. There can be more than one right answer to almost any question.

   ○ Agree
   ○ Don't Know
   ○ Disagree

3. I try not to allow my emotions to get in the way of making the right decision.

   ○ Agree
   ○ Don't Know
   ○ Disagree

4. Good critical thinkers listen to all sides of an argument before taking a position.

   ○ Agree
   ○ Don't Know
   ○ Disagree

How do your answers here compare to your responses to the quiz you took at the start of the chapter? Which sections of this chapter left a strong impression on you? What strategies for critical thinking have you started to use? Are they working? What other strategies will you commit to trying?

08

121
Understanding Information Literacy

123
Choosing, Narrowing, and Researching a Topic

125
Using the Library

128
Evaluating Sources

131
Synthesizing Information and Ideas

Developing Information Literacy

Domofon/Shutterstock.

Developing the skills to locate and use information will increase your ability to keep up with what is going on in the world, participate in activities that interest you, and succeed in college, your career, and your community. When you think of information literacy, you might assume that it's all about learning how to use your college library. While the library is a great place for you to learn, study, relax, and make connections, information is available in many locations and, of course, on the Internet. But as you probably know already, the Internet poses real challenges to anyone who is looking for the best information source.

Whatever career you choose, the research skills you learn and use as a student will serve you well as a successful professional. Whether you're a nursing, criminal justice, business, or engineering student, you are managing information, and in a few years, when you're working as a nurse, a probation officer, an accountant, or an engineer, you will again be managing information. To make sense of the enormous amount of information at your fingertips—whether in a library or online, at school or at work—and to do so in a reasonable amount of time, you'll need to develop information literacy and research skills.

This chapter will introduce you to the meaning of information literacy, the importance of information skills in today's world, and the strategies for finding and using information while you're in college and after you graduate. It will help you understand the difference between just retrieving information and going one step further — conducting research. Because the array of available information is mind-boggling, this chapter will also help you discriminate between information that is relevant or irrelevant to your needs as well as sources that are valid or biased.

How do you measure up?

1. Doing a thorough search for information for a class paper should include using both the Internet and the college library.

   ○ Agree
   ○ Don't know
   ○ Disagree

2. If an instructor assigns a broad topic for an assigned paper, students should narrow their research focus to something manageable.

   ○ Agree
   ○ Don't know
   ○ Disagree

3. When searching online for information, it's important to select resources that are most relevant, not just those that are first in a list on a search engine.

   ○ Agree
   ○ Don't know
   ○ Disagree

4. In choosing resources for a paper or project, it's important to avoid biased sources—those based on opinions that aren't backed up with solid evidence.

   ○ Agree
   ○ Don't know
   ○ Disagree

Review the items you marked "Don't know" or "Disagree." Pay special attention to these topics in this chapter—you will find motivating strategies to develop in these areas.

The Early Bird Gets the A

△ **Analee Bracero**

When I was looking into going to college, Ocean County College in New Jersey had everything I wanted—online courses, off-campus sites, transfer opportunities, and a variety of student clubs. The college also has a good library system that allows me to conduct research and write papers while on campus. Plus, I can access the databases I need from my laptop when I'm off campus.

Writing what were considered good papers in high school is much different from writing college papers. In high school, teachers didn't emphasize how important it was to avoid plagiarism. In college, instructors want you to use your critical-thinking skills, research your work, and cite as many sources as you can. I start researching my topic for an assignment as soon as possible, look for more data every day, and take additional notes. This way I don't procrastinate, and I can pull together a good paper gradually, working through the writing process, and without a lot of stress. I do most of my research online, and I am careful about checking the validity of material I find, especially on sites like Wikipedia.

As Analee's story illustrates, developing good habits for writing college papers provides many benefits, including less stress, better grades, and solid information literacy skills, all of which will help Analee succeed in the job market. What can you learn from Analee's story?

Understanding Information Literacy

What is information literacy? It is the ability to find, interpret, and use information to meet your needs; it includes computer literacy, media literacy, and cultural literacy.

- **Computer literacy:** The ability to use electronic tools for conducting searches and for communicating and presenting to others what you have found and analyzed. This ability encompasses the use of different computer programs, digital video and audio tools, and social media.

- **Media literacy:** The ability to think deeply about what you see, read, and hear through television, film, advertising, radio, magazines, books, and the Internet.

- **Cultural literacy:** Knowing what has gone on and is currently going on around you. This ability involves such things as understanding the difference between the American Revolutionary War and the Civil War, U2 and YouTube, and Eminem and M&Ms, so that you can keep up with everyday conversation with your peers and with your college reading material.

Information matters. It helps people make good, informed choices—choices that can sometimes determine their chances of career success, their happiness as friends and family members, and their well-being as citizens of this planet.

▷ **Information Literacy**
In today's world, information literacy is essential to success in college and at work. This means developing computer, media, and cultural literacy, along with learning how to find, interpret, and use the information you need.

Information matters. It helps people make good choices.

People are amazed at the amount of information available everywhere, especially on the Internet. Many of us think that because we found links using a search engine, we are informed or can easily become informed. Most of us, though, are unprepared for the vast number of available sources and the enormous amount of information we can find at the press of a button. What can we do when we're faced with information overload? To become an informed and successful user of information, keep three basic goals in mind:

1. **Know how to find the information you need.** Once you have figured out where to look for information, you'll need to ask good questions and learn how to search information systems such as the Internet, libraries, and databases. You'll also want to get to know the librarians at your college, who can help you formulate the right questions, decide what sources you need to investigate, and find the information you need.

2. **Learn how to interpret the information you find.** Finding information is very important, but making sense of that information is even more important. What does the information mean? Have you selected a source you can understand? Is the information correct? Can the source be trusted?

3. **Have a purpose.** Even the best information won't do you much good if you don't know what to do with it. True, sometimes you'll hunt down a fact simply to satisfy your own curiosity. But more often you'll need to communicate what you've learned to someone else. You should know not only how to put your findings into a particular format—a research paper for a class or a presentation at a meeting—but also what you want to accomplish. Will you use the information to make a decision, to solve a problem, to share an idea, to prove a point, or to do something else?

In this chapter we'll explore ways to work toward each of these goals. ◼

Choosing, Narrowing, and Researching a Topic

Assignments that require the use of library materials can take many forms and will likely be a part of most of your classes. We'll consider several ways to search for information later in the chapter. Before you start searching, however, you need to have an idea of exactly what you're looking for. Choosing a topic is often the hardest part of a research project. Even if an instructor assigns a general topic, you'll need to narrow that topic down to a particular area that interests you enough to research it. Imagine, for example, that you have been assigned to write a research paper on the topic of global warming. What steps should you take?

Your first job is to get an overview of your topic. You can begin by conducting an Internet search. Once you've found some basic information to guide you toward an understanding of your topic, you have a decision to make: What aspects of the subject will you research? As soon as you start researching your topic, you may realize that it is really large (for example, simply typing "global warming" into Google will return millions of hits) and that it includes many related subtopics. You can use this new information to create key words. A key word is a word or phrase that tells an online search tool what you're looking for. You can create a list of key words by brainstorming various terms and subtopics within your general topic. For example, key words for the topic "global warming" may include "climate change," "greenhouse effect," "ozone layer," "smog," or "carbon emissions." Even those terms, however, will generate a large number of hits, and you will probably need to narrow your search several times.

What you want are twelve or so focused and highly relevant hits on a particular aspect of the topic, which you can use to write a coherent, well-organized essay. Begin by figuring out what you already know and what you would like to learn more about. Perhaps you know a little about the causes and effects of global warming, and you're curious about its impacts on animals and plants; in that case you might decide on a two-part topic: impacts on animals, impacts on plants. By consulting a few general sources, you'll find that you can narrow a broad topic to something that interests you and is a manageable size. You may end up focusing on the impact of global warming on a particular animal or plant in a specific geographic area.

If you are having trouble coming up with key words, write out your topic or problem as a statement or question. Doing so will help you identify potentially useful key words. As you brainstorm key words, think about synonyms, related terms, and people or historical events that connect to your topic. Then you'll have some backup terms on hand if your first search does not result in any useful hits.

Take advantage of encyclopedias that provide general overviews of topics. An encyclopedia can help you understand the basics of a concept or an event and thus is a great place to start your research, but you will need to use other resources for most college-level research projects. You have probably used an encyclopedia recently—you may use one all the time without thinking about it: Wikipedia. A *wiki* is a type of Web site that allows many different people to edit its content. This means that information on wikis is constantly evolving. Wikipedia is controversial in college work. Many instructors feel that the information on Wikipedia cannot be guaranteed to be reliable because anyone can change it; they instead want students to use sources that have gone through a formal editing and reviewing process. Your instructors might even forbid the use of Wikipedia; if so, avoid it altogether. Even if an instructor permits the use of Wikipedia, it's best to consult it only as a *starting point* for your research. Do not plan on citing Wikipedia in your final paper. Rather, check the references at the bottom of Wikipedia pages, or otherwise verify claims made at Wikipedia on a trustworthy Web site.

Even with an understanding of various types of sources, it can be difficult to determine exactly what you need for your assignment. The information time line shown here provides an overview of when to use different common research sources and gives examples of what you'll find in each type of source.

Figure 8.1 ▽ Information Time Line

This information time line helps identify when and how to use each type of source, whether for classwork or for your personal life. Where would you go to find information about an environmental issue affecting your neighborhood?

INFORMATION TIME LINE

Topic: Environmental Issue: Effects of BP/Deepwater Horizon oil spill on the brown pelican, the state bird of Louisiana

Source	When to access information	What it offers
Newspapers (print and online)	Daily/hourly after an event	Primary-source, firsthand discussions of a current event, and of what happened at the time of the event; short articles
Magazines	Weekly/monthly after an event	Analysis by a journalist or reporter of an event days or weeks after it occurred; longer articles than in newspapers; informally credits sources; might include more interviews or research as well as historical context
Scholarly articles	Months after an event	In-depth analyses of issues; research-based scientific studies with formally credited sources, written and reviewed by experts; contains graphs, tables, and charts
Books	Months/years after an event	A comprehensive overview of a topic with broad and in-depth analyses

Check Your Engine

If you understand the basics of online research but don't know how to apply them to an academic setting, learn what research is considered scholarly: peer-reviewed academic journals (e.g., the *Harvard Business Review*), government Web sites (the Web addresses for U.S. government–sponsored Web sites usually end in .gov), and newspaper Web sites (like the *New York Times* or the *Washington Post*). Unlike these examples, much of the information you'll find online isn't objective or factual; it's a digital free-for-all out there. When looking for academic research, you need to filter out the garbage.

Your college library offers free access to many academic databases, LexisNexis, e-journals, and so on. If you have questions about how to use these resources (and about what kinds of materials qualify as academic research in general), make an appointment with a reference librarian. Within half an hour you'll probably be smarter than anyone else in your class. As an example, visit the University Libraries Web site for Bowling Green State University (http://libguides.bgsu.edu/library_basics) to find helpful guides to getting started in online research and to work on honing your online research skills.

- **Consult the Help or FAQ links.** The first time you use any catalog, database, or search engine, check the Help or Frequently Asked Questions (FAQ) links to learn specific searching techniques. You will get the best results if you use the tips and strategies suggested by the database provider.

- **Use search operators.** A particular database or search engine may use a set of search operators, which are symbols (such as quotation marks, asterisks, or colons) or words (such as *and, not,* or *or*) added to key words to narrow the results of a search. Check the database or site for basic and advanced search tips.

- **Know when and how to limit/narrow your search.** You can often limit a search by date, language, journal name, full text, or words in the title. If you still get too many hits, add more search terms. Think about limiting your topic by geographic region, time period, or a specific population. For example, instead of just using the key word "poverty," you can use "poverty" and "United States" and "children" and "Great Depression."

- **Search more than one database or engine.** Different databases and search engines might pull up very different sources.

- **Check your library's electronic resources page.** Here you will see what else is available online. Most libraries have links to other commonly used electronic reference tools. These include online encyclopedias, dictionaries, almanacs, style guides, biographical and statistical resources, and news sources.

Using the Library

Whenever you have research to do—whether for a class, your job, or your personal life—visit a library. We can't stress this enough. Although the Internet is loaded with billions of pages of information, you should not be fooled into thinking it will serve all of your needs. For one thing, you'll have to sort through a lot of junk to find your way to quality online sources. More important, if you limit yourself to the Web, you'll miss out on some of the best materials. Although we are prone to think that everything is digitized and can be found through a computer, a great deal of valuable information is still stored only in traditional print formats and is most easily found in a library.

Every library has books and journals, as well as a great number of items in electronic databases, that aren't available on public Web sites. Librarians at your college work with your instructors to determine the kinds of materials that support their teaching and research. Most libraries also have other types of information, such as government documents, microfilm, photographs, historical documents, maps, music, and films. A key component of being information literate is determining the kinds of sources you need to satisfy your research questions.

Before you begin your library research, it's important to recognize what research is and isn't. In the past, you might have completed assignments that asked you to find a book, journal article, or Web page related to a particular topic. If so, what you accomplished was to find information—an essential part of research, but just a single step. Research isn't just copying a paragraph from a book or patching together bits and pieces of information from a number of sources. In fact, such behavior could be considered cheating. Good research *is* about evaluating and interpreting sources, organizing and citing them, and drawing your own conclusions.

A college library is far more than a document warehouse, however. For starters, most campus libraries have Web sites that offer lots of help for students. Some provide guidelines for writing research papers, conducting online searches, or navigating the stacks (the area of a library in which most of the books are shelved).

△ **Library of the Future? No, the Present!**
College libraries are evolving as information goes digital and space for collaboration becomes a priority. Sectional furniture can be pulled apart and outlets moved to accommodate different activities. This facility contains quiet spaces for individuals or groups and a digital classroom. Have you explored your college library? Are you making the most of this important academic resource? Learning Commons, 2012, Atlanta University Center Robert W. Woodruff Library Photographs, Atlanta University Center Robert W. Woodruff Library.

Of course, a single library cannot possibly own every resource or enough copies of each item, so groups of libraries share their materials. If your library does not have a particular journal or book that looks promising for your project, or the item you need is checked out, you can use what is called an interlibrary loan, a service that allows you to request an item at no

TRY IT!

FEELING CONNECTED ▷ A Library Is a Terrible Thing to Waste

As you're learning in this chapter, your college library is an amazing resource. Have a discussion with a group of your classmates in which you answer these questions: How am I making use of my college library? How can I make even better use of it? Make a list of ways that students are taking advantage of the library, especially their specific successes. Share your group's ideas with others in the class.

College librarians are dedicated to helping students like you.

charge from another library at a different college or university. The request process is simple, and the librarians can help you get started.

If getting to your college library is difficult because of commuting, family, or work concerns or because you are an online student who lives a long way from the actual campus and its library, you will still have off-campus access to library materials through a school-provided ID number and password. You can also have online chats with librarians who can help you in real time. To learn more, poke around your library's Web site, or e-mail or phone the library's reference desk. And be sure to use the handouts and guides that are available online or at the reference desk. You will also find tutorials and virtual tours that will help you become familiar with the collections, services, and spaces available at your library.

The 20-Minute Rule

If you have been trying to locate information for a research project and after 20 minutes haven't found what you need, stop and ask a librarian for help. Let the librarian know what searches you've tried, and he or she will be able to help you figure out new strategies to get to the books, articles, and other sources you need. In addition, the librarian can help you develop strategies to improve your research and writing skills. Doing research without a librarian is like driving cross-country without a map or GPS—technically you can do it, but you will likely get lost along the way and may not get to your destination on time. Get to know at least one librarian as your go-to expert. College librarians are dedicated to helping students like you.

Scholarly Articles and Journals

Many college-level research projects will require you to use articles from scholarly journals, collections of original, peer-reviewed research articles written by experts or researchers in a particular academic discipline. Examples are the *Journal of Educational Research* and the *Social Psychology Quarterly*. The term *peer-reviewed* means that other experts in the field read and evaluate the articles in the journal before it is published. Some of your instructors may use the term *peer-reviewed* or *academic* to refer to scholarly articles or journals. Be sure to clarify what your instructor expects of your sources before you begin your work.

Scholarly articles focus on a specific idea or question and do not usually provide a general overview of a topic. For example, for the topic of climate change you might find scholarly articles that compare temperature data over a certain time period, analyze the effect of pollution, or explore public and political conversations on the topic. Scholarly articles always include a reference list that cites other sources related to the topic; you may find those sources useful as well.

The most popular way to find scholarly articles is to use an online database, a searchable set of information often organized by certain subject areas. Some databases are specific to one subject, such as chemistry, while others include articles from a wide variety of disciplines. Many libraries have dozens, if not hundreds, of databases. Figuring out which ones you should use can be difficult; your librarian can help you determine which databases are best for your research.

Many of the sources you will need to use for college-level research are accessible only through subscription databases. When you use a database, you can easily add filters to ensure that your search results include only scholarly articles, and you can clearly see who the authors are. Your database search should result

---

TRY IT!

MAKING DECISIONS ▷ Put the 20-Minute Rule to the Test

Sometime this term, you will be required to write a major paper or conduct a research project. This assignment might be for your college success course or for another class. Make a decision now to follow the advice in this chapter: If you have spent 20 minutes looking for a particular source of information and are not making good progress, ask a librarian for help. Your college or university library might even have a special librarian assigned to help first-year college students. Ask your college success instructor for suggestions about which librarian can be most helpful to you.

in article and journal titles, descriptions, and, on occasion, full articles.

The second most popular way to find scholarly articles is to use your library's catalog, an online resource that is accessible on or off campus. Sometimes off-campus access requires you to log in with your college ID number and password. When searching the library catalog, you are more likely to find only the names of journals and *not* the titles of the articles within each journal. You might find a link to the electronic version of a journal. You may also be able to find scholarly articles by using Google Scholar as your search engine. This is a specific part of Google that searches only within scholarly journal articles.

Periodicals

You may have heard the word *periodical* before. Many sources that we use in both academic research and our personal lives are periodicals. A periodical is a resource—a journal, magazine, or newspaper—that is usually published multiple times a year. Specific issues of a periodical are designated either by their date of publication or by annual volume numbers and issue numbers (which vary according to the number of issues published in a given year).

Peer-reviewed scholarly journals, as described in the preceding section, are of course periodicals, but most periodicals are classified as popular rather than scholarly. The articles in *Rolling Stone*—a periodical with a focus on politics and popular culture that is published twice each month—do not go through a peer-review process. Lack of peer review does *not* disqualify magazines as legitimate sources for your research, unless your assignment specifically requires all sources to be scholarly articles or books. Look back at the information time line (Fig. 8.1) for a breakdown of different types of sources.

Books

Books are especially useful for research projects. Often students in introductory classes must write research papers on broad topics like the Civil War. While many scholarly articles have been written about the Civil War, they will not provide the kind of general overview of the topic that is available in books.

Searching the library catalog for a book is a lot like searching a database. When you find a

source that looks promising, check to see whether it is currently available or checked out to another student. If it's available, write down the book's title, author, and call number. The call number tells you where the book is located in the library. After you have this information, head into the stacks to locate your book. If the book is checked out or if your library doesn't own the item, ask about interlibrary loan. One big benefit of searching for a book in the stacks is the ability to browse. When you find your book on the shelf, look at the other books around it—they will be on the same topic. ▪

TRY IT!

SETTING GOALS ▷ **Cozy Up to Your College Library**

Set a goal to get comfortable with all of the resources in your college or university library. Start by thinking about a book you love that was turned into a movie (for example, *The Lord of the Rings*, *The Hunger Games*, or the Harry Potter series). Search your library catalog to find the print copy of the book—also see if it's available as an audiobook or in a language other than English. Find the movie DVD and soundtrack in your library's media collection. Use a newspaper database to find movie reviews or interviews with the book's author. Look for magazine articles or reviews of the book or movie. How many different kinds of media can you find related to the book/movie that you selected?

Evaluating Sources

Both the power and the pitfalls of doing research on the Internet relate to the importance of knowing how to evaluate sources properly. The Internet makes research easier in some ways and more difficult in others. Through Internet search engines such as Google and Bing, you have immediate access to a great deal of free information. Keep in mind that many of the entries on any topic are not valid sources for serious research, and the order of the search results is determined not by their importance but by search formulas that depend both on popularity and on who pays for certain Web pages to be at the top of the list. Anybody can put up a Web site, which means you can't always be sure of the Web site owner's credibility and reliability. A Web source may be written by a person with little knowledge about the topic.

Some students might be excited at first about receiving 243,000,000 hits from a Google search on global warming, but they may be shocked when they realize the information they find is

"It's a new syndrome we're seeing more of . . . 'Google-itis'."

△ **Google-itis**
Search engines such as Google have made finding immediate answers to any question easier than ever before. Be careful, though: Some Google hits may be authentic and valuable, but others may take you to advertisements or biased reports that don't give you exactly the answer you were looking for. www.CartoonStock.com.

not sorted or organized. Think carefully about the usefulness of the information, keeping in mind these three important factors: relevance, authority, and bias.

Relevance

The first thing to consider in looking at a possible source is whether it is relevant. Decide whether the source relates to your subject in an appropriate way and whether it fits your needs. Your evaluation will depend on your research project and the kind of information you are seeking. Consider the following questions:

- **Is the source introductory?** Introductory information is very basic and elementary. It does not require prior knowledge about the topic. Introductory sources can be useful when you're first learning about a subject. They are less useful when you're drawing conclusions about a particular aspect of the subject.

- **Is it definitional?** Definitional information provides some descriptive details about a subject. It might help you introduce a topic to others or clarify the focus of your investigation.

- **Is it analytical?** Analytical information supplies and interprets data about origins, behaviors, differences, and uses. In most cases it's the kind of information you want.

- **Is it comprehensive?** The more detail, the better. Avoid unconfirmed opinions, and look instead for sources that consider the topic in depth and offer plenty of evidence to support their conclusions.

- **Is it current?** You should usually give preference to recent sources, although older ones can sometimes be useful (for instance, primary sources for a historical topic, or a source that is still cited by others in the field).

- **Can you conclude anything from it?** Use the "So what?" test: So what does this information mean?

Research Wisely

One of the best things about the Internet is that it allows people to be both consumers and creators of content. You have the power to publish your thoughts, creative writing, or artwork. On the flip side, so does everyone else. Don't assume that information you find on the Internet is necessarily accurate or unbiased. Get some context for the information that you find by developing an understanding of the different types of Web sites:

- **Portals:** One-stop shops that serve up a full range of cyberservices. Expect to find search engines; news, weather, and news updates; stock quotes; reference tools; and even movie reviews. (Bonus: Most services are free.) Prime examples: Google and Yahoo.

- **News:** Sites that offer news articles and analysis of current events, politics, business trends, sports, entertainment, and so on. These sites are often sponsored by magazines, newspapers, and radio stations and include online-only extras. Prime examples: NYTimes .com, Harvard Business Review (hbr.org), and CNN.com.

- **Corporate and marketing:** Promotional sites for businesses. Some of these sites let you order the company's products or services online; others even list job openings. Prime examples: Ford .com and BenJerry.com.

- **Informational:** Fact-based sites, often created by government agencies. Go to these sites for information on everything from city bus schedules to passports and health and safety tips. Examples: NYCsubway.org, Travel.State.gov, and cdc.gov, as shown here.

Courtesy Centers for Disease Control and Prevention.

- **Blogs:** Web sites where people can air their views and opinions. Some businesses create blogs to connect with their customers; other blogs are strictly personal, designed to be shared with family and friends. Prime examples: Gawker.com and thelawsonspilltheirguts.blogspot .com.

- **Wikis:** Informational Web sites that allow for open editing by registered users, or in some cases by the general public. Prime examples: Wikipedia.com and TechCrunch .com.

Keep in mind that there's a big difference between the *Journal of the American Medical Association* and a journal written by Fred from Pomona. And no, you can't use an ad for the Shake Weight as a source for a fitness article: It's an ad. Be discerning; use your critical-thinking skills. To make sure that the research you use is unbiased and current, look for tip-offs. Most reputable Web sites are easy to navigate, contain little advertising, and list author names and credentials.

Authority

Once you have determined that a source is relevant to your project, check that its author is someone who is qualified to write or speak on the subject and whose conclusions are based on solid evidence. This, too, will depend on your subject and the nature of your research — a fifth grader would generally not be considered an authority, but if you are writing about a topic such as bullying in elementary schools, a fifth grader's opinion might be exactly what you're looking for.

Make sure you can identify the author, and be ready to explain why that author is qualified to write on the subject. Good qualifications might include academic degrees, other research and writing on the subject, or related personal experience.

Understand as well whether your project calls for you to use scholarly publications, periodicals such as magazines and newspapers, or both. As mentioned above, you don't necessarily have to dismiss popular periodicals as sources. Many journalists and columnists are extremely well qualified, and their work might be appropriate for your needs. As a general rule, a scholarly source will have been thoroughly reviewed, giving the work credibility in a college research project. Refer to the information time line earlier in this chapter (Fig. 8.1) to review different types of sources and what each type offers.

Bias

When you are searching for sources, you should realize that every source has an author with personal beliefs or opinions that affect the way he or she views the world and approaches a topic. Because personal opinions are unavoidable, researchers have adopted methods to ensure that their own views don't get in the way of accuracy. However, many sources will be heavily biased toward a specific viewpoint or ideology. Although nothing is wrong with someone having a particular point of view, as a researcher you will want to know that the bias exists.

Research consists of considering multiple perspectives on a topic, analyzing the sources, and creating something new from your analysis. Signs of bias such as overly positive or overly harsh language, hints of a personal agenda, or a stubborn refusal to consider other points of view indicate that you should question the credibility and accuracy of a source and possibly exclude it from your research. For example, the reality of global warming is a topic that is debated by many scientists based on their research and agendas. ■

Synthesizing Information and Ideas

Ultimately, the point of conducting research is that the process contributes to the development of new knowledge. As a researcher, you tried to find the answer to a question. Now is the time to formulate that answer and share it.

Many students satisfy themselves with a straightforward report that only summarizes what they found. Sometimes, that's enough. More often, though, you'll want to apply the information to ideas of your own. To do that:

- First consider all of the information you found and how your sources relate to one another. What do they have in common, and where do they disagree?

- Ask yourself these questions: What conclusions can I draw from those similarities and differences? What new ideas did they spark?

- Consider how you can use the information you have on hand to support your ideas and conclusions.

Essentially, what you're doing at this stage of your research project is processing information, an activity known as synthesis—accepting some ideas and rejecting others, combining related concepts, assessing the implications, and pulling everything together to create new information and ideas that other people can use.

Once your research has reached the point of synthesis, you are ready to begin putting your ideas into writing. The next chapter provides you with guidelines and strategies for using your research when communicating in writing, in speeches, or interpersonally. ■

TRY IT!

MANAGING TIME ▷ Be the Early Bird

Think back to Analee at the start of this chapter. How does she use time to her advantage in tackling writing assignments? Analee never waits until the last minute to begin an important research project or paper. She knows that dealing with the anxiety that comes from last-minute efforts can sap her energy and ultimately her time and also result in a poor grade.

Remember to start an assignment right after you get it, and spread the work over several weeks. Do a little bit each day, and don't forget to make use of your library's resources, including the librarian whose job it is to help you. Analee started her research with Wikipedia. Unless your instructor doesn't allow you to use Wikipedia as a starting point, this site can help you get a broad overview and identify some initial sources for further investigation.

Chapter Review

Steps to Success: Developing Information Literacy

○ **Work to learn "information literacy" skills.** These skills include the abilities to find, evaluate, and use information. They are important not only for college but also for your career because you will be working in the information economy, which uses and produces information.

○ **Become comfortable in your campus library.** Use it as a place to read, relax, study, or just be by yourself.

○ **Accept that research projects and papers are part of college life.** Learn how to do them well. Doing so will teach you how to "research" the information you'll need after you've finished college. After all, modern professional life is one big term paper after another!

○ **Get to know your college librarians.** They are anxious to help you find the information you need. Ask them for help even if they look busy. If possible, get to know one as your personal "library consultant."

○ **Become familiar with as many new electronic sources as possible.** You must be able to do research and seek the information you need in ways other than just using Google or Wikipedia.

○ **Take courses early in college that require you to do research and use your library skills.** Yes, these classes, and especially the writing assignments, will demand more of you, but you will be thankful for them later. Go ahead—bite the bullet.

○ **When you use the ideas of others, be sure to give them credit; then create your own unique synthesis and conclusions.** Someday you will create your own "intellectual property," and you will want others to give you credit for your ideas.

Applying what you've learned . . .

Now that you have read and discussed this chapter, consider how you can apply what you have learned to your academic and personal lives. The following prompts will help you reflect on chapter material and its relevance to you both now and in the future.

1. It is important to get familiar with all the resources in your campus library. Think about a book that you love that was turned into a movie (e.g., *Twilight* or *The Hunger Games* series). Search your library catalog to find the print copy and an e-book version. See if the library has it as an audiobook or in a language other than English. Find the DVD and soundtrack in your library's media collection, or see if you can download the music. Take a moment to appreciate what is available at your campus library!

2. The importance of using information literacy skills in college is a no-brainer, but think beyond your college experience. How will improving your information literacy skills help you once you are out of college?How will you be applying these skills?

Create Community

GO TO ▷ Your instructor: If you need help understanding his or her expectations for a writing assignment. Talk to your instructor after class, drop by during office hours, or make a one-on-one appointment.

GO TO ▷ The library: If you need help working on an assignment. Check out the library's Web site or ask to see a calendar of upcoming events. Many libraries have drop-in classes or workshops to help you learn specific skills. Head over to the reference desk and talk with a librarian about the assignment you are working on.

GO TO ▷ The writing center: If you need help finding effective writing and research tools.

GO TO ▷ The library's main Web site: If you need help finding specialized libraries, collections, or information specific to your major. These specialized collections might come in handy, especially as you advance in your coursework. Visit the ones that are most relevant to your needs.

GO TO ▷ Your institution's computer services office: If you need help dealing with a computer problem. Get familiar with this office *before* you are in the middle of a crisis.

GO TO ▷ Purdue University's Online Writing Lab (http://owl.english.purdue.edu/owl/resource/584/02): If you need help with documenting print or electronic sources or with understanding forms of citation.

GO TO ▷ http://www.plainlanguage.gov/howto/guidelines/FederalPLGuidelines/index.cfm: If you need help with converting government jargon into plain language.

GO TO ▷ Bedford/St. Martin's, the publisher of this textbook, at http://bcs.bedfordstmartins.com/rewriting2e/#t_526483____: If you need help finding inspiration, building a bibliography, learning about citation styles, and more.

NOW . . . How do you measure up?

1. A thorough search for information for a class paper should include using both the Internet and my college library.

   ○ Always
   ○ Occasionally
   ○ Never

2. If an instructor assigns a broad topic for an assigned paper, the first step to take is to narrow one's research focus to something manageable.

   ○ Always
   ○ Occasionally
   ○ Never

3. When searching online for information, it's important to select resources that are most relevant, not just those that are first in a list on a search engine.

   ○ Always
   ○ Occasionally
   ○ Never

4. In choosing resources for a paper or project, it's important to avoid biased sources—those based on opinions that aren't backed up with solid evidence.

   ○ Always
   ○ Occasionally
   ○ Never

How do your answers here compare to your responses to the quiz you took at the start of the chapter? Which sections of this chapter left a strong impression on you? What strategies for developing information literacy have you started to use? Are they working? What other strategies will you commit to trying?

09

137
Understanding the Basics of Writing

142
Citing Your Sources

144
Speaking

Communicating Clearly

PureSolution/Shutterstock.

Many people can write, but few can write really well. The same is true of speaking: Some people can speak with authority, while others seem disorganized and uncomfortable.

The ability to write and speak clearly, persuasively, and confidently makes a tremendous difference in how the rest of the world perceives you and how well you will communicate throughout your life. In almost every conceivable occupation, you will be expected to think, create, manage, lead—and communicate. That means you will have to write and speak well. To participate in the information age, you will need to be both a good thinker and an excellent communicator.

In the preceding chapter, we learned what it means to be information literate, the importance of information skills in today's world, and the strategies for finding and using information while you're in college and after you graduate. The chapter ended with a discussion of synthesis, the stage of a research project in which you process information, pulling ideas and concepts together to create new information and ideas that other people can use. You'll present this new information through writing and speaking.

Most people look at writing and speaking as tasks to be mastered and then forgotten. Nothing could be further from the truth. Writing is both a process (a step-by-step method for reaching your final goal) and a product (such as a final paper, answers to an essay exam, or a script). Similarly, speaking is a skill that involves the mastery of several basic steps.

How do you measure up?

1. I allow myself plenty of time to do a first draft and make revisions before submitting essays or major papers to my instructors.
   - ○ Always
   - ○ Occasionally
   - ○ Never

2. I consider who is in my audience before deciding whether to use formal or informal language.
   - ○ Always
   - ○ Occasionally
   - ○ Never

3. I am careful to cite all my sources accurately.
   - ○ Always
   - ○ Occasionally
   - ○ Never

4. When giving a speech, I avoid using filler words such as *like*, *um*, and *you know*.
   - ○ Always
   - ○ Occasionally
   - ○ Never

Review the items you marked "Occasionally" or "Never." Paying attention to all these aspects of your college experience can be important to your success. A follow-up quiz at the end of the chapter will prompt you to consider what you have learned.

The Truth Hurts, but It Also Helps

△ **Hilary Braddock**

© Jim Craigmyle/Corbis.

The first and best thing I learned about my Philosophy 101 course? No exams. "Your grade will depend entirely on your essay scores," said our instructor, Professor Mann. I always earned A's on my papers back in high school. So when the time came to work on our first big assignment, a paper on Plato's Five Dialogues, I felt pretty sure that my first draft was flawless. Professor Mann thought the opposite: He ripped it apart with negative comments. That was rough.

When I went to talk to him about my paper in his office after class, he looked it over again for a minute and gave me criticism that was hard to hear but, in the end, helpful. "I just don't see much effort here," he told me. "Your paper isn't well researched, and it has a considerable number of grammatical errors and no clear thesis statement. And your bibliography cites Wikipedia more than the actual source material."

"Oh, is that wrong?" I asked, surprised.

"Yes, that's wrong." Professor Mann studied me. "How long did you spend on this, anyway?"

"I don't know," I said. "A couple of hours at least."

"Well, most of your classmates probably spent four times that amount of time on their papers." Professor Mann's tone softened a little. "It's possible that your former teachers had a different standard. You will need to get your writing up to the level expected in college. I can help, and so can the campus writing center, but the decision to put the work into improving is up to you."

Not everyone arrives at college with the same expectations or the same level of preparedness. Some students haven't learned what it takes to earn high grades in college. What did Hilary learn about the amount of time she should have spent on her paper? What did she learn about the difference between primary sources and Wikipedia? What could Hilary do next to build on what she learned through this first assignment?

Understanding the Basics of Writing

Your writing tells others how well you think and how well you understand the ideas you are learning in the courses you are taking. Your writing is your chance to show what you've discovered through your research and to demonstrate your ability to analyze and synthesize sources into a new product that is uniquely your own. Like research, writing takes practice, and asking for help is always a good idea. This section will get you started by walking you through the writing process with step-by-step guidelines for effective and efficient writing.

Steps to Good Writing

The writing process typically includes the following steps: (1) prewriting, (2) drafting, and (3) revising. Let's look more in depth at each of these steps.

Step 1: Prewrite to Discover What You Want to Say.
Engaging in prewriting activities is the first step in the writing process. Prewriting means writing things down as they come to mind based on information from the sources you found through your research, along with your own ideas. It can involve filling a page or screen with words, phrases, or sentences.

The most commonly used prewriting activity is called freewriting. Freewriting means writing without worrying about punctuation, grammar, spelling, and background. In this step, you are writing without trying to organize your thoughts, to find exactly the right words, or to think about structure. Freewriting also helps you avoid the temptation to try to write and edit at the same time. It's impossible to write well and at the same time try to organize, check your grammar and spelling, and offer intelligent thoughts to your readers.[1] If you are freewriting on your computer or tablet, turn off the grammar and spelling checkers.

When you freewrite, you might notice that you have more ideas than can fit into one paper—this is very common. Fortunately, freewriting helps you choose, narrow, and investigate a topic. It helps you figure out what you really want to say as you make connections between different ideas. When you freewrite, you'll see important issues more clearly—issues that you can use as key words in developing your theme. Remember, key words are synonyms, related terms, or subtopics that you can use to find materials for research papers.

[1]Peter Elbow, *Writing without Teachers,* 2nd ed. (New York: Oxford University Press, 1998).

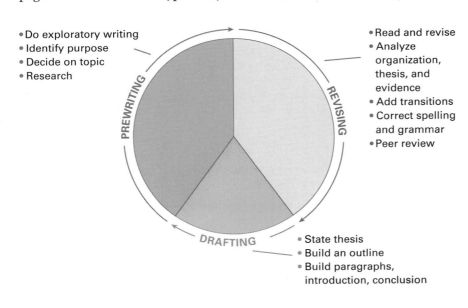

- Do exploratory writing
- Identify purpose
- Decide on topic
- Research

PREWRITING

- Read and revise
- Analyze organization, thesis, and evidence
- Add transitions
- Correct spelling and grammar
- Peer review

REVISING

DRAFTING

- State thesis
- Build an outline
- Build paragraphs, introduction, conclusion

Figure 9.1 ◁ The Writing Process

Step 2: Drafting. Once you have completed your research with the help of your librarian, gathered a lot of information sources and ideas, and done some prewriting, it's time to move to the drafting stage. Before you start writing your draft, you need to organize all the ideas you generated in the prewriting step and form a **thesis statement,** a short statement that clearly defines the purpose of the paper (see Figure 9.2).

Many students find that creating an outline helps them organize their thoughts, resulting in a clear structure from thesis to conclusion (see Figure 9.3). Once you've set the structure for your paper, you can then support the sections with analysis and synthesis of your research

findings, at which point you're well on your way to a final draft. Now, with your workable outline and thesis, you can begin to pay attention to the flow of ideas from one sentence to the next and from one paragraph to the next, adding headings and subheadings where needed. If you have chosen the thesis carefully, it will help you check to see that each sentence relates to your main idea. When you have completed this stage, you will have the first draft of your paper in hand.

Step 3: Revising. The key to good writing is rewriting or revising, which is the stage at which you take a good piece of writing and do your best to make it great. After you draft your

Figure 9.2 ▷ Example of a Thesis Statement

Thesis: Napoleon's dual personality can be explained by examining incidents throughout his life.
1. Explain why I am using the term "dual personality" to describe Napoleon.
2. Briefly comment on his early life and his relationship with his mother.
3. Describe Napoleon's rise to fame from soldier to emperor. Stress the contradictions in his personality and attitudes.
4. Describe the contradictions in his relationship with Josephine.
5. Summarize my thoughts about Napoleon's personality.
6. Possibly conclude by referring to opening question: "Did Napoleon actually have a dual personality?"

Figure 9.3 ▷ Example of an Outline

An outline is a working document; you do not need a complete outline to begin writing. Note how this author has a placeholder for a second example; she has not yet decided which example from her research to use.

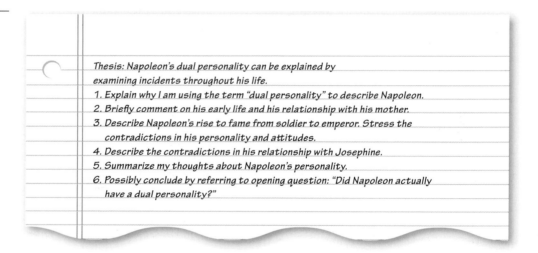

Outline for Napoleon Paper

I. Thesis—Napoleon's dual personality can be explained by examining incidents in his life
II. Dual Personality
    a. What is it?
    b. How does it apply to Napoleon?
III. Napoleon's Rise to Fame
    a. Contradictions in his personality and attitudes
        i. Relationship with Josephine
        ii. Example #2 (to come)
IV. Summary of my thoughts about Napoleon's personality
V. Conclusion
    a. Restate and answer thesis
        i. Yes, he had a dual personality because:
            1. Josephine
            2. Example #2

paper, read it once. You may need to reorganize your ideas, add smoother transitions, cut unnecessary words from sentences and paragraphs, rewrite some sentences or paragraphs, or use stronger words.

After you revise your paper, put it aside for at least a day and then reread it. Distancing yourself from your writing for a while allows you to see it differently. You will probably find and correct more grammatical and spelling errors, reorganize your ideas, and make your writing stronger as a result.

It also might help to share your paper with one or more of your classmates or family members to get their feedback. You should also check to see whether your college provides any writing or editing assistance. Many community colleges have a writing center or learning center where students can get help during any stage of the writing process: finding a topic, narrowing a topic, creating a thesis, outlining, drafting, and rewriting and revising. Once you have talked with your reviewers about your paper, you will have to decide whether to accept or reject their suggested changes.

At this point, you are ready to finalize your writing and turn in your paper. Reread the paper one more time, and double-check spelling and grammar.

△ **Write. Revise. Repeat.**
Good writers spend more time revising and editing their written work than they spend writing the original version. Never turn in your first draft; spend the necessary time to reread and improve your work.
© Radius Images/Corbis.

TRY IT!

MANAGING TIME ▷
The Importance of Time in the Writing Process

Many students turn in poorly written papers because they skip the first step (prewriting) and the last step (revising) and make do with the middle one (drafting). The best writing is usually done over an extended period of time, not as a last-minute task.

When planning the amount of time that you'll need to write your paper, make sure to factor in enough time for the following:

- Asking your instructor to clarify the assignment
- Seeking help from a librarian or from writing center staff or trained peers in academic support/learning centers
- Narrowing or expanding your topic, which might require finding some new sources and so doing more research.
- Balancing other assignments and commitments
- Dealing with technology problems

Writing for class projects might be a challenge at first, but when you plan properly, you'll see a much better result. The research and writing that you do in the first year can also open up possible areas of interest for you to pursue later in your college experience.

Know Your Audience

Before you came to college, you probably spent much more time writing informally than writing formally. Think about all the time that you've spent writing e-mails, Facebook posts, text messages, and tweets. Now think about the time that you've spent writing papers for school or work. The informal style that you use in writing an e-mail, a text, or a post can become a problem when you try to write a formal research paper. Be sure that you know when it's OK to use abbreviations and when you have to write out an entire word or phrase. When you write research papers in college, you should assume that your audience is composed of instructors and other serious students—people who will make judgments about your knowledge and abilities based on your writing. You should not be sloppy or casual when writing a formal paper.

Being aware of the differences between formal writing and informal writing will help you build appropriate writing skills for college work. How would you write an e-mail to friends telling them about the volunteer work you did this past weekend? How would you write that same e-mail to a potential employer who might hire you for your first job after college? How would you write about volunteer work in a research paper? (Read "E-mail Etiquette" below for more on writing e-mails. The section "Communicating in a Digital Age" in Chapter 10 will help you become more competent in various types of online communication.)

Consider your audience when you make a public presentation of your work. Taking your work from research to writing to delivering a speech to a group of people is a series of steps you'll likely take in your first year of college. You will probably take a course in public speaking soon, or maybe you are already taking one. When preparing for a presentation, you need to understand the people who are in your audience. Ask yourself the following questions:

- **What do they already know about my topic?** If you're going to give a presentation on the health risks of fast food, you'll want to find out how much your listeners already know about fast food so that you don't risk boring them or wasting their time.

E-mail Etiquette

Whether your class is online or face-to-face, at some point you will need to communicate with your instructor via e-mail. Although you may prefer to use Facebook, Twitter, or Instagram, use e-mail to communicate with your instructors unless they tell you otherwise. Writing e-mails to your instructors is different from writing e-mails to your friends.

If you need help with an assignment and have to send your professor an e-mail, but you've never sent an e-mail to a teacher before, take a few minutes to figure out exactly what you need to ask, jot down your main points, and then construct a clear and concise e-mail. Here's how to do it:

1. **Look at the example shown here and follow its format in your e-mail.** It's best to use your college e-mail address so that your professor immediately recognizes you as a student. If you have to use another e-mail address, use a professional, simple address that includes your name.
2. **Make the subject line informative.**
   Your instructor might receive hundreds of e-mails every day; a subject line that includes the name of the course or the assignment helps him or her prioritize your e-mail. A subject line that just says "Class" or "Question" isn't helpful; an e-mail with a blank subject line usually goes to the instructor's spam folder.
3. **Address your instructor with respect.** Think about how you address your instructor in class, or look at your syllabus to see his or her preference. If an instructor uses *Doctor*, then you should use *Doctor*. If you don't know the proper or preferred title, you can never go wrong with *Dear Professor*, followed by your instructor's last name.
4. **Sign every e-mail with your full name, course number, and e-mail address.**
5. **When attaching files to your e-mail (a skill you should have), use widely accepted file formats** such as .doc, .docx, or .pdf. Also, be sure your last name is included in the file name you use. See the example shown.

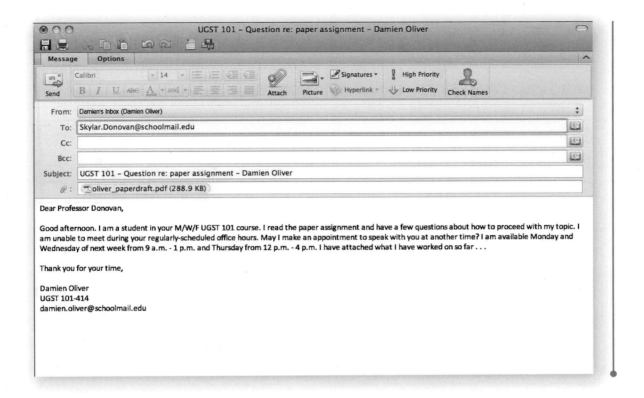

The informal style that you use in writing an e-mail, a text, or a post can become a problem when you try to write a formal research paper.

- **What do they want or need to know?** If your presentation will be about fast food and health, how much interest do your listeners have in nutrition? Would they be more interested in some other aspect of college life?

- **Who are my listeners?** What do the members of your audience have in common with you? How are they different from you?

- **What are their attitudes toward me, my ideas, and my topic?** How are your listeners likely to feel about the ideas you are planning to present? For instance, what are their attitudes about fast food? ■

Citing Your Sources

Whether you are writing an essay, a formal research paper, a script for a presentation, a page for a Web site, or something else, at some point you'll present your findings. Remember that for each source you quote, paraphrase, or summarize, you must include a complete citation, a reference that enables a reader to locate the source based on information such as the author's name, the title of the work, and the publication date.

Citations: Why and How?

Citing your sources serves many purposes. For one thing, acknowledging the information and ideas you've borrowed from other writers distinguishes their ideas from your own and shows respect for their work. Source citations show your audience that you have based your conclusions on good, reliable evidence. They also provide a starting place for anyone who would like more information about the topic or is curious about how you reached your conclusions. Most important, citing your sources is the simplest way to avoid *plagiarism*—taking another person's ideas or work and presenting it as your own—which we will turn to next.

Source citations show your audience that you have based your conclusions on good, reliable evidence.

Source citation includes many details and can get complicated, but it all comes down to two basic rules. As you write, just remember these two points:

1. If you use somebody else's exact words, you must give that person credit.

2. If you use somebody else's ideas, *even if you use your own words to express those ideas*, you must give that person credit.

Your instructors will tell you their preferred method for citation: footnotes, references in parentheses included in the text of your paper, or endnotes. If you are not given specific guidelines for composing citations, or if you simply want to be sure that you cite your sources correctly, use a handbook or writing style manual. The *MLA Handbook for Writers of Research Papers,* published by the Modern Language Association (http://www.mlahandbook.org), is a standard manual. Another is the *Publication Manual of the American Psychological Association* (http://www.apastyle.org). You can now download MLA and APA apps on your mobile devices from Google Play or iTunes.

About Plagiarism

Plagiarism is taking another person's ideas or work and presenting it as your own. Plagiarism is unacceptable in a college setting. Just as taking someone else's property is considered physical theft, taking credit for someone else's ideas is considered intellectual theft. In written reports and papers, you must give credit any time you use (a) another person's actual words; (b) another person's ideas or theories, even if you don't quote the person directly; or (c) any other information that is not considered common knowledge.

Occasionally, writers and journalists who have plagiarized have jeopardized their careers. In 2012, columnist Fareed Zakaria was suspended for a week from *Time* and CNN for plagiarizing material from *The New Yorker*, an oversight for which he took full responsibility. In spring 2013, Fox News analyst Juan Williams was criticized for plagiarizing material from a Center for American Progress report in a column he wrote for a political insider publication, but he blamed his research assistant for the transgression. Also in 2013, Republican senator Rand Paul of Kentucky found himself in trouble over accusations that he plagiarized portions of his book and several speeches. Even a few college presidents have been found guilty of borrowing the words of others and using them as their own in speeches and written documents. Such discoveries may result not only in embarrassment and shame but also in lawsuits and criminal actions.

Plagiarism can be a problem on any college campus, and research finds that first-year students are more likely to plagiarize than others. Some students contemplate plagiarizing because they think that doing so will help them get a better grade, but you can avoid the temptation if you keep in mind the high likelihood of getting caught as well as the serious consequences if you do get caught.

Because there is no universal rule about plagiarism, ask your instructors about the guidelines they set in their classes. Once you know the rules, plagiarism is easy to avoid. Keep careful notes as you do your research, so that later on you don't mistake someone else's words or ideas for your own. Finally, be sure to check out your college's official definition of what constitutes plagiarism, which you will find in the student handbook, college catalog, college Web site, course syllabi, or first-year course materials. If you have any questions about what is and isn't acceptable, be sure to ask someone in charge. "I didn't know" is not a valid excuse if you get caught plagiarizing.

It should go without saying (but we'll say it anyway) that intentional plagiarism is a bad idea on many levels. Aside from the possibility of being caught and the potential for punishment—a

failing grade, suspension, or even expulsion— submitting a paper you purchased from an Internet source, copying and pasting passages from someone else's paper, or lifting material from a published source will cause you to miss out on the discovery and skill development that research assignments are meant to teach. ■

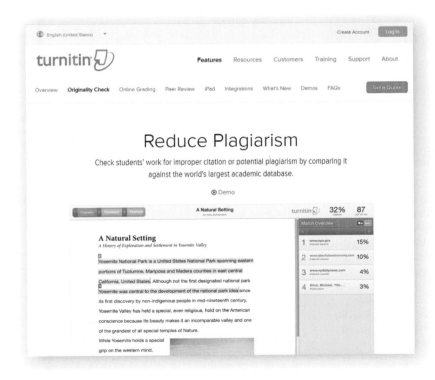

Speaking

What you have learned in this chapter about writing also applies to public speaking—each is a process that you can learn and master, and both result in a product. Since the fear of public speaking is a common one (it is more common, in fact, than the fear of death), you might be thinking along these lines: What if I plan, organize, prepare, and rehearse my speech, but as I'm about to begin my mind goes completely blank, I drop my note cards, or I say something totally embarrassing? Remember that people in your audience have been in your position and will understand your anxiety. Your audience wants you to succeed. Just be positive, rely on your wit, and keep speaking. Your recovery is what they are most likely to recognize; your success is what they are most likely to remember.

△ **They Make It Look So Easy**

Can you imagine speaking in front of a live audience at an event being broadcast to millions of people around the world? When television icon Ellen DeGeneres hosted the eighty-sixth Academy Awards ceremony in March 2014, she surprised everybody by having pizza delivered during the show to the hungry celebrity audience. While this comedian's use of humor and creativity to engage with the audience seems effortless, she wasn't always so comfortable onstage. "I got so nervous I would choke," she has said when talking about her early days doing stand-up comedy. When you feel nervous about speaking in front of others, consider taking a cue from Ellen: How can you work some audience interaction into your presentation? © Getty Images.

Guidelines for Successful Speaking

Just as there is a process for writing a paper, there is a process for developing a good speech. The following guidelines can help you greatly improve your speaking skills and lose your fear of speaking publicly.

Step 1: Clarify Your Objective Begin by identifying the goals of your presentation. Do you want to persuade your listeners that your campus needs additional student parking? Do you want to inform your listeners about the student government? What do you want your listeners to know, believe, or do when you are finished?

Step 2: Understand Your Audience To help you understand the people you'll be talking to, ask yourself the following questions:

- What do they already know about my topic?
- What do they want or need to know?
- Who are my listeners?
- What are their attitudes toward me, my ideas, and my topic?

Step 3: Organize Your Presentation Now comes the most important part of the process: building your presentation by selecting and arranging blocks of information so that you will guide your listeners through ideas they already have to the new knowledge, attitudes, and beliefs you would like them to have. You can use the suggestions given earlier for creating an outline to actually write an outline for a speech.

Step 4: Choose Appropriate Visual Aids You might use presentation software, such as Prezi or PowerPoint, to prepare your presentations. When creating PowerPoint slides or Prezi templates, you can insert images and videos to support your ideas while making your presentations animated, engaging, and interactive. You might also choose to prepare a chart, write on the board, or distribute handouts. As you

△ **Reach for the Stars**
A planetarium probably won't be available to you when you're giving a speech about astronomy, but you can still use dynamic visual aids that grab your audience's attention and support your major points. © Hill Street Studios/Blend Images/Corbis.

select and use your visual aids, consider these guidelines:

- Make visuals easy to follow. Make sure that words are large enough to be read, and don't overload your audience by including too much information on one slide.

- Use font colors to make your slides visually attractive. Use light colors for text on a dark background or dark colors on a light background.

- Explain each visual clearly.

- Give your listeners enough time to process visuals.

- Proofread carefully. Misspelled words do not make you seem knowledgeable.

- Maintain eye contact with your listeners while you discuss the visuals. Don't turn around and address the screen.

A fancy slide show can't make up for a lack of careful research or sound ideas, but using clear, attractive visual aids can help you organize your material and help your listeners understand what they're hearing. The quality of your visual aids and your skill in using them can help make your presentation effective.

Step 5: Prepare Your Notes If you are like most speakers, having an entire written copy of your speech in front of you may tempt you to read much of your presentation. But a speech that is read word for word will often sound artificial. A better strategy is to memorize your introduction and conclusion, and then use a carefully prepared outline to guide you in between the beginning and end of your speech. You should practice in advance. Because you are speaking mainly from an outline, your choice of words will be slightly different each time you give your presentation, with the result that you will sound prepared but natural. Since you're not reading, you will be able to maintain eye contact with your listeners. Try using note cards (number them in case you accidentally drop the stack on your way to the front of the room). After you become more experienced, your visuals can serve as notes. A handout or a slide listing key points can provide you with a basic outline.

Step 6: Practice Your Delivery Practice delivering your speech before an audience—a friend, your dog, even the mirror. Use eye contact and smile. As you rehearse, form a mental image of success rather than failure. Practice your presentation aloud several times to control your anxiety. Begin a few days before your speech date, and make sure you rehearse out loud, as thinking through your speech and talking through your speech have very different results. Consider making an audio or video recording of yourself on your cell phone or mobile device so you can hear or see your mistakes. If you ask a practice audience (friends or family) to give you feedback, you'll have some idea of what changes you might make.

Step 7: Pay Attention to Word Choice and Pronunciation As you reread your presentation, make sure that you have used the correct words to express your ideas. Get help ahead of time with words you aren't sure how to pronounce. Try your best to avoid *like*, *um*, *uh*, *you know*, and other filler words.

Step 8: Dress Appropriately and Give Your Presentation Now you're almost ready to give your presentation. But don't forget one last step: Dress appropriately. Leave the baseball cap, the T-shirt, and the tennis shoes at home. Don't overdress, but do look professional. Experts suggest that your clothes should be a little nicer than what your audience is wearing. Some speakers find that when they dress professionally, they deliver a better presentation!

Step 9: Request Feedback from Someone in Your Audience After you've completed your speech, ask a friend or your instructor to give you some honest feedback. If you receive written evaluations from your audience, read them and pay attention to suggestions for ways you can improve. ■

TRY IT!

SETTING GOALS ▷
Seek Out Chances to Speak

What experience do you have as a public speaker in school, church, or organizations? Do you enjoy public speaking, or is it your worst nightmare? Wherever you are on the continuum of public speaking skills—from unsure to really confident—set a goal to seek out public speaking opportunities in your first year of college. These could include presentations at your former high school, a church, or a civic group, in addition to your college classes. Don't run away from speaking opportunities; avoiding them can get in the way of attaining your academic and career goals. If you think your anxiety about public speaking is out of control, however, seek help from your campus counseling center.

Chapter Review

Steps to Success: Communicating Clearly

○ **When you use the ideas of others, be sure to give them credit; then create your own unique synthesis and conclusions.** Someday you will create your own "intellectual property," and you will want others to give you credit for your ideas.

○ **Take the time and effort to develop your writing and speaking skills.** Effective writing and speaking are skills for success in college and in life after college. They are skills that employers desire for all employees.

○ **Understand the differences between formal and informal communication.** When you are in doubt about what's appropriate, use a more formal writing style.

○ **Learn and practice the three distinct stages of writing.** Prewriting, drafting, and revising are separate steps. Going through each step will improve the finished product. Ask for feedback on your writing. Accepting criticism and praise will make you a better writer.

○ **Learn and practice the guidelines for effective speaking.** Clarify your objective, analyze your audience, organize your presentation, choose appropriate visual aids, prepare your notes, and practice your delivery. Pay attention to word choice and pronunciation, dress appropriately for your presentation, and request feedback from someone in your audience afterward.

Applying what you've learned . . .

Now that you have read and discussed this chapter, consider how you can apply what you have learned to your academic and personal lives. The following prompts will help you reflect on the chapter material and its relevance to you both now and in the future.

1. Develop a five-slide PowerPoint presentation to introduce yourself to your classmates in a new way. You might include slides that contain points about your high school years, your hobbies, your jobs, your family, and so forth. Use the effective speaking strategies in this chapter to help you outline your presentation. In addition to text, use visuals such as photos, video clips, and art to engage your audience.

2. Before reading this chapter, had you considered the differences between writing an exam response and writing a blog post or a response to someone on Facebook? Think about your online communications in the past week. Can you say for certain that you knew exactly who your audience was each time? Did you send or post anything that could be misinterpreted or read by someone outside your intended audience? What advice about online communications would you give to other students?

Create Community

GO TO ▷ The writing center: If you need help with your writing assignments in any of your courses. Most campuses have a writing center—it's frequently in the English department. Students at every level benefit from taking advantage of the campus writing center.

GO TO ▷ The learning assistance center: If you need help with a wide range of learning issues, including problems with writing.

GO TO ▷ The departments of speech, theater, and communications: If you need help finding resources and specific courses to help you develop your speaking skills.

GO TO ▷ The student activities office: If you need help learning and practicing speaking skills. Becoming active in student organizations, especially those such as your student government association and your college's debate club, can provide opportunities to practice public speaking.

GO ONLINE TO ▷ The OWL, Purdue University's Online Writing Lab (http://owl .english.purdue.edu/owl/): If you need help with your writing assignments and want some writing tips. The OWL houses writing resources to assist with many writing projects.

GO ONLINE TO ▷ PLAIN, the Plain Language Action and Information Network (http://www.plainlanguage.gov/howto/guidelines/FederalPLGuidelines/TOC.cfm): If you need help deciphering government gobbledygook. This link will take you to guidelines for federal employees to use in writing user-friendly documents.

GO ONLINE TO ▷ Toastmasters International's public speaking tips (http://www .toastmasters.org/MainMenuCategories/FreeResources/NeedHelpGivingaSpeech/ TipsTechniques.aspx): If you need help developing your public speaking skills.

NOW... How do you measure up?

1. I allow myself plenty of time to do a first draft and make revisions before submitting essays or major papers to my instructors.
   - ○ Always
   - ○ Occasionally
   - ○ Never

2. I consider who is in my audience before deciding whether to use formal or informal language.
   - ○ Always
   - ○ Occasionally
   - ○ Never

3. I am careful to cite all my sources accurately.
   - ○ Always
   - ○ Occasionally
   - ○ Never

4. When giving a speech, I avoid using filler words such as *like*, *um*, and *you know*.
   - ○ Always
   - ○ Occasionally
   - ○ Never

How do your answers here compare to your responses to the quiz you took at the start of the chapter? Which sections of this chapter left a strong impression on you? What strategies for writing and speaking have you started to use? Are they working? What other strategies will you commit to trying?

10

151
Connecting with Instructors

154
Personal Relationships

155
The Ties That Bind: Family

157
Communicating in a Digital Age

159
Thriving in Diverse Environments

163
Connecting through Involvement

Connecting with Others in a Diverse World

WonderfulPixel/Shutterstock.

What does success in college have to do with connecting with others? Very simply, the quality of the relationships you develop and maintain in college will have an important effect on your success.

Not only will you develop relationships with students who look, act, and think like you, you also have the opportunity to get to know other students whose life experiences and worldviews are different. A college or university serves as a microcosm of the real world—a world that requires us all to live, work, and socialize with people from diverse ethnic, cultural, and economic groups. In few real-world settings do members of these different groups interact in such close proximity as they do on a college campus.

One important set of relationships you develop will be with your instructors. You can choose to get to know them or ignore them, but the quality and frequency of your interactions with instructors—especially interactions out of class—will affect how well you do in college.

You will also maintain relationships with members of your family, although those relationships may change in some ways. It will be important for you to keep the lines of communication open with family members to increase their understanding of your college experience.

How do you measure up?

1. One of the best parts of college is getting to know people who are different from me in terms of ethnicity, religion, or life experience.
   ○ Agree
   ○ Don't Know
   ○ Disagree

2. Some of the most important relationships I develop in college will be with my instructors.
   ○ Agree
   ○ Don't Know
   ○ Disagree

3. It will be beneficial for me to select at least one college course that exposes me to other cultures.
   ○ Agree
   ○ Don't Know
   ○ Disagree

4. Being involved in college life outside of class will probably help me get a good job after graduation.
   ○ Agree
   ○ Don't Know
   ○ Disagree

Review the items you marked "Don't Know" or "Disagree." Pay special attention to these topics in this chapter—you will find motivating strategies to develop in these areas. A follow-up quiz at the end of the chapter will prompt you to consider what you have learned.

Finding a Niche

△ Jenna Tidwell

© Steve Hix/Somos Images/Corbis.

Last week when I went to visit my psych instructor, Professor Velez, during office hours with some questions about the lecture, I noticed a family photo on her desk, and we ended up having a really nice talk about our families. She told me that going to college was really tough for her; her family was poor, so she had borrowed money for school, and she was still paying it back. It's funny—now that I know something about her life, I can relate to my instructor more than I can relate to most of my fellow students.

I'm on financial assistance, whereas the other students in my study group are always talking about the trips they're taking and sporting new shoes, haircuts, and iPads. I'm hardly about to volunteer that I've never really left the state and that I live at home to save on rent. I was expecting to meet a lot of people at college who are different than I am. I just didn't picture our differences being so much about money.

Professor Velez invited me to help with child development research that she is doing. I'm considering psychology as my major, so this is an exciting opportunity. We've already scheduled a follow-up meeting to talk more about her research. She told me about the other students she had invited to participate in the research team. "Marty just got out of the military, where he counseled soldiers, and Sunita is a first-year student like you who is interested in psych. She has a work-study job in the library." I felt excited to meet them. My dad is a veteran, so I immediately had respect for Marty, and it would probably be helpful to explore psychology with Sunita. Suddenly I could feel a little niche for myself starting to form. I also wondered whether I could find something in common with those in my study group if I tried a little harder.

What challenges do college students who are trying to connect with others often face? What are some strategies for meeting these challenges? How will Jenna's involvement in this research opportunity benefit her? What kind of diversity have you experienced in college thus far?

Connecting with Instructors

One of the most important types of relationships you can develop in college is with your instructors. The basis of such relationships is mutual respect. Instructors who respect students treat them fairly and are willing to help them both in and outside of class. Students who respect instructors come to class regularly and take their work seriously.

What Your Instructors Expect from You

Although instructors' expectations may vary depending on the particular course, most instructors will expect their students to exhibit attitudes and behaviors that are central to student success. First, and quite simply, students should get to class on time. In college, punctuality is a virtue. If you repeatedly arrive late for class or leave before class periods have officially ended, you are breaking the basic rules of etiquette and politeness, and you are intentionally or unintentionally showing a lack of respect for your instructors and your classmates. Being on time might be a difficult adjustment for some students, but you need to be aware of faculty members' expectations at your college or university.

Arrive early enough to shed your coat, shuffle through your backpack, and have your assignments, notebooks, and writing utensils or devices (only those that you need for class) ready to go. Likewise, be on time for scheduled appointments. Avoid behaviors that show a lack of respect for both the instructor and other students, such as leaving class to feed a parking meter or to answer a non-emergency call and then returning five or ten minutes later, thus disrupting class twice. Similarly, text messaging, sending instant messages, doing homework for another class, falling asleep, or talking to other students (even if you whisper) disrupts the class. Make adequate transportation plans in advance, get enough sleep at night, wake up early enough to be on time for class, and complete assignments prior to class.

Your instructors expect you to come to class promptly, do the assigned work to the best of your ability, listen and participate, think critically about course material, and *persist*—that is, not give up when a concept is difficult to master. Instructors also expect honesty and candor. Many instructors will invite you to express your feelings about the course anonymously in writing through one-minute papers or other forms of class assessment.

Generally speaking, college instructors expect that you're going to be self-motivated to do your best. Your grade school and high school teachers might have spent a great deal of time thinking about how to motivate you, but college instructors usually consider motivation to be your personal responsibility.

College instructors expect that you're going to be self-motivated to do your best.

What You Can Expect from Your Instructors

The expectations you have for college instructors may be based on what you have heard, both positive and negative, from friends, fellow students, and family members, but you will find that instructors vary in personality and experience. You might have instructors who are in their first year of teaching, either as graduate students or as new professors. Other instructors

△ **Exchanging Ideas**

Most college instructors have a passion for their field and love to exchange ideas. Many successful college graduates can name a particular instructor who made a positive difference in their lives and influenced their academic and career paths. Embrace opportunities to develop meaningful relationships with your instructors. Doing so could change your life for the better. © John Stanmeyer/VII/Corbis.

might be seasoned professors who have taught generations of new students. Some will be introverted and difficult to approach; others will be open, friendly, and willing to talk to you and your classmates.

You may find that your instructors have differing viewpoints on a single topic. Don't let it confuse you. This "intellectual diversity" is one of the special features of almost all higher education environments and can help you understand that there is seldom one right answer to any complex question.

No matter what their personality, viewpoint, or level of experience or skill as a lecturer, however, you should expect your instructors to grade you fairly and provide meaningful feedback on your papers and exams. They should be organized, prepared, and enthusiastic about their academic field, and they should be accessible. You should always be able to approach your instructors if you need assistance or if

you have a personal problem that affects your academic work.

Maximizing the Learning Relationship

Most college instructors appreciate your willingness to ask for appointments. This may seem a little scary to some students, but most instructors welcome the opportunity to establish appropriate relationships with their students and to get to know them. As discussed in the first chapter of this book, it's up to you to take the initiative to visit your instructors during their office hours. Most instructors are required to keep office hours, so don't worry that you are asking for a special favor. Even part-time instructors, who are not required to have office hours, can be available to help you with your coursework or answer your questions. You can visit your instructors, either in real

So What *Is* Academic Freedom?

Colleges and universities have promoted the advancement of knowledge by granting instructors *academic freedom*, the virtually unlimited freedom of speech and inquiry as long as human lives, rights, and privacy are not violated. Such freedom is not usually possible in other professions.

Most college instructors believe in the freedom to speak out, whether in a classroom discussion about economic policy or at a political rally. Think of where education would be if instructors were required to keep their own ideas to themselves. You won't always agree with your instructors, but you will benefit by listening to what they have to say and respecting their diverse ideas and opinions.

Academic freedom also extends to students. Within the limits of civility and respect for others you will be free to express your opinions in a way that might be different from your experience in high school or work settings.

time or online, anytime during the term, to ask questions, seek help with a difficult topic or assignment, or discuss a problem. If you have a problem with the instructor, the course, or your grade, set up a meeting with your instructor to work things out. If the problem is a grade, however, keep in mind that your instructors have the right to assign you a grade based on your performance, and no one can force them to change that grade.

People who become college faculty members do so because they have a real passion for learning about a particular subject. If you and your professor share an interest in a particular field of study, you will have the opportunity to develop a true friendship based on mutual interests. The relationships you develop with instructors can be valuable to you both now and in the future. Instructors who know you well can also write that all-important letter of reference when you are applying to graduate school or looking for your first job after college.

Handling Conflict between You and an Instructor

Although there is potential in any environment for things to go wrong, only rarely are problems between students and instructors irresolvable. If you have a conflict with an instructor, you should first ask the instructor for a meeting to discuss your problem. See whether the two of you can work things out. If the instructor refuses, go up the administrative ladder, starting at the bottom: department head to dean, and so on. Above all, don't let a bad experience sour you on college. Even the most trying instructor will be out of your life by the end of the term. When all else fails, resolve to stick with the class until the final exam is behind you. Then shop carefully for instructors for your next term by getting recommendations from fellow students, your academic adviser, and others whose advice you can trust. ■

Personal Relationships

One of the best things about going to college is meeting new people. In fact, scholars who study college students have found that students learn as much—or more—from other students as they learn from instructors. Although not everyone you meet in college will become a close friend, you will likely find a few special relationships that may even last a lifetime. Some relationships will be with people with whom you don't share a common background.

Roommates

Adjusting to a roommate is a significant transition experience. You might make a lifetime friend or end up with an exasperating acquaintance you wish you'd never known. A roommate doesn't have to be a best friend, just someone with whom you can share your living space comfortably.

Perhaps your current roommate is someone you wouldn't have selected if given a choice. Although it's tempting to room with your best friend from high school, that friend might not make the best roommate. In fact, many students lose friends by rooming with them. Many students end up developing a lasting relationship with someone who at first was a total stranger.

It's important for roommates to establish in writing their mutual rights and responsibilities. Many colleges provide contract forms that you and your roommate might find useful if things go wrong. If you have problems with your roommate, talk them out promptly. Talk directly—politely, but plainly. If the problems persist or if you don't know how to talk them out, ask your residence hall adviser for help.

Romantic Relationships

You may already be in a long-term committed relationship as you begin college, or you might have your first serious romance with someone you meet on campus. Given that college allows you to meet people from different backgrounds who share common interests, you might find it easier to meet romantic partners in college than it ever was before. Whether you commit to one relationship or you keep yourself open for meeting others, you'll grow and learn about yourself and those with whom you become involved.

If you are thinking about getting married or entering a long-term commitment, consider this: Studies show that the younger you are when you marry, the lower your odds are of enjoying a successful marriage. It is important not to marry before both you and your partner are certain who you are and what you want.

Breaking Up Is Hard to Do

Breaking up is hard, but if it's time to end a relationship, do it cleanly and calmly. Explain your feelings and talk them out. If you don't get a mature reaction, take the high road; don't join someone else in the mud.

Almost everyone has been rejected or "dumped" at one time or another. Let some time pass, be open to emotional support from your friends and family, and, if necessary, visit your college counselor or a chaplain. These professionals have assisted many students through similar experiences, and they can be there for you as well.

Relationship No-Nos

It is never wise to become romantically involved with an instructor or with someone who works above or for you. Imagine how you will feel if the relationship ends and your ex still has control over your grades or your job! If you date someone who works for you and the relationship ends, you might find yourself being fired, sued, or accused of sexual harassment, which refers to any kind of unwanted sexual advances or remarks. Even dating a coworker is risky: If it goes well, the relationship may take your attention away from your job; if it does not go well, things may be awkward if you continue to work together. ■

The Ties That Bind: Family

Almost all first-year students, no matter their age, are connected to other family members. Your family might be a spouse and children, a partner, or your parents and siblings. The relationships that you have with family members can be a source of support throughout your college years, and it's important to do your part to maintain those relationships.

If you come from a cultural background that values family relationships and responsibilities above everything else, you will also have to work to balance your home life and college. In some cultures, if your grandmother or aunt needs help, that might be considered just as important—or more important—than going to class or taking an exam.

Negotiating the demands of college and family can be difficult. However, most college instructors will be flexible with requirements if you have genuine problems with meeting a deadline because of family obligations. But it's important that you explain your situation to your instructors; don't expect them to be able to guess what you need. As the demands on your time increase, it's also important that you talk with family members to help them understand your role and responsibilities as a student.

Marriage and Parenting during College

Can marriage and parenting coexist positively with being a college student? The answer, of course, is yes, although meeting everyone's needs—your own, your spouse's, your children's—is not easy. If you are married, whether or not you have children, you need to become an expert at time management. If you do have children, make sure you find out what resources your college offers to help you with child care.

◁ **Sweet Success**
Whether you are single or have a spouse or partner, being a parent while being a college student is one of the most challenging situations you can face. Find other students who have children so that you have a support system—it can make all the difference. You may not believe it now, but you are functioning as an important role model for your children. They will learn from you that education is worth striving for, even in the face of many obstacles. © Paul Barton/Corbis.

Sometimes going to college can create conflict between you and your spouse or partner as you take on a new identity and new responsibilities. Financial problems are likely to put extra pressure on your relationship, so both you and your partner have to work hard at paying attention to each other's needs. Be sure to involve your spouse and children in your decisions. Bring them to campus at every opportunity, and let your spouse (and your children, if they are old enough) read your papers and other assignments. Finally, set aside time for your partner and your children just as carefully as you schedule your work and your classes.

Relationships with Parents

Your relationship with your parents will never be quite the same as it was before you began college. On the one hand, you might find it uncomfortable when your parents try to make decisions on your behalf, such as choosing your major, determining where and how much you work, and setting rules for what you do on weekends. On the other hand, you might find that it's hard to make decisions on your own without talking to your parents first. While communication with your parents is important, don't let them make all your decisions. Your college can help you draw the line between which decisions should be yours alone and which decisions your parents should help you make. Many college students are living in blended families, so more than one set of parents is involved in their college experience. If your father or mother has remarried, you might have to negotiate with both family units.

So how can you have a good relationship with your parents during this period of transition?

A first step in establishing a good relationship with them is to be aware of their concerns. Your parents may be worried that you'll harm yourself in some way. They might still see you as young and innocent, and they don't want you to make the same mistakes that they might have made or experience situations that have been publicized in the media. They might be concerned that your family or cultural values will change or that you'll never really come home again, and for some students, that is exactly what happens.

Remember, though, that parents generally mean well. Most of them love their children even if their love isn't always expressed in the best way. Your parents have genuine concerns that you will understand even better if and when you become a parent yourself. To help your parents feel more comfortable with your life in college, try setting aside regular times to update them on how things are going for you. Ask for and consider their advice. You don't have to take it, but thinking about what your parents suggest can be useful as one of the many factors that will help you make decisions.

Even if you're successful in establishing appropriate boundaries between your life and your parents' lives, it's hard not to worry about what's happening at home, especially when your family is in a crisis. If you find yourself in the midst of a difficult family situation, seek help from your campus's counseling center or from a chaplain. And whether or not your family is in crisis, if they are not supportive, reach out to others who can offer the emotional support that you need. With your emotional needs satisfied, your reactions to your real family will be much less painful. ■

Communicating in a Digital Age

So much of our communication with others occurs online, through e-mail, text messaging, mobile apps, instant messaging, photo messaging, and posting on social networking sites such as Facebook. Online communication enables us to connect with others, whether we're forming new friendships or romantic relationships or maintaining established ones. Online communication also gives us a broad sense of community. Whereas people used to gather around the proverbial water cooler to chat, new media continually offer new virtual gathering places. Given how often we use technology to communicate with others, it becomes critically important to use it properly. Here are some helpful suggestions.[1]

1. **Match the seriousness of your message to your communication medium.** Know when to communicate online versus offline. Texting a friend to remind her of a coffee date that you've already set up likely makes more sense than going to her home, and it's probably quicker and less disruptive than calling her. E-mail may be best when dealing with problematic people or trying to resolve certain types of conflicts. That's because you can take time to think and carefully draft and revise your responses before sending them—something that isn't possible during face-to-face interactions.

   Use face-to-face interactions for in-depth, lengthy, and detailed explanations of professional or personal problems or important relationship decisions. Although online communication is common, many people still expect important news to be shared in person. Most of us would be surprised if our spouse revealed a long-awaited pregnancy through e-mail, or if a friend disclosed a serious illness through a text message.

2. **Don't assume that online communication is always more efficient.** Issues that may cause

[1]Adapted from Steven McCornack, *Reflect & Relate: An Introduction to Interpersonal Communication*, 3rd ed., pp. 24–27. © 2013 Bedford/St. Martin's. Boston, MA.

Given how often we use technology to communicate with others, it becomes critically important to use it properly.

an emotional reaction are more effectively and ethically handled in person or over the phone. So are many simple things—like deciding when to meet or where to go to lunch. Often a one-minute phone call or a quick face-to-face exchange can save several minutes of texting.

3. **Presume that your posts are public.** You may be thinking of the laugh you'll get from friends when you post the funny picture of you drunkenly hugging a houseplant on Facebook. But would you want family members, future in-laws, or potential employers to see the picture? Even if you have privacy settings on your personal page, what's to stop friends from downloading your photos and posts and distributing them to others? Keep this rule in mind: Anything you've sent or posted online can potentially be seen by anyone.

4. **Remember that your posts are permanent.** What goes online or is shared through a mobile app lives on forever, despite some sites' claims to the contrary. Old e-mails, photos, videos, tweets, blogs, you name it—all of these may still be accessible years later. As just one example, everything you have ever posted on Facebook is stored on the Facebook server, whether or not you delete it from your profile. And Facebook legally reserves the right to sell your content, as long as they first delete personally identifying information (such as your name). Think before you post.

Table 10.1 ▽ Important Points to Keep in Mind

Online Communication Suggestion	Best Practices Suggestions
1. Match the gravity of your message to your communication medium.	*Online* is best for quick reminders, linear messages, or messages that require time and thought to craft. *Offline* is best for important information: engagements, health issues, etc.
2. Don't assume that online communication is always more efficient.	If your message needs a quick decision or answer, a phone call or a face-to-face conversation may be best. Use online communication if you want the person to have time to respond.
3. Presume that your posts are public.	If you wouldn't want a message published for public consumption, don't post/send it online.
4. Remember that your posts are permanent.	Even after you delete something, it still exists on servers and may be accessible.
5. Practice the art of creating drafts.	Don't succumb to the pressure to answer an e-mail immediately. Taking time to respond will result in a more competent message.
6. Protect your online identity and yourself when online correspondence turns into face-to-face communication.	Choose passwords carefully and limit the personal information you put online. Exercise caution and common sense when meeting in person people whom you've met online.

Source: Adapted from Steven McCornack, *Reflect & Relate: An Introduction to Interpersonal Communication*, 3rd ed., pp. 24–27. © 2013 Bedford/St. Martin's. Boston, MA.

5. **Practice the art of creating drafts.** Get into the habit of saving text and e-mail messages as drafts, then revisiting them later and editing them as needed for appropriateness, effectiveness, and ethics. Because online communication makes it easy to flame, many of us impetuously fire off messages that we later regret.

6. **Protect your online identity and yourself when online correspondence turns into face-to-face communication.** Choose secure passwords for your social networking sites and for course sites where your grades might be listed. Limit the amount of personal information available on your Facebook profile, ratchet up your security settings, and accept friend requests only from people you know. Exercise caution and common sense when meeting in person someone you've met online. Keep in mind that some people tell lies on their profiles and posts. Select a public meeting place, and be sure a friend, family member, or roommate knows about your plans. ■

Thriving in Diverse Environments

So far in this chapter, you have learned about various ways to connect with others while in college and also about how being in college changes many of the relationships in your life. A logical next step is to increase your awareness of differences and similarities across people, which is an important component of your ability to connect with others and to build and maintain healthy relationships. Colleges and universities attract students with different backgrounds; the ethnicity, cultural background, economic status, and religion of students may vary widely on these college campuses. These differences provide opportunities for students to experience diversity.

Diversity is the difference in social and cultural identities among people living together. Through self-assessment, discovery, and open-mindedness, you can begin to understand your perspectives on diversity. This work, although difficult at times, will add to your educational experiences, personal growth, and development. Thinking critically about your personal values and belief systems will allow you to have a greater sense of belonging and to make a positive contribution to our multicultural society.

Stereotyping: Why We Believe What We Believe

Many of our beliefs are the result of our personal experience. Others are a result of a *stereotype*, a generalization—usually exaggerated or oversimplified and often offensive—that is used to describe or distinguish a group. A negative experience with members of a particular group may result in the stereotyping of people in that group. We may acquire stereotypes about people we have never met before or may have bought into a stereotype without even thinking about it. Children who grow up in an environment in which dislike and distrust of certain types of people are openly expressed might adopt those judgments even if they have had no interaction with those being judged.

◁ **Expand Your Worldview**
How has going to college changed your experience with diversity? Are you getting to know people of different races or ethnic groups? Do your classes have both traditional-aged and older students? Are you seeking out people who are different from you and sharing personal stories and worldviews? © 2/Ocean/Corbis.

△ Can You Find Yourself?

Are you a student who has recently come to the United States from another country? Perhaps you have immigrated to the United States with family members, or perhaps you came on your own. Whatever your particular situation, learning the unique language, culture, and expectations of a U.S. college can be a challenge. Do instructors' expectations and student behaviors seem different from what you experienced in your home country? Seek out English as a second language (ESL) courses or programs if you need help with your English skills. You can also visit the international student counselors at your college to find out how you can continue to increase your understanding of life in the United States, both on and off campus. © Elaine Thompson/AP/Corbis.

TRY IT!

MAKING DECISIONS ▷ Resist Prejudice

All of us have been guilty of stereotyping people at some point in our lives. College is a good time to challenge your prejudices—beliefs or opinions you hold that are based not on reason or actual experience but on someone's ethnicity, religion, sexual orientation, political viewpoint, or other defining characteristic. The first step is to be aware of these prejudices. Then decide to challenge these prejudices by getting to know people as individuals, rather than making assumptions about them because they are members of certain groups. Spending time with people who view the world differently than you do will contribute to your college experience and help you avoid stereotyping.

Other Differences You Will Encounter in College

When we hear the word *diversity*, most of us immediately think of differences in race or ethnic group. But you will experience many other kinds of human difference during your years in college.

Age. Although some students enter college around age eighteen, others choose to enter or return to college in their thirties and beyond. Age diversity in the classroom gives everyone the opportunity to learn from others who have different life experiences. Many factors come into play when students enter higher education for the first time, stop, and then reenter.

Economic status. The United States is a country of vast differences in wealth. This considerable economic diversity can be either a positive or a negative aspect of college life. On the positive side, you will be exposed to, and can learn from, students who present you with a wide range of economic differences. Meeting others who have grown up with either more or fewer opportunities than you did is part of learning how to live in a democracy.

Try to avoid developing exaggerated feelings of superiority or inferiority. What matters now is not what you had or didn't have before you came to college; what matters is what you do in college. You have more in common with other students than you think. Now your individual efforts, dreams, courage, determination, and ability to stay focused can be your success factors.

Religion. Many students come to college with deeply held religious views. Some will create faith communities on campus. Their religions will be not only those with a common Judeo-Christian heritage but also Islam, Hinduism, and Buddhism. Learning about different faith perspectives is another way you can explore human difference.

Some students and instructors may consider themselves atheists or agnostics, either denying or doubting the existence of a divine creator. Whatever *your* religious views may be, it is important that you respect the views of others. Learning more about world religions can help you better understand your own faith perspective.

Learning and physical challenges.

Although the majority of college students have reasonably average learning and physical abilities, the numbers of students with physical or learning challenges are rising on most college campuses, as are the services that are available to them. Physical challenges can include hearing impairment, visual impairment, paralysis, or specific disorders such as cerebral palsy or multiple sclerosis. As discussed earlier in this book, many students have some form of learning disability that makes college work a challenge.

A person with a physical or learning challenge wants to be treated just as you would treat anyone else—with respect. If a student with such a challenge is in your class, treat him or her as you would any student; too much eagerness to help might be seen as an expression of pity.

If you have, or think you might have, a learning disability, visit your campus learning center for a diagnosis and advice on getting extra help for learning problems. Unlike in high school, college students with disabilities need to inform the appropriate office if they require accommodations.

Sexuality. The word *sexuality* refers to the people to whom you are romantically attracted. You are familiar with the terms *gay, straight, homosexual, heterosexual,* and *bisexual.* In college you will likely meet students, staff members, and instructors whose sexual orientation may

◁ **Role Model**
He spent only three months on Capitol Hill, but Zach Ennis, a deaf college intern in the office of Representative Kevin Yoder (R-KS), developed a video to help the congressman reach out to his deaf constituency that could be a model for others. How can Zach's achievements inspire you to overcome challenges that you face? © MCT via Getty Images.

△ Commit to Coexist

In a college or university environment, students often learn that there are more commonalities than differences between themselves and others who have been on the opposite side of the fence for centuries. By learning to coexist respectfully and peacefully, students can take the first step toward building a better world. Jamie Smith—Skinny Genes Photography.

TRY IT!

SETTING GOALS ▷
Make a New and Different Friend

College will give you the opportunity to expand your horizons. And if you want college to be more than a repeat of high school, you have to be willing to branch out, to try new things, to meet new people. Set a goal of befriending someone who you think is different from you based on what you observe. Pay attention to what other students say in class and get an idea of which students think differently from you and hold different values. Strike up a conversation with one of these students and find out more about his or her background and what the two of you have in common in spite of your differences. Is this person as different from you as you originally thought? What have you learned about the assumptions you make about people?

differ from yours. While some people are lucky enough to come from welcoming environments, for many students, college is the first time they have been able to openly express their sexual identity. Sexual orientation can be difficult to talk about, and it is important that you respect all individuals with whom you come in contact. Check to see if your campus has a center for the lesbian, gay, bisexual, and transgendered (LGBT) community. Consider going to hear some speakers, and expand your worldview.

Creating a Welcoming Environment on Your Campus

Colleges are working to provide a welcoming and inclusive campus environment for all students. Because of acts of violence, intimidation, and stupidity occurring on campuses, college administrations have established policies against any and all forms of discriminatory actions, racism, and insensitivity. Many campuses have adopted zero-tolerance policies that prohibit verbal and nonverbal harassment as well as hate crimes such as physical assault, vandalism, and intimidation.

Whatever form these crimes might take on your campus, it is important to examine your thoughts and feelings about their occurrence. The most important question to ask yourself is: Will you do something about it, or do you think it is someone else's problem? Commit to becoming involved in making your campus a safe place for all students.

If you have been the victim of a racist, insensitive, or discriminatory act, report it to the proper authorities. ■

Connecting through Involvement

A college or university can seem to be a huge and unfriendly place, especially if you went to a small high school or grew up in a small town. So that you will feel comfortable in this new environment, it is important for you to get involved in campus life. Getting involved is not difficult, but it will take some initiative on your part. Consider your interests and the high school activities you enjoyed most, and choose some activities to explore. You might be interested in joining an intramural team, performing community service, running for a student government office, or getting involved in your residence hall. Or you might prefer to join a more structured campuswide club or organization.

While involvement is the key, it's important to strike a balance between finding a niche where you are immediately comfortable and challenging yourself to have new and different interactions with others. Having an open mind and experiencing diversity will prepare you for the workforce you will be entering after you graduate. Also challenge yourself to learn about various cultural groups in and around your college and home community, and participate in campus ethnic and cultural celebrations to learn about unique traditions, ideas, and viewpoints.

Almost every college has numerous organizations you can join; usually, you can check them out through activity fairs, printed guides, open houses, Web pages, and so on. If a particular organization interests you, consider attending one of the organization's meetings before you decide to join. Find out what the organization is like, what the expected commitment is in terms of time and money, and whether you feel comfortable with the members. Students who become involved with at least one organization are more likely to complete their first year and remain in college.

Be careful not to overextend yourself when it comes to campus activities. Although it is important to get involved, joining too many clubs or organizations will make it difficult to focus on any one activity and will interfere with your studies. Future employers will see a balance in academics and campus involvement as a desirable quality in prospective employees. Don't fall into the trap of thinking that more is better. In campus involvement as in many things, quality is much more important than quantity.

Working

One of the best ways to develop meaningful relationships on your campus is to get an on-campus job, either through the federal work/study program or directly through the college. Generally, your on-campus supervisors will be much more flexible than off-campus employers in helping you balance your study demands and your work schedule. You might not make as much money working on campus as you would in an off-campus job, but the relationships that you'll develop with influential people who care about your success in college and who will write those all-important reference letters make

TRY IT!

MANAGING TIME ▷
How Involved Is Too Involved?

How many clubs and organizations have you joined? Do you think you are too involved in campus activities? As you develop your term schedule, include your out-of-class activities and obligations. Be careful not to overextend yourself when it comes to campus activities. If you are spending more time participating in extra-curricular activities than studying, you probably should cut back, at least for the first year. And if you think you are not involved enough, remember that future employers will consider a healthy balance between academics and campus involvement to be an important quality in applicants.

on-campus employment well worth it. Consider finding a job related to your intended major. For instance, if you are a premed major, you might be able to find on-campus work in a biology or chemistry lab. That work could help you gain knowledge and experience as well as make connections with faculty experts in your field.

If an on-campus job is not available or you don't find one that appeals to you, an off-campus job can allow you to meet new people in the community. If you already had a job before starting college, talk to your employer about the new demands on your time. Also keep in mind that some employers offer tuition assistance in certain circumstances; ask whether any such opportunities are available to you.

Wherever you decide to find a job, it's important that you limit work to a reasonable number of hours per week. Although some students have to work to pay their tuition or living expenses, many college students work too many hours just to support a certain lifestyle. Be careful to maintain a reasonable balance between work and study. Don't fall into the trap of thinking, "I can do it all." Too many college students have found that trying to do it all means not doing anything well.

Limit work to a reasonable number of hours per week.

Community Service

As a first-year student, one way to expand your experience with diversity is to consider volunteering for a community service project such as serving the homeless at a soup kitchen or helping to build or renovate homes for needy families. Your campus's division of student affairs might have a volunteer or community service office that offers other service opportunities such as working with elementary school students who are learning to read, tutoring in an after-school program, participating in a campus cleanup, or working in a local animal shelter. You can also check Volunteer Match (http://www.volunteermatch.org) for opportunities in your area. Simply enter your ZIP code and, if you wish, key words to help you find volunteer work in your field of interest. ▪

Chapter Review

Steps to Success: Connecting with Others in a Diverse World

○ **Seek out relationships with instructors outside of class.** In particular, visit them during their posted office hours.

○ **Be open to new relationships.** College may be a great time for you to test out serious relationships, including romantic ones.

○ **Don't hesitate to get help from your campus counseling center.** When counselors are asked, "What is the most common type of problem you help students address?" the answer is "relationships."

○ **Work to have a good relationship with your family during the college years.** Family members have your best interests at heart, and college is a time to become closer to them while also setting boundaries.

○ **Get involved.** Join other students in groups sponsored by your educational institution. Students who are involved are more likely to graduate from college than those who are not. Getting involved is fun, easy, free, and rewarding, and employers will be interested in your extracurricular activities.

○ **Look for the right on- or off-campus job.** Working during college is a good thing, depending on where you work, how much you work, and what you do. Get help on this important decision from your adviser and career center.

○ **Consider performing some kind(s) of service during college.** By doing so, you will develop meaningful relationships that will help you clarify your career choice.

Applying what you've learned . . .

Now that you have read and discussed this chapter, consider how you can apply what you have learned to your academic and personal lives. The following prompts will help you reflect on the chapter material and its relevance to you both now and in the future.

1. If you are not already involved in on-campus activities and clubs, visit your campus's Web site or activities office to learn more about the kinds of clubs, organizations, service learning opportunities, sports teams, and volunteer work that are offered. Find at least one activity that seems interesting to you and learn more about it. When does the group meet and how often, and how many students are involved?

2. Check out some of your fellow students' profiles on Facebook or Twitter. What kinds of personal information do they share? What kinds of issues are they writing about? Do they use the privacy settings that are available? Do you think that it is important for college students to be careful about the kinds of information they post on social networking sites? Why or why not?

Create Community

GO TO ▷ The counseling center: If you need help thinking and talking about your relationships and making the most appropriate decisions. It is normal to seek such assistance. This kind of counseling is strictly confidential (unless you are a threat to yourself or others) and usually is provided at no charge, which is a great benefit.

GO TO ▷ A campus chaplain: If you need help from a member of the clergy in dealing with a relationship problem. Many public and private colleges have religiously affiliated chaplains, most of whom have specialized training in pastoral counseling. They also organize and host group activities in campus religious centers that you might want to take advantage of.

GO TO ▷ Student organizations: If you need help getting into a small group with other students that share the same interests with you.

GO ONLINE TO ▷ The University of Chicago's Student Counseling Virtual Pamphlet Collection (http://www.dr-bob.org/vpc/): If you need help finding Web sites devoted to relationship problems. Browse among the many links to see whether any information applies to you.

GO ONLINE TO ▷ "Healthy Romantic Relationships during College" (http://cmhc .utexas.edu/romrelations/romrelations.html): If you need help dealing with the ups and downs of romantic relationships. The University of Texas Counseling & Mental Health Center offers this online brochure that discusses important aspects of healthy romantic relationships.

GO ONLINE TO ▷ Diversity Web (http://www.diversityweb.org): If you need help finding resources related to diversity on campus.

GO ONLINE TO ▷ Teaching Tolerance (http://www.tolerance.org): If you need help accessing resources for dealing with discrimination and prejudice both on and off campus.

NOW... How do you measure up?

1. One of the best parts of college is getting to know people who are different in terms of ethnicity, religion, or life experience.
- ○ Agree
- ○ Don't Know
- ○ Disagree

2. Some of the most important relationships that students develop in college will be with their instructors.
- ○ Agree
- ○ Don't Know
- ○ Disagree

3. It is beneficial to select at least one college course that exposes students to other cultures.
- ○ Agree
- ○ Don't Know
- ○ Disagree

4. Being involved in college life outside of class helps students get good jobs after graduation.
- ○ Agree
- ○ Don't Know
- ○ Disagree

How do your answers here compare to your responses to the quiz you took at the start of the chapter? Which sections of this chapter left a strong impression on you? What strategies for connecting with others have you started to use? Are they working? What other strategies will you commit to trying?

169
Living on a Budget

172
Understanding Financial Aid

176
Achieving a Balance between Working and Borrowing

178
Managing Credit Wisely

Managing Money

artizarus/Shutterstock.

Whether we like it or not, we can't ignore the importance of money. Money is often symbolically and realistically the key ingredient to independence and even, some people have concluded, to a sense of freedom. You probably know of instances in which money divided a family or a relationship or seemed to drive someone's life in a direction that person would not have taken otherwise. Money can also affect people's specific academic goals, causing them to select or reject certain academic majors or degree plans.

Sometimes parents will insist that students major in a field that is more likely to yield a good job and a good salary. Given the cost of college today, these attitudes are understandable.

Although your primary goal in college should be to achieve a strong academic record, the need for money can be a significant distraction, making it more

difficult to complete your degree. Sometimes, in their attempt to survive financially, students will overuse credit cards and get themselves in serious financial trouble. Educators recognize that not understanding personal finances can hinder a student's progress, and mandatory personal finance classes are now being added in high schools and are available as options at some colleges. The purpose of this chapter is to provide basic information and suggestions so that money issues will not be a barrier to your success in college. There are sources of financial assistance through loans, grants, and work study, and this chapter will help you develop a strategy for investigating your options. Think of this chapter as a summary of needed financial skills; if you want more information, consider taking a personal finance class at your college or in your community.

How do you measure up?

1. A budget should guide how much money I spend each month.
   - ○ Agree
   - ○ Don't Know
   - ○ Disagree

2. I know how many courses I have to take to receive or maintain financial aid.
   - ○ Agree
   - ○ Don't Know
   - ○ Disagree

3. I understand the disadvantages of working too many hours a week off campus.
   - ○ Agree
   - ○ Don't Know
   - ○ Disagree

4. I am working to build a good credit score while I'm in college.
   - ○ Agree
   - ○ Don't Know
   - ○ Disagree

Review the items you marked "Don't Know" or "Disagree." Pay special attention to these topics in this chapter—you will find motivating strategies to develop in these areas. A follow-up quiz at the end of the chapter will prompt you to consider what you have learned.

Eating Your Words

△ **Jeff Zisa**

Monkey Business Images/Shutterstock.

My first two years at college, it was easy to figure out my budget, because so many of my expenses were fixed. But this year I have a car and an off-campus apartment, so I decided to get off the meal plan and buy my own food.

"This is a bad idea," said my mother when I told her of my plan. "What are you going to eat?"

"Stuff I cook," I said. "It'll be cheaper in the long run. All my roommates and I are taking turns."

We did take turns, for the first week or so. Sam made pizza. Nick made burritos. I made my famous spaghetti. Occasionally, we made more pizza or spaghetti. Then classes started and sports and clubs kicked in, and I guess no one really had time to go to the grocery store anymore. In fact, it was hard to even eat a bowl of cereal in the morning because we were always out of milk. It got to the point where we ate out all the time, and even the cheapest meal out costs $10. So within months, I had to call and tell my parents that I'd maxed out my credit card, drained my bank account, and run up over $200 in penalties—all on food.

"I know I should have kept track of what I was spending," I admitted. "It just added up so fast."

"See, I warned you?" my mother said. "You learned a painful lesson." An ominous pause followed. "So . . . what kind of job are you planning to get?"

Why is it so important to track your spending in college? What steps could Jeff take to manage his money more carefully? Going to college may give some students their first experience of living on a budget, or they may already be very good at living within their means. Some students make it a habit to track their income and expenses precisely, but other students seem to be unaware of how much money they are spending. If they run out, which they often do, they rely on credit cards to get them to the end of the month. Getting in the habit of spending more money than you have can sabotage not only your college experience but also your life after college.

Living on a Budget

Face it: College is expensive, and most students have limited financial resources. Not only is tuition a major cost, but day-to-day expenses can also add up quickly. No matter what your financial situation, a budget for college is a must. Although a budget might not completely eliminate debt after graduation, it can help you become realistic about your finances so that you will have a basis for future life planning.

A budget is a spending plan that tracks all sources of income (student loan disbursements, money from parents, etc.) and expenses (rent, tuition, etc.) during a set period of time (a week, a month, etc.). Creating and following a budget will allow you to pay your bills on time, cut costs, put some money away for emergencies, and finish college with as little debt as possible.

Creating a Budget

A budget will condition you to live within your means, put money into savings, and possibly invest down the road. Here are a few tips to help you get started.

Gather income information. To create an effective budget, you need to learn more about your income and your spending behaviors. First, determine how much money is coming in and when. Sources of income might include a job, your savings, gifts from relatives, student loans, scholarship dollars, or grants. List all your income sources, making note of how often you receive each type of income (weekly or monthly paychecks, quarterly loan disbursements, one-time gifts, etc.) and how much money you can expect each time. Knowing when your money is coming in will help you decide how to structure your budget. For example, if most of your income comes in on a monthly basis, you'll want to create a monthly budget. If you are paid every other week, a biweekly budget might work better.

Gather expense information for your college or university. Your expenses will include tuition; residence hall fees if you live on campus; and the costs of books and course materials, lab fees, and membership fees for any organizations you might join. Some institutions offer a separate January or May term. Although your tuition for these one-month terms is generally covered in your overall tuition payment, you would have extra expenses if you wanted to travel to another location in the United States or abroad.

Gather information about living expenses. First, get a "reality check." How do you *think* that you are spending your money? To find out for sure where your money is going and when, track your spending for a few weeks—ideally, for at least a full month—in a notebook or in a table or spreadsheet. The kinds of expense categories you should consider will vary depending on your situation. If you are a full-time student who lives with your parents or other family members, your living expenses won't be the same as those of a student living in a campus residence hall or in an off-campus apartment. If you are a returning student holding down a job and have a family of your own to support, you will calculate your expenses differently. Whatever your situation, keeping track of your expenses and learning about your spending behaviors are important habits. Consider which of the following expense categories are relevant to you:

- Rent/utilities (electricity, gas, water)
- Cell phone/cable/Internet/wi-fi
- Transportation (car payment, car insurance, car repairs, gas, public transportation)
- Child care
- Groceries
- Medical expenses (prescriptions, doctor visits, hospital bills)
- Clothing/laundry
- Entertainment (dining out, hobbies, movies)
- Personal grooming (haircuts, toiletries)
- Miscellaneous (travel, organization dues)

MAKING DECISIONS ▷
Miscellaneous Expenses

Trying to get a handle on your "miscellaneous" expenses can be a challenge. Make a decision to write down everything you purchase over a two-week period, and see how many of those expenses don't fit in any of the categories listed on page 169. Which of your miscellaneous expenses really are necessary, and which aren't? The unnecessary expenses are places to reduce money you spend. Make some tough choices to cut back, and start immediately. Track your spending for another two weeks. Can you tell the difference?

Be sure to recognize which expenses are fixed and which are variable. A *fixed expense* is one that will cost you the same amount every time you pay it. For example, your rent is a fixed expense because you owe your landlord the same amount each month. A *variable expense* is one that may change. Your textbooks are a variable expense because the number and cost of them will be different each term.

Find out how you are doing. Once you have a sense of how your total income compares to your total weekly or monthly expenses, you can get a clearer picture of your current financial situation.

Make adjustments. Although your budget might never be perfect, you can strive to improve it. In what areas did you spend much more or much less than expected? Do you need to reallocate funds to better meet the needs of your current situation? Be realistic and thoughtful in how you spend your money, and use your budget to help meet your goals, such as planning for a trip or getting a new pair of jeans.

Whatever you do, don't give up if your bottom line doesn't turn out to be what you expected. Budgeting is a lot like dieting; you might slip up and eat a pizza (or spend too much buying one), but all is not lost. If you stay focused and flexible, your budget can lead you to financial stability and independence.

Cutting Costs

Once you have put together a working budget and have tried it out and adjusted it, you're likely to discover that your expenses still exceed your income. Don't panic. Simply begin to look for ways to reduce those expenses. Here are some tips for saving money in college:

Recognize the difference between your needs and your wants. A *need* is something you must have. For example, tuition and textbooks are considered *needs.* On the other hand, your *wants* are goods, services, or experiences that you wish to purchase but could reasonably live without. For example, concert tickets and mochas are *wants.* Your budget should always provide for your *needs* first.

Share expenses. Having a roommate (or several) can be one of the easiest ways to cut costs on a regular basis. In exchange for giving up a little bit of privacy, you'll save hundreds of dollars on rent, utilities, and food. Make sure, however, that you work out a plan for sharing expenses equally and that everyone accepts his or her responsibilities.

Use low-cost transportation. If you live close to campus, consider whether or not you need a car. Take advantage of lower-cost options such as public transportation or biking to class to save money on gasoline and parking. If you live farther away, check to see whether your institution hosts a ride-sharing program for commuter students, or carpool with someone in your area.

Seek out discount entertainment options. Take advantage of discounted or free programming through your college. Most institutions use a portion of their student fees to provide affordable entertainment options such as discounted or free tickets to concerts, movie theaters, sports events, or other special activities.

△ **Go Vintage**

Saving money doesn't mean you have to deprive yourself. Shopping at thrift stores for your clothes or apartment furnishings is a fun, affordable way to get one-of-a-kind pieces and not break the bank. © ANDREW WINNING/Reuters/Corbis.

Embrace secondhand goods. Use online resources such as Craigslist and thrift stores such as Goodwill to expand your wardrobe, purchase extras such as games and sports equipment, or furnish and decorate your room, apartment, or house.

Avoid unnecessary fees. Making late payments on credit cards and other bills can lead to expensive fees and can lower your credit score (which in turn will raise your interest rates). You might want to set up automated online payments to avoid this type of costly mistake. ■

TRY IT!

SETTING GOALS ▷ **Develop a Personal Budget**

Using an online tool such as Bankrate's Student Budget Calculator (http://www.bankrate.com/calculators/smart-spending/college-student-budget-calculator.aspx), develop a budget for this term. Don't put this off! Unexpected financial problems can be a major source of stress and can sabotage your academic progress. Get a clear understanding of your income and expenditures right away.

Understanding Financial Aid

Few students can pay the costs of college tuition, academic fees, books, room and board, bills, and random expenses without some kind of help. Luckily, financial aid—student loans, grants, scholarships, work-study programs, and other sources of money to support your education—is available to help cover your costs.

Few students can pay the costs of college tuition, academic fees, books, room and board, bills, and random expenses without help.

Types of Aid

While grants and scholarships are unquestionably the best forms of aid because they do not have to be repaid, the federal government, states, and colleges offer many other forms of assistance, such as loans, work-study opportunities, and cooperative education. A student loan is a form of financial aid that must be paid back with interest.

Grants are funds provided by the government to help students pay for college and do not need to be repaid. They are given to students based on their financial needs. Some grants are specific to a particular academic major. Grants are awarded by the federal government, state governments, and the educational institutions themselves. Students meet academic qualifications for grants by being admitted to a college and maintaining grades that are acceptable to the grant provider.

A scholarship is money from your college or another institution that supports your education and does not have to be repaid. Some scholarships are need-based—that is, they are awarded on the basis of both talent and financial need. *Talent* can refer to your past accomplishments in the arts or athletics, your potential for future accomplishments, or even where you are from. Some colleges and universities place importance on admitting students from other states or countries. "Need" in this context means the cost of college minus a federal determination of what you and your family can afford to contribute toward that cost. Your institution might provide scholarships from its own resources or from individual donors. Donors themselves sometimes stipulate characteristics of scholarship recipients, such as age or academic major.

Other scholarships are known as merit scholarships. These are based on talent as defined above but do not require you to demonstrate financial need. It can be challenging to match your talent with merit scholarships. Most of them come through colleges and are part of the admissions and financial aid processes, which are usually described on the college's Web site. Web-based scholarship search services are another good source to explore. Be certain that the Web site you use is free, will keep your information confidential unless you release your name, and will send you a notice (usually through e-mail) when a new scholarship that matches your qualifications is posted. Also be sure to ask your employer, your family's employers, and social, community, or religious organizations about any available scholarships.

Work-study means that students who receive financial aid can also have part-time jobs to earn extra money if their aid amount is not enough to cover all their education costs. Students receive work-study notices as part of the overall financial aid notice and then can sign up to be interviewed for work-study jobs. Although some work-study jobs are relatively menial, the best options provide experience related to your academic studies while allowing you to earn money for college. Your salary is based on the skills required for a particular position and the hours involved. Keep in mind that you will be expected to accomplish specific tasks while on duty, although some employers might permit you to study during any downtime.

Cooperative (co-op) education allows you to alternate a term of study (a semester or quarter) with a term of paid work. Engineering co-op opportunities are among the most common, and the number of co-op programs in health care fields is growing. Colleges make information about co-ops available through admissions and academic departments.

Navigating Financial Aid

Financial aid seems complex because it can come from so many different sources. Each source may have a different set of rules about how to receive the money and how not to lose it. The financial aid office at your college can help you find the way to get the largest amount of money that doesn't need to be repaid, the lowest interest rate on loans, and work

possibilities that fit your academic program. Do not overlook this valuable campus resource. The financial aid office and its Web site are the best places to begin looking for all types of assistance. Other organizations that can help students find the right college and money to help them attend are located throughout the United States. Many of these organizations are members of the National College Access Network (which helps manage the National College Access Program Directory at http://www.collegeaccess.org/accessprogramdirectory) or participate in a national effort called KnowHow2Go (http://knowhow2go.acenet.edu). You might also be able to obtain funds from your employer, a local organization, or a private group.

The majority of students pay for college through a combination of various types of financial assistance: scholarships, grants, loans, and paid employment. Financial aid professionals refer to this combination as a *package.*

△ **Show Me the Money**
Don't let the paperwork scare you away. If you're not already receiving financial aid, be sure to investigate all the available options. And remember that your institution may also offer scholarships or grants that you don't have to repay. © Riza Liu/PSU Vanguard.

Qualifying for Aid

Most financial assistance requires some form of application. The application used most often is the Free Application for Federal Student Aid (FAFSA). All students should complete the FAFSA by the earliest submission deadline among the colleges they are considering. The FAFSA Web site is very informative: https://fafsa.ed.gov/. If additional forms are also required, such as the College Board's PROFILE form (http://student.collegeboard .org/css-financial-aid-profile) and individual scholarship applications, they will be listed in colleges' financial aid or admissions materials or by organizations that offer scholarships.

Read "Steps to Qualify for Financial Aid," which outlines the steps you must take to qualify for most scholarships and grants, especially those sponsored by the federal government or state governments. The amount of financial aid you receive will depend on the cost of your academic program and what you or your family can pay as

determined by the FAFSA. The cost includes average expenses for tuition and fees, books and supplies, room and board, transportation, and personal expenses. The financial aid office will subtract from that cost the amount you and your family are expected to pay. In some cases that amount can be as little as zero. Financial aid is designed to make up as much of the balance or "need" as possible.

How to Keep Your Funding

If you earn average or better grades, complete your courses each term, and finish your program or degree on time, you should have no trouble maintaining your financial aid. It's a good idea to check with the financial aid office before you drop classes to make sure you will not lose any aid.

Some types of aid, especially scholarships, require that you maintain full-time enrollment and make satisfactory academic progress.

Steps to Qualify for Financial Aid

1. Enroll half-time or more in a certificate or degree program at one of the more than 4,500 colleges and universities certified to distribute federal financial aid. A few aid programs are available for less than half-time study; check with your department or college.

2. Complete the FAFSA. The first FAFSA you file is intimidating, especially if you rush to complete it right before the deadline. Completing the FAFSA in subsequent years is easier because you only need to update items that have changed. To make the process easier, get your personal identification number (PIN) a few weeks before the deadline. This PIN will be the same one you'll use throughout your college career. Try to do the form in sections rather than tackling all of it at once. Most of the information is basic: name, address, driver's license number, and things you will know or have in your personal files and records. For many undergraduates the financial section will require your own and your parents' information from tax materials. However, if you are at least twenty-four, are a veteran, or have dependents, you do not need to submit your parents' tax information. If you are married, your spouse's tax information will be needed.

3. If your school or award-granting organization requires it, complete the College Board PROFILE form. Review your college's admission information, or ask a financial aid adviser to determine whether this form is required.

4. Identify any additional applications that are required. These are usually scholarship applications with personal statements or short essays. The organizations, including the colleges that are giving the money, will provide instructions about what is required. Most have Web sites with complete information.

5. Follow instructions carefully, and submit each application on time. Financial aid is awarded from a fixed pool of funds. Once money is awarded, there is usually none left for those who file late.

6. Complete the classes for which you were given financial aid with at least a minimum grade point average as defined by your academic department or college or the organization that provided you the scholarship.

Dropping or failing a class might jeopardize all or part of your financial aid unless you are enrolled in more credits than the minimum required for financial aid. For full-time financial aid that minimum is often defined as twelve credit hours per term. If you initially enrolled in fifteen credit hours and dropped one three-hour course, your aid should not change. Even so, talk with a financial aid counselor before making the decision to drop a course, just to be sure. Remember that, though the financial aid office is there to serve you, you must take the following steps to be your own advocate.

- **File for financial aid every year.** Even if you don't think you will receive aid for a certain year, you must file annually in case you become eligible in the future.

- **Meet all filing deadlines.** Students who do not meet filing deadlines risk losing aid from one year to the next.

- **Talk with a financial aid officer immediately if you or your family experience a significant loss** (such as the loss of a job or the death of a parent or spouse). Don't wait for the next filing period; you might be eligible for funds for the current year.

- **Inquire every year about criteria-based aid.** Many colleges and universities have grants and scholarships for students who meet specific criteria. These might include grants for minority students, grants for students in specific academic majors, and grants for students from single-parent families.

- **Inquire about campus jobs throughout the year,** as these jobs might be available at any time, not just at the beginning of the term. If you do not have a job and want or need to work, keep asking.

- **Consider asking for a reassessment of your eligibility for aid.** If you have reviewed your financial aid package and think that your circumstances deserve additional consideration, you can ask the financial aid office to reassess your eligibility. The office is not always required to do so, but the request might be worth your effort. ▪

TRY IT!

SETTING GOALS ▷ **Exhaust All Avenues**

Learn about possible sources of financial support on your campus in addition to those you may already be receiving. The best single source for this information is your institution's financial aid office. You may also want to check with your employer (if you work off campus), your parents' employers, churches, and civic organizations such as the Rotary Club or Kiwanis club in your hometown.

Achieving a Balance between Working and Borrowing

After you have determined your budget, decided what (if anything) you can pay from savings, and taken your scholarships and grants into consideration, you may find that you still need additional income. Each term or year, you should decide how much you can work while maintaining good grades and how much you should borrow from student loans.

Advantages and Disadvantages of Working

The majority of students today find that a combination of working and borrowing is the best way to gain experience, finance college, and complete their educational goals on time. Paid employment while you are in college has benefits beyond the money you earn. Having a job in a field related to your major can help you develop a credential for graduate school and make you more employable later because it shows you have the capability to manage several priorities at the same time. Working while you are in college can help you determine whether a particular career is what you will really want after you complete your education. And students who work a moderate amount (15 hours per week) typically get better grades than students who do not work at all.

On the other hand, it's almost impossible to get great grades if you work full-time while also trying to be a full-time student. Some first-year students prefer not to take a job while they're making adjustments to a new academic environment. You might find that you're able to work some terms but not others while you are a student. And family obligations or challenging classes can sometimes make the added burden of work impractical or impossible.

Part-time off-campus jobs that relate to your major or career plan are hard to come by. You'll likely find that most part-time employment has little or no connection to your career objectives. A better option may be to seek a job on campus. Students who work on campus develop relationships with instructors and staff members who can help them negotiate the academic and social sides of campus life and make plans for the future. While off-campus employers are often unwilling to allow their student employees time off for study and exam preparation, college employers will want you to put your studies and exam preparation first. The downside to on-campus employment is that you'll likely earn less than you would in an off-campus job, but if success in college is your top priority, the upside of working on campus outweighs the downside.

Student Loans

Although you should be careful not to borrow yourself into a lifetime of debt, avoiding loans altogether could delay your graduation and your progress up the career ladder. For most students, some level of borrowing is both necessary and prudent.

The following list provides information about the most common types of student loans. The list reflects the order in which you should apply for and accept loans to get the lowest interest rates and best repayment terms.

- **Subsidized federal student loans** are backed by the government, which pays the loan

---

TRY IT!

MANAGING TIME ▷ Be Realistic

Once you realize that you need extra income, you may immediately assume that you need to find a job. However, many college students try to do the impossible by taking on too many time commitments—working one or even two jobs while maintaining a full load of courses. Be realistic about what you can do in 24 hours a day, 7 days a week. The better alternative might be reducing your expenses instead of adding more time commitments.

interest on your behalf while you are enrolled in undergraduate, graduate, or professional school. These loans require at least half-time enrollment and a submitted FAFSA application.

- **Unsubsidized federal student loans** may require that you make interest payments while you are enrolled. If not, the interest is added to the amount you owe; this is called *capitalization.*

- **Parent Loan for Undergraduate Students (PLUS) loans** are applied for and owed by parents but disbursed directly to students. The interest on PLUS loans is usually higher than the interest on federal student loans but lower than that on private loans. Parents who apply must provide information on the FAFSA.

- **Private student loans** are offered through banks and credit unions. Private loans often have stricter credit requirements and higher interest rates than federal loans do, and interest payments on private loans begin immediately.

Student loans are a very important source of money for college, but like paid employment,

TRY IT!

FEELING CONNECTED ▷ **Search Party**

Connect with other students in your class who need or want to find jobs. Investigate what on-campus and part-time off-campus jobs are available for students, and share ideas for searching for jobs that make sense considering the competing responsibilities of working, being in college, and meeting other personal and family commitments. Compare the wages, hours, and working conditions of available jobs. Share leads. Share your perspectives with one another and with your whole class.

loans should be considered carefully. Loans for costs such as textbook purchases and tuition fees are good investments. Loans for a more lavish lifestyle are likely to weigh you down in the future. As one wise person put it, if by borrowing you live like a wealthy graduate while you're a student, you'll live like a student after you graduate. Student loans can be a good way to begin using credit wisely, a skill you are likely to need throughout your life. ■

Plan for the Future

It's never too early to begin thinking about how you will finance your life after graduation and whether you will begin working immediately or pursue a graduate or professional degree. Your work, whether on or off campus, will help you make that decision. Here are some tips that will help you plan now for your future.

- **Figure out your next step—more education or work?** If you are working on campus, get to know faculty or staff members and seek their advice about your future plans. If you are working off campus, think carefully about whether your current job is one that you would want to continue after you graduate. If not, keep your options open and look for part-time work in a field that more closely aligns with your career plans or long-term educational objectives.
- **Keep your address current with the registrar.** Even when you have finished your degree or program, and especially if you stop classes for a term, alert the registrar of any changes in address. This is doubly important if you have a student loan; you don't want to get a negative report on your credit rating because you missed information about your loan.
- **Establish a savings account.** Add to it regularly, even if you can manage to deposit only a few dollars a month. The sooner you start, the greater your returns will be.

Your education is the most productive investment you can make for your future and that of your family. Research shows that the completion of programs or degrees after high school increases earnings, opens up career options, leads to greater satisfaction in work, results in more engaged citizenship such as voting and community service, and greatly increases the probability that your children will go on to college. Although college is a big investment of time and money, it's an investment you'll be glad you made.

Managing Credit Wisely

When you graduate, you will leave your institution with two significant numbers. The first is your grade point average (GPA), which represents the level of academic success you attained while in college. The second, your credit score, is a numerical representation of your fiscal responsibility. Although this second number might be less familiar to you than the first, it could be a factor that determines whether you get your dream job, regardless of your GPA. In addition, twenty years from now you're likely to have forgotten your GPA, while your credit score will be more important than ever.

Your credit score is derived from a credit report that contains information about accounts in your name. These accounts include credit cards, student loans, utility bills, cell phones, and car loans, to name a few. This credit score can determine whether or not you will qualify for a loan (car, home, student, etc.), what interest rates you will pay, how much your car insurance will cost, and your chances of being hired by certain organizations. Even if none of these things are in your immediate future, now is the time to start thinking about your credit score.

Although using credit cards responsibly is a good way to build credit, acquiring a credit card has become much more difficult for college students. In May 2009, President Barack Obama signed legislation that prohibits college students under the age of twenty-one from obtaining a credit card unless they can prove that they are able to make the payments or unless the credit card application is cosigned by a parent or guardian.

Understanding Credit

Even if you can prove that you have the means to repay credit card debt, it is important for you to thoroughly understand how credit cards work and how they can both help and hurt you. Simply put, a credit card allows you to buy something now and pay for it later. Each month you will receive a statement listing all purchases you made with your credit card during the previous thirty days. The statement will request a payment toward your balance and will set a payment due date. Your payment options will vary: You can pay your entire balance, pay a specified portion of the balance,

◁ **In Case of Emergency**
Having a credit card for emergencies is a good practice. Circumstances that might warrant the use of credit include paying critical expenses to care for yourself or your family, dealing with an auto accident or an unforeseen medical expense, or traveling on short notice to handle a crisis. But remember that spring break is *not* an emergency. © Britt Erlanson/cultura/ Corbis.

or make only a minimum payment, which may be as low as $10.

Beware: If you pay only the minimum required, the remaining balance on your card will be charged a finance fee, or interest charge, causing your balance to increase before your next bill arrives even if you don't make any more purchases. Paying the minimum payment is almost never a good strategy and can add years to your repayment time. In fact, assuming an 18 percent interest rate, if you continually pay only $10 per month toward a $500 credit card balance, it will take you more than seven years to pay it off! And you'll pay an extra $431 in interest, almost doubling the amount you originally charged.

Avoid making late payments. Paying your bill even one day late can result in a finance charge of up to $30, and it can raise the interest rate not only on that card but also on any other credit accounts you have. If you decide to use a credit card to build credit, you might want to set up automated online payments to avoid incurring expensive late fees. Remember that the payment due date is the date that the payment should be received by the credit card lender, not the date that you send it.

If you decide to apply for a credit card while you're in college, remember that it should be used to build credit and for emergencies. Credit cards should not be used to fund a lifestyle that you cannot otherwise afford or to buy wants (see the section "Living on a Budget" in this chapter). On the other hand, if you use your credit card just once a month and pay the balance as soon as the bill arrives, you will be on your way to a strong credit score in just a few years.

Debit Cards

Although you might wish to use a credit card for emergencies and to establish a good credit rating, you might also look into the possibility of applying for a debit card (also called a checkcard). The big advantage of a debit card is that you don't always have to carry cash and thus don't run the risk of losing it. Because the amount of your purchases will be limited to the funds in your bank account, a debit card is also a good form of constraint on your spending.

The only real disadvantage is that a debit card provides direct access to your checking account, so it's very important to keep your card in a safe place and away from your personal identification number (PIN). The safest way to protect your account is to commit your PIN to memory. If you lose your debit card or credit card, notify your bank immediately. ∎

◁ **Don't Let This Happen to You**
The 2013 comedy *Identity Thief* tells the story of an identity theft victim (played by Jason Bateman) who confronts the thief (played by Melissa McCarthy). In the movie, the victim answers questions about vital personal information in a phone call that he did not initiate—a big no-no—and his life is turned upside down. If identity theft happens to you, it's not so funny. Bob Mahoney/ ©Universal/courtesy Everett Collection.

Frequently Asked Questions about Credit Cards and Identity Theft

- **I have a credit card with my name on it, but it is actually my parents' account number. Is this card building credit for me?** No. You are considered an authorized user on the account, but your parents are the primary account holders. To build credit, you must be the primary account holder or at least a joint account holder.

- **I have a credit card and am the primary account holder. How can I resist abusing it?** Use your credit card to help you build credit by making small charges and paying them off each month. Stick to two expense categories only, such as gas and groceries, and don't make any exceptions unless you have a serious emergency.

- **I choose the "credit" option every time I use my debit card. Is this building credit for me?** No. Using the credit function of your debit card is more like writing an electronic check because you are still taking money directly out of your checking account. Even if your debit card has a major credit card (Visa, MasterCard, etc.) logo on it, it is not building credit for you.

- **I have a few store credit cards (Target, Best Buy, etc.). Are these accounts included on my credit report?** Yes. However, though they will affect your credit score, store credit cards do not carry as much weight as major credit cards (Visa, MasterCard, etc.). It is OK to have a few store credit cards, but a major credit card will do more to help you build credit.

- **Where can I apply for a major credit card?** A good place to begin is your bank or credit union. Remember that you might have to prove your ability to make payments in order to obtain a card. Use your credit card to build credit by making small charges and paying them off each month.

- **If one credit card will help me build credit, will several build my credit even more?** Research shows that there is no benefit to having more than two major credit cards. And even if you're able to pay the required monthly amounts, having too many accounts open can make you appear risky to the credit bureaus determining your credit score.

- **What if I forget and make a late payment? Is my credit score ruined?** Your credit report reflects at least the past seven years of activity but puts the most emphasis on the most recent two years. In other words, the farther you get from your mistakes, the less impact they will have on your credit score. There is no quick fix for improving a credit score, so beware of advertisements that say otherwise.

- **If building credit is a wise decision, what's so bad about using credit cards to buy some things that I really want but can't afford right now?** It is not wise to use credit cards to purchase things that you cannot afford. Living within your means is always the way to go.

- **What is identity theft?** In this insidious and increasingly common crime, someone assumes your identity, secretly opens up accounts in your name, and has the bills sent to another address.

- **How can I protect myself from identity theft?** *Be password savvy.* The more sensitive the information, the stronger your password should be. Aim for passwords with eight to fourteen characters, including numbers, both uppercase and lowercase letters, and, if allowed, a few special characters like @ and #. Never use an obvious number like your birthday or wedding anniversary. Don't use the same username and password for every site. Change the password to your online credit card or bank account at least once a year. If you must keep a written record of your usernames and passwords, keep the list in a secure place at home, not in your wallet.
  Beware of scams. Lots of them are out there. Don't make yourself vulnerable. A few tips: Research a company or organization before submitting your résumé. Don't e-mail any personal information (social security number, bank details, credit or debit card numbers, passwords, etc.) that could put you at risk of identity theft. Don't answer questions about vital personal information over the phone if you didn't originate the call. Don't reply to e-mails, pop-ups, or text messages that ask you to reveal sensitive information. Don't send sensitive data by e-mail. Call instead and deal only with businesses you trust. Never click on links in unsolicited e-mails or paste URLs or lines of code into your browser bar. If an offer sounds too good to be true, it probably is.

- **Where can I get my credit report?** You can keep an eye on your credit report by visiting the free (and safe) Web site http://www.annualcreditreport.com at least once a year. Regularly reviewing your credit history pays off in major ways. It alerts you to any new accounts that might have been opened in your name. It also lets you catch unauthorized activity on accounts that you've closed or haven't used lately. Everyone is entitled to one free credit report a year from each of the three major credit bureaus.

Chapter Review

Steps to Success: Managing Money

- ○ **Make financial literacy a key college success skill.** Financial literacy is a specialized form of information literacy.

- ○ **Create a budget and then live on it.** Remember that it's your budget, tailor-made by and for you.

- ○ **Act on some of the suggestions offered in this chapter for cutting your costs.** For most college students, cutting costs is even more important than increasing their income.

- ○ **Learn as much as you can about the different types of financial aid.** Find out what is offered to U.S. college students and by your particular college, even though the term has already started. It's never too late to take advantage of these opportunities.

- ○ **Consider the pros and cons of working while in college.** If you do plan to work, consider how much and where you will work. Realize that students who borrow money and attend college full-time are more likely to attain their degrees than those who use a different strategy.

- ○ **Remember that you will finish college with two key numbers: your GPA and your credit score.** Potential employers will be checking your transcripts *and* your credit reports.

- ○ **Learn the strategies in this chapter for wise credit card management.** College is a time to learn how to use credit wisely.

- ○ **Protect yourself from identity theft.** Be password savvy and avoid scams.

- ○ **Take advantage of help offered on your campus to learn financial management skills.** You can't help it if you didn't learn these skills before; you may not have had any money to manage!

Applying what you've learned . . .

Now that you have read and discussed this chapter, consider how you can apply what you have learned to your academic and personal lives. The following prompts will help you reflect on the chapter material and its relevance to you both now and in the future.

1. Sometimes planning for the future is hard. Why not start small? Describe at least two things you can do each week to save money. For example, using public transportation when possible can help reduce the expense of owning a car.

2. Money can be a difficult subject to talk about, and sometimes it seems easier not to worry about it. Ask yourself some hard questions. Do you spend money without much thought? Do you have a lot of debt and not much to show for it? Describe what you want your financial picture to look like.

Create Community

GO TO ▷ Your institution's financial aid office: If you need help understanding financial aid opportunities and how to apply for scholarships.

GO TO ▷ Your local United Way office: If you need credit counseling. Many communities have credit counseling agencies within the local United Way.

GO TO ▷ Your college campus: If you need help finding programs on money management. These programs are often offered in residence halls or through the division of student affairs.

GO TO ▷ The business school or the college or division of continuing education: If you need help finding a course in personal finance. Check your college catalog or Web site, or call the school, college, or division office.

GO TO ▷ The counseling center: If you need help managing money problems that are related to compulsive shopping or gambling.

GO TO ▷ Your campus library or bookstore: If you want additional print resources about money management. A good book to look for is Susan Knox's *Financial Basics: A Money-Management Guide for Students* (Columbus: Ohio State University Press, 2004).

GO ONLINE TO ▷ The Budget Wizard (http://budget.cashcourse.org): If you want to use a free, secure budgeting tool from the National Endowment for Financial Education (NEFE).

GO ONLINE TO ▷ The Free Application for Federal Student Aid (https://fafsa.ed.gov): If you want to access the online application for federal student aid. You can set up an account, complete the application electronically, save your work, and monitor the progress of your application.

GO ONLINE TO ▷ FastWeb (http://www.FastWeb.com): If you are interested in using a free scholarship search service and discovering sources of educational funding you never knew existed.

GO ONLINE TO ▷ Bankrate (http://www.bankrate.com): If you are interested in unbiased information about the interest rates, fees, and penalties associated with major credit cards and private loans. This site also provides calculators that let you determine the long-term costs of different kinds of borrowing.

NOW... How do you measure up?

1. A budget should guide how much money a person spends each month.

   ○ Agree
   ○ Don't Know
   ○ Disagree

2. To receive or maintain financial aid, students often have to take a set number of courses or credit hours each term.

   ○ Agree
   ○ Don't Know
   ○ Disagree

3. Working too many hours a week off campus has several disadvantages.

   ○ Agree
   ○ Don't Know
   ○ Disagree

4. College provides students with an opportunity to begin building a good credit score.

   ○ Agree
   ○ Don't Know
   ○ Disagree

How do your answers here compare to your responses to the quiz you took at the start of the chapter? Which sections of this chapter left a strong impression on you? What strategies for managing money have you started to use? Are they working? What other strategies will you commit to trying?

185
Managing Stress

188
Paying Attention to Nutrition and Weight Management

190
Maintaining Sexual Health

192
Using Alcohol Responsibly

Staying Healthy

The first year of college can be one of life's most interesting and challenging transition periods. Much of what you experience will be new—new friends, new freedoms, and new responsibilities. You will notice that many students use sensible and healthy coping strategies to handle the transition to college successfully. They watch what they eat and drink, exercise regularly, and get enough sleep. However, some students go in the opposite direction; they stay up late, drink too much, smoke, overeat, or engage in risky sexual behaviors. Many students, especially men, gain weight during the college years, and much of that weight gain happens in the first year.

This chapter explores the topic of staying healthy, which includes taking care of your mind, body, and spirit, making healthy choices, and achieving balance. The college experience shouldn't only be about studying. To make the most of the college years, it's also important to spend time with friends and enjoy all the activities your college has to offer.

The freedoms you experience in this new environment bring challenges and risks, and your success in college will depend on your ability to make sensible decisions about your personal habits and behaviors. If you maintain both your physical and mental well-being, you will be more likely to achieve your goals for being in college.

How do you measure up?

1. When I feel overwhelmed, I deal with my stress in healthy ways, like exercising or taking control of my schedule to make time to tackle my top priorities.

   ○ Agree
   ○ Don't Know
   ○ Disagree

2. Exercising regularly will help me manage my weight and stay fit.

   ○ Agree
   ○ Don't Know
   ○ Disagree

3. I have adequate information about sex and contraception.

   ○ Agree
   ○ Don't Know
   ○ Disagree

4. I know the difference between responsible and irresponsible alcohol use.

   ○ Agree
   ○ Don't Know
   ○ Disagree

Review the items you marked "Don't Know" or "Disagree." Pay special attention to these topics in this chapter—you will find motivating strategies to develop in these areas. A follow-up quiz at the end of the chapter will prompt you to consider what you have learned.

Some People Make It Look So Easy

△ **Sofia Gavi**

Denise Lett/Shutterstock.

Week 5 at college: My roommate, Julia, slips on a pair of elegant heels with the air of a movie heroine. To look at perfectly manicured Julia, you would never guess at her complex life—taking fifteen credits, playing on the field hockey team, and working part-time in the math department, all while maintaining a 3.8 GPA.

"Why so bummed out?" she says. "C'mon, get dressed."

Julia and I share a major in business administration. We both have part-time academic jobs. Sadly, the similarities end there.

"How do you always manage to channel Penélope Cruz?" I ask her. "Look at me: I'm like someone who's been hiding in a Pepperidge Farm warehouse." It's not much of an exaggeration: I'm so stressed out by school and work that I've embraced every brownie I can get my hands on. I no longer fit into anything in my wardrobe that doesn't involve an elastic waist. The weight gain then makes me more stressed. I can't sleep. I feel totally disorganized.

Julia shifts a basket of dirty laundry from my bed and sits down beside me. "Don't be silly," she says sympathetically.

"I just don't know how you get everything done and stay so Zen," I tell her. "I feel like I'm running as fast as I can just to keep up."

What can Sofia learn from Julia? What steps could Sofia take to manage stress better? Why is it important for students to eat properly, get regular exercise, and maintain a regular sleep schedule? Do you have more in common with Sofia or Julia? What strategies do you use to stay healthy? When do you slip up?

Managing Stress

One of the biggest challenges facing college students is stress. Many students report that stress negatively affects their ability to concentrate and their scores on exams and tests.[1] When you are stressed, your body undergoes physiological and psychological changes. Your breathing becomes rapid and shallow; your heart rate increases; the muscles in your shoulders, your forehead, your neck, and perhaps your chest tighten; your hands become cold or sweaty; your hands and knees may shake; your stomach becomes upset; your mouth goes dry; and your voice may sound strained.

The psychological changes you might experience include a sense of confusion, trouble focusing on your work, an inability to remember things, and poor problem solving. As a result of stress, you may make snap decisions that you regret later. Emotions such as anger, anxiety, depression, fear, frustration, and irritability are common, and you also might either be unable to go to sleep at night or wake up frequently.

Stress has many sources, but the following three seem to be the most important ones:

1. **Life events such as a death in the family, the loss of a job, or an illness.** Repeated stress from life events can cause physical and mental health problems, especially if many such events happen within a short time period.

2. **Too many responsibilities at home, work, or college.** When there is not enough time to attend to family, meet deadlines, and prepare for tests and projects, the level of stress increases.

3. **Daily hassles.** Minor things that we experience every day, such as losing the car keys, getting stuck in traffic, having three tests on the same day, arguing with a roommate or spouse, or worrying about money, can result in major stress.

The best starting point for handling stress is to be in good physical and mental shape. This

[1]American College Health Association, *National College Health Assessment, Undergraduate Reference Group Executive Summary, Spring 2012* (Hanover, MD: American College Health Association, 2012).

The best starting point for handling stress is to be in good physical and mental shape.

means you need to pay attention to your diet, your exercise and sleep habits, and your mental health.

Evaluate Your Diet and How Much You Exercise

There is a clear connection between what you eat and drink, your overall health and well-being, and stress. So when you feel stressed, stop and think about what you have been eating and drinking and also how active you have or haven't been. Eating a lot of junk food will add pounds and reduce your energy level. And if you can't keep up with your work because

△ **Nothing but Blue Skies**

When you are feeling stressed, take a moment to breathe. This strategy sounds simple, but it gets overlooked. Focusing on inhaling and exhaling slowly and picturing a serene scene like a blue sky or a sunny beach can help slow your heart rate and calm you down. You might also picture yourself succeeding at the task that is currently stressing you out. Breathing and visualization techniques can be powerful tools. Filipe Frazao/Shutterstock.

TRY IT!

SETTING GOALS ▷ **Are You Losing It?**

Are there times in college when you feel like you're losing it? Perhaps you're so stressed out that you can't concentrate or study, or maybe you're irritable with your roommate or best friend for no good reason. Set a goal to use some time-tested strategies to calm down. A first step is to read the material on pages 000–00 and apply these strategies. If your worry or anxiety is still out of control, visit your college counseling center and get the help you need. Staff members there are trained to help you. By reducing or eliminating your stress and worry, you can improve your academic performance and even your relationships with others.

Aerobic exercise is the best recreation for both stress management and weight management.

you're sluggish or tired, you might experience more stress. One dietary substance that can be directly linked to high stress levels is caffeine.

Caffeine increases alertness and reduces feelings of fatigue if used moderately—50 to 200 milligrams per day, equivalent to one to two cups of regular coffee. Even at this low dosage, however, caffeine can make you more energetic during part of the day but more tired

later. Too much caffeine can cause nervousness, headaches, a bad temper, an upset stomach, and sleeplessness—all symptoms of stress. Instead of drinking caffeinated drinks, consider drinking water, decaf coffee, caffeine-free soft drinks, or herbal tea.

Exercise is an excellent stress-management technique, the best way to stay fit, and a critical part of losing weight. When you feel your stress level is high, bring it down by ramping up your activity level. While any kind of recreation benefits your body and spirit, aerobic exercise is the best for both stress management and weight management. In aerobic exercise,

△ **Get Moving!**
Whether it means running, walking, or playing a sport, every student needs to get moving. What are your exercise habits? Remember that daily exercise can be a great no-cost way to reduce stress while keeping you in good physical and mental shape.

MANAGING TIME ▷ It's All in Your Hands

One way to reduce stress is to do a good job of managing your time. Remember that time is your most precious resource, and when you waste it, it's gone. Many college students become frantic when they realize they haven't allowed enough time to study for an upcoming test or write a paper. Use the time-management strategies and tools you learned about in this book. When you plan your schedule and allow enough time for your academic work, you will reduce your stress.

△ **Catch Some Z's**

When you aren't getting enough sleep, you cannot do your best. A brief nap of 20 minutes or so can revive you when you're feeling tired during the day. Establish good sleeping habits and grab opportunities for power naps when you can.
© Randy Faris/Corbis.

you work until your heart rate is in a "target zone," and then you keep it in this zone for at least 30 minutes. You can reach your target heart rate through a variety of exercises: walking, jogging, running, dancing, playing basketball, swimming, biking, and using a stair-climber. Choose activities that you enjoy so you will look forward to your exercise time. That way, it's more likely to become a regular part of your routine.

Get Enough Sleep

Getting adequate sleep is another way to protect yourself from stress. According to the National Sleep Foundation, 63 percent of American adults do not get the recommended eight hours of sleep per night. Lack of sleep can lead to anxiety, depression, and academic problems. Researchers found that students who studied all week but then stayed up late partying on the weekends forgot as much as 30 percent of the material they had learned during the prior week. Try the following suggestions to establish better sleep habits:

- Avoid long daytime naps that last more than 30 minutes.

- Try reading or listening to a relaxation tape before going to bed.

- Exercise during the day.

- Get your clothes, school materials, and food together for the next day before you go to bed.

- Sleep in the same room and bed every night.

- Stick to a regular schedule for going to bed and getting up.

Take Control

Modifying your lifestyle is the best overall approach to stress management. You have the power to change your life so that it is less stressful. Lifestyle modification involves identifying the parts of your life that do not serve you well, making plans for change, and then carrying out those plans. For example, if you are stressed because you are always late for classes, get up 10 minutes earlier. If a certain negative classmate makes you nervous on test-taking days, avoid him or her. Learn test-taking skills (available in this book) so that you have more confidence and can manage test anxiety better.

Check your college Web site, counseling center, health center, student newspaper, or fitness center for classes that teach relaxation. You'll find apps, Web sites, books, and other resources that guide you through relaxation techniques. Learning new techniques for managing stress takes knowledge and practice. ■

You have the power to change your life so that it is less stressful.

Paying Attention to Nutrition and Weight Management

"You are what you eat" is more than a catchphrase; it's an important reminder of the vital role that diet plays in our lives. You've probably read news stories about the obesity epidemic in the United States, especially among young people. College is a good time to establish lifelong healthy behaviors.

If you are gaining weight and losing energy, what can you do about your eating habits? Think about what, when, and how much you eat day to day. Altering your eating habits might not be easy at first, but if you start making small positive changes, you can build toward a new way of eating. You not only will feel better but also will be healthier and probably happier. If you're responsible for feeding your family, then all of you will benefit from establishing healthy habits. The MyPlate icon in Figure 12.1 proposes one set of guidelines for healthy eating, and here are some commonsense suggestions as well:

- Limit snacks to healthy options—for example, fruit, vegetables, yogurt, and small portions of nuts such as pistachios, almonds, cashews, or walnuts.

- Eat plenty of vegetables and fruits daily. Opt for these over fruit juices, which tend to be high in sugar.

- Drink plenty of water. Aim for about 64 ounces each day.

- Restrict your intake of red meat, butter, white rice, white bread, and sweets. Instead, eat a sensible amount of nuts and beans, which will add to your fiber intake.

- Avoid fried foods. Choose grilled or broiled lean meat and fish instead.

- Watch your portion sizes. Avoid large, jumbo, or king-size fast-food items and all-you-can-eat buffets.

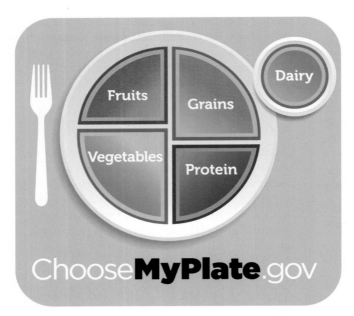

Figure 12.1 ◁ MyPlate Eating Guidelines
In 2011 the federal government introduced the MyPlate icon to replace the Food Guide Pyramid. The Web site ChooseMyPlate.gov provides tips and recommendations for healthy eating and for understanding the plate's design.
Courtesy USDA.

- Eat breakfast! Your brain will function better if you eat a power-packed meal first thing in the morning.

- Always read the nutrition label on packaged foods, and use this information to guide your decisions about what to eat. Look for the number of grams of fat and carbohydrates as well as the calorie total. Check the sodium content: Sodium (table salt) will make you gain weight and may also increase your blood pressure.

- If possible, take time to shop for groceries and cook your own food; making a meal at home is almost always healthier than eating out or buying food on the fly. Fast food might be fast, but it carries a high calorie cost while offering little nutritional value. ■

Eating Disorders

Although we advise you to think about what you are eating from day to day, we also advise you not to overthink it. Remember that the key to good health is achieving balance, and an obsession with food intake may be a sign that things are out of balance. Over the last few decades, an increasing number of male and female college students have been developing eating disorders such as anorexia nervosa (an extreme fear of gaining weight), bulimia (overeating followed by self-induced vomiting or laxative use), or binge eating disorder (compulsive overeating long past the feeling of being full).

Anyone who is struggling with an eating disorder should seek medical attention. Eating disorders can be life-threatening if they are not treated by a health care professional. Many colleges and universities have eating disorder case management teams to help individuals on campus. Contact your student health center for more information, or contact the National Eating Disorders Association (http://www.nationaleatingdisorders.org or 1-800-931-2237) to find a professional in your area who specializes in the treatment of eating disorders.

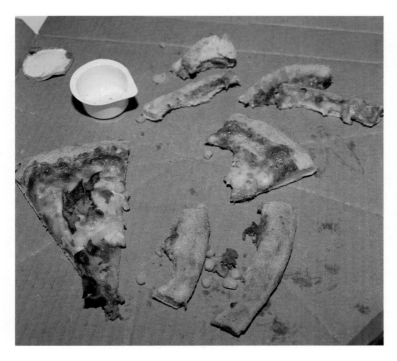

◁ **A Serving Is a Slice, Not an Entire Pizza**

Have you ever found yourself staring at the remains of a pizza and realizing that you're a bit out of control? Start to rein yourself back in that second. Stop at the grocery store on the way home to pick up some healthy snacks. Throw out half-eaten bags of chips. Take a long walk or give yourself an extra half hour in the morning to take another walk or jog. It's never the wrong time and never too late to take better care of yourself, and no step in the right direction is too small. © Image Source/Corbis.

Maintaining Sexual Health

Numerous studies indicate that about 75 percent of traditional-age college students have engaged in sexual intercourse at least once. Whether or not you are part of this percentage, it can be helpful to explore your sexual values and to consider whether sex is right for you at this time. If it is the right time, you should choose a good birth control method and adopt strategies for avoiding sexually transmitted infections (STIs) and unplanned pregnancies.

Avoiding Sexually Transmitted Infections

The problem of STIs on college campuses has received growing attention in recent years as epidemic numbers of students have become infected. STIs are usually spread through genital contact. Sometimes, however, these infections can be transmitted mouth-to-mouth.

One particularly common STI is the human papillomavirus (HPV), a sexually transmitted infection that is closely linked to cervical cancer. Gardasil, a vaccine, provides protection for both men and women against the types of HPV that cause genital warts, anal cancer, and cervical cancer. For more information about this vaccine, contact your college or university health services or local health care provider.

Communicating about Safe Sex

If you are sexually active, it's important to talk with your partner about ways to protect against sexually transmitted infections and unwanted pregnancies. Communicating with your partner about safe sex can be difficult and even embarrassing initially, but it can make your relationship stronger and more meaningful.

You can avoid STIs and unwanted pregnancies by avoiding sex entirely. Apparently, 25 percent of college students choose this option, according to national research. For many people, masturbation is a reasonable alternative to sex with a partner.

If you're in the remaining 75 percent, you'll be safer (in terms of STIs) if you have only one partner. Whether you're monogamous or not, you should always protect yourself by using a condom or being sure your partner uses one.

In addition to being a contraceptive, a condom can help prevent the spread of STIs, including HIV. A condom's effectiveness against disease holds true for anal, vaginal, and oral intercourse. The most current research indicates that the rate of protection provided by a condom against STIs is similar to its rate of protection against pregnancy (90–99 percent) when used correctly and consistently for every act of intercourse or oral sex. Note that only latex rubber condoms and polyurethane condoms—not lambskin or other types of natural membrane condoms—provide this protection. The polyurethane condom is a great alternative for individuals who have allergies to latex. Use a water-based lubricant (such as K-Y Jelly) rather than an oil-based lubricant, which can cause a latex condom to break.

Using Birth Control

Sexually active heterosexual students have to take steps to prevent unwanted pregnancies. Planning is the key. What is the best method of contraception? It is any method that you use correctly and consistently each time you have intercourse. Always discuss birth control with your partner so that you both feel comfortable with the option you have selected. For more information about a particular method, consult a pharmacist, your student health center, a local family planning clinic, or your private physician. The important thing is to resolve to protect yourself and your partner each and every time you have sexual intercourse.

What if the condom breaks or you forget to take your birth control pill? Emergency contraceptive pills can reduce the risk of pregnancy. According to the Planned Parenthood Federation of America, if the pills are taken within 72 hours of unprotected intercourse, they can significantly reduce the risk of pregnancy. Most campus health centers and local health clinics dispense emergency contraception to individuals in need. ■

Protecting against Sexual Assault

The occurrence of sexual assault on college campuses is a problem that has existed for many years. Although colleges have addressed this issue with some success, the problem remains: Today 20 to 25 percent of female college students report experiencing a rape or attempted rape.[2] Anyone is at risk for being raped, but the majority of victims are women. An estimated one out of four college women will be the victim of attempted rape, and one out of six will be raped.[3] Most are raped by someone they know—a date or an acquaintance—and most will not report the crime. Alcohol is a factor in nearly three-fourths of the incidents. Whether raped by a date or by a stranger, a victim can suffer long-term traumatic effects. Below is some advice from Tricia Phaup, Director, Medical Case Management at University of South Carolina School of Medicine, on avoiding sexual assault:

- Know what you want and do not want sexually.
- Go to social gatherings with friends, and leave with them.
- Avoid being alone with people you don't know very well.
- Trust your intuition.
- Be alert to subtle and unconscious messages you may be sending and receiving.

- Be aware of how much alcohol you drink, if any.
- Avoid putting yourself in a vulnerable position because you have consumed too much alcohol.

If you are ever tempted to force another person to have sex:

- Realize that it is never OK to force sex on someone.
- Never assume that you know what your date wants.
- If you're getting mixed messages, ask for clarification.
- Don't have sex with someone who is too drunk to know what they are doing.
- Remember that rape is morally and legally wrong.

If you have been raped, regardless of whether you choose to report the rape to the police or get a medical exam, it is very helpful to seek counseling by contacting resources such as a campus sexual assault coordinator, a local rape crisis center, the campus police department, student health services, women's student services, a local hospital emergency room, or a campus chaplain.

In 2014, the federal government established the "Campus Sexual Violence Elimination" (SaVE) Act to ensure that all colleges and universities have policies for reporting and responding to issues of sexual violence. SaVE requires that incidents of domestic violence, dating violence, sexual assault, and stalking be disclosed in annual campus crime statistics reports required of each college and university. Also students or employees who report being victims will get assistance from campus authorities, a change in living or working situations as needed, the ability to obtain a "no contact" or restraining order, knowledge about their college's disciplinary process, and information about counseling, health, and legal services.

SaVE ensures that there will be a prompt and fair investigation by officials who are trained in matters to do with sexual violence. SaVE also requires colleges and universities to provide programming for students and employees addressing these issues that specifically targets new students and new employees. Don't keep silent if you are a victim.

[2]Clery Center for Security on Campus, "The Campus Sexual Violence Elimination (SaVE) Act" http://clerycenter.org/campus-sexual-violence-elimination-save-act (accessed 23 July 2014).

[3]Ibid.

Using Alcohol Responsibly

Our purpose in this section is not to make judgments but to warn you about irresponsible use of two substances that can have a strongly negative impact on your college experience and your life: alcohol and tobacco. While you're in college, you will likely be exposed to the reckless use of one or both of these substances. We hope that this information will help you think twice and avoid the trouble that can come from substance abuse.

Even if you don't drink, you should read this information, because 50 percent of college students reported helping a drunken friend, classmate, or study partner in the previous year.

△ **Consider the Consequences**
This party looks like fun. But if you drink too much, you may find yourself hooking up with someone you hardly know. What started off as a good time could end up being your worst nightmare. © 2/Ocean/Corbis.

Alcohol can turn even people who don't drink into victims, such as people who are killed by drunk drivers or family members who suffer from the behavior of an alcoholic. Over the course of one year, about 20 to 30 percent of students report serious problems related to excessive alcohol use. You might have heard news reports about college students who died or were seriously or permanently injured as a result of excessive drinking. Just one occasion of heavy or high-risk drinking can lead to problems.

How alcohol affects behavior depends on the dose of alcohol, which is best measured by blood alcohol content, or BAC. Most of the pleasurable effects of alcoholic beverages are experienced at lower BAC levels, when alcohol acts as a behavioral stimulant. For most people, the stimulant level is around one drink per hour. Usually, problems begin at an intake higher than .05, when alcohol acts as a sedative and begins to slow down areas of the brain. Most people who have more than four or five drinks at one occasion feel "buzzed," show signs of impairment, and are likely to be at higher risk for alcohol-related problems. However, significant impairment at lower doses can occur.

How fast you drink makes a difference, too. Your body gets rid of alcohol at a rate of about one drink, or one ounce, an hour. (Home remedies for sobering up like drinking coffee or water or taking a cold shower don't work.) Drinking more than one drink an hour may cause a rise in BAC because the body is absorbing alcohol faster than it can eliminate it.

At BAC levels of .025 to .05, a drinker may feel animated and energized. At a BAC level of around .05, a drinker may feel rowdy or boisterous. This is where most people report feeling a buzz from alcohol. At a BAC level between .05 and .08, alcohol starts to act as a depressant. So as soon as you feel that buzz, remember that you are on the brink of losing coordination, clear thinking, and judgment.

Driving is measurably impaired even at BAC levels lower than the legal limit of .08. In fact, an accurate safe level for most people may be half the legal limit, or .04. As BAC levels climb past .08, people become progressively less coordinated and less able to make good decisions. Most people become severely uncoordinated with BAC levels higher than .08 and may begin falling asleep, falling down, or slurring their speech.

Most people pass out or fall asleep when their BAC level is above .25. Unfortunately, even after you pass out and stop drinking, your BAC level can continue to rise as alcohol in your stomach is released to the intestine and absorbed into the bloodstream. Your body may try to get rid of alcohol by vomiting, but you can choke if you are unconscious, semiconscious, or severely uncoordinated. Worse yet, at BAC levels higher than .30, most people will show signs of severe alcohol poisoning, such as

TRY IT!

FEELING CONNECTED ▷
Sharing and Comparing Experiences

List three ways that your quality of life has been influenced by another person's drinking or smoking. In small groups, share your lists. What did you find out when you compared your experiences with theirs? What did you learn about handling situations that involve drinking and smoking?

an inability to wake up, slowed breathing, a fast but weak pulse, cool or damp skin, and pale or bluish skin. Anyone exhibiting these symptoms needs medical assistance immediately. ■

Tobacco—the Other Legal Drug

Tobacco use is clearly the cause of many serious medical conditions, including heart disease, some forms of cancer, and lung ailments. Over the years, tobacco has led to the deaths of hundreds of thousands of individuals. Unfortunately, many college students smoke. The University of Michigan's Monitoring the Future Survey published by the National Institute on Drug Abuse estimates that rates of smoking have declined among college students and were at 20 percent as of 2007.[4] But one concern is "social smoking." This term describes smoking by students who do so only when hanging out with friends, drinking, or partying. Most college students feel they will be able to give up their social smoking habit once they graduate, but after four years of college, some find that they are addicted to cigarettes.

The chemicals in tobacco are highly addictive, making it hard to quit smoking. Young people may not worry about long-term effects such as lung cancer and emphysema, but increased incidence of respiratory infections, worsening of asthma, bad breath, stained teeth, and the high cost of cigarettes should be motivations not to start smoking at all. Many institutions and local hospitals offer smoking cessation programs to help people quit smoking. If you smoke, contact your campus health center for more information about how to quit.

[4] L. D. Johnston, P. M. O'Malley, J. G. Bachman, and J. E. Schulenberg, *Monitoring the Future: National Survey Results on Drug Use, 1975–2007*, vol. 2, *College Students and Adults Ages 19–45* (NIH Publication No. 08-6418B) (Bethesda, MD: National Institute on Drug Abuse, 2008).

Chapter Review

Steps to Success: Staying Healthy

○ **Remember that managing stress is a key college success strategy.** College, by its very demanding nature, increases stress. Use the strategies from your college success course to learn how to reduce stress in college and beyond.

○ **Get in touch with your own stress levels and sources.** Heightened awareness is the first step in learning how to manage and reduce stress.

○ **Consider the powerful connections between things you control through your decisions.** Make good decisions concerning diet, exercise, sleep, your schedule, and your stress levels.

○ **Practice good sexual health decision making.** Make wise choices to protect yourself against sexually transmitted infections, develop and maintain respectful relationships, and avoid unplanned pregnancies.

○ **Practice moderation.** Successful college students can still have a good time in college and not let alcohol use interfere with their academic success or personal health. Contrary to prevalent stereotypes, it is not the norm for students to abuse alcohol.

○ **Don't get hooked!** Many young adults acquire what become lifetime behaviors during their college years. It would be a shame if one of the consequences of your college experience were an addiction to tobacco, with its long-term expense and negative health effects.

○ **Avoid experimenting with dangerous behaviors.** Keep thinking about your purpose(s) for being in college and for your life, and try to make decisions that help you work toward achieving your goals rather than take you farther from them.

Applying what you've learned . . .

Now that you have read and discussed this chapter, consider how you can apply what you have learned to your academic and personal lives. The following prompts will help you reflect on the chapter material and its relevance to you both now and in the future.

1. Identify one area in your life in which you need to make changes to become healthier. How do you think becoming healthier will improve your performance in college? What are the challenges you face in becoming healthier?

2. If you could make only three recommendations to an incoming first-year college student about managing stress in college, what would they be? Use your personal experience and what you have learned in this chapter to make your recommendations.

Create Community

GO TO ▷ **The counseling center:** If you need help with anxiety and stress. Professionals here will offer individual and group assistance and lots of information. Remember that their support is confidential, and you will not be judged.

GO TO ▷ **The campus health center or online to Planned Parenthood Federation of America (http://www.plannedparenthood.org):** If you need help with STI prevention or birth control. You should be able to receive treatment for an STI as well.

GO TO ▷ **Health education and wellness programs:** If you need help with problems and challenges with alcohol or other drugs or with sexual decision making. Student peer health educators who are trained and supervised by professionals can provide support. Taking part in such peer leadership is also a great way to develop and practice your own communication skills.

GO TO ▷ **Campus support groups:** If you need help dealing with problems related to excessive alcohol and drug use, abusive sexual relationships, and other issues.

GO ONLINE TO ▷ **Go Ask Alice! (http://goaskalice.columbia.edu):** If you need advice about health issues related to being in college. This Web site, sponsored by Columbia University, has answers to many health questions.

GO ONLINE TO ▷ **The American Institute of Stress (http://www.stress.org):** If you need help combating stress.

GO ONLINE TO ▷ **The Academy of Nutrition and Dietetics (http://www.eatright.org) or Shape Up America! (http://www.shapeup.org):** If you need help finding information on healthy eating and nutrition.

GO ONLINE TO ▷ **The National Eating Disorders Association (http://www .nationaleatingdisorders.org):** If you want to learn more about online screening, treatment, and support for an eating disorder that you or someone you care about is struggling with.

GO ONLINE TO ▷ **The American Cancer Society (http://www.cancer.org):** If you want to learn more about the health effects of tobacco.

NOW... How do you measure up?

1. When I feel overwhelmed, I deal with my stress in healthy ways, like exercising or taking control of my schedule to make time to tackle my top priorities.
   - ○ Agree
   - ○ Don't Know
   - ○ Disagree

2. Exercising regularly will help me manage my weight and stay fit.
   - ○ Agree
   - ○ Don't Know
   - ○ Disagree

3. I have adequate information about sex and contraception.
   - ○ Agree
   - ○ Don't Know
   - ○ Disagree

4. I know the difference between responsible and irresponsible alcohol use.
   - ○ Agree
   - ○ Don't Know
   - ○ Disagree

How do your answers here compare to your responses to the quiz you took at the start of the chapter? Which sections of this chapter left a strong impression on you? What strategies for staying healthy have you started to use? Are they working? What other strategies will you commit to trying?

199
Careers and the New Economy

203
Self-Exploration in Career Planning

207
Planning for Your Career

209
Getting Experience

211
Job Search Strategies

214
Skills Employers Seek

216
Staying on the Path to Success

Considering Majors & Careers

VoodooDot/Shutterstock.

College is a time for gaining academic knowledge and exploring career opportunities with the goal of developing from a student into a productive member of the global economy. However, you don't have to be sure about your academic and career goals as you begin or return to college. Rather, you can use your first classes and even your first year of college to explore your interests and see how they might connect to various academic programs. You may discover interests and opportunities you never imagined.

Depending on your academic strengths, you can major in almost anything. As this chapter emphasizes, how you integrate your classes with extracurricular pursuits and work experiences will prepare you for a first career—or, if you have been in the labor force for some time, for advancement in your current job or even a new career. Try a major that you think you will like or that you feel drawn toward, and see what develops. But keep an open mind, and don't pin all your hopes for finding a career on that major alone. Your selection of a major and a career ultimately has to fit with your overall life goals, purposes, values, and beliefs. This chapter provides you with tips and resources for career planning. Visiting your college career center can help you build on the information in this chapter.

How do you measure up?

1. The world economy is changing, and how it changes will probably affect my job prospects.
   - ○ Agree
   - ○ Don't Know
   - ○ Disagree

2. There is no guarantee that anyone's first career choice will be permanent.
   - ○ Agree
   - ○ Don't Know
   - ○ Disagree

3. I know my strengths and interests and how they might influence my career choice.
   - ○ Agree
   - ○ Don't Know
   - ○ Disagree

4. One of the most important things college students can do in the first year is visit the campus career center.
   - ○ Agree
   - ○ Don't Know
   - ○ Disagree

Review the items you marked "Don't Know" or "Disagree." Pay special attention to these topics in this chapter—you will likely find new ways of thinking about these questions. A follow-up quiz at the end of the chapter will prompt you to consider what you have learned.

Build Your Résumé from Day One

△ **Brett Kossick**

Monkey Business Images/Shutterstock.

"I really admire your focus," said Dr. Woloshyn, my academic adviser, when I dropped by his office to talk about my course schedule. Many people study a whole gamut of things until they settle on a major and don't specialize until graduate school. That's so not me.

"I've wanted to be an engineer for as long as I can remember," I said. "So I'm a little confused about the courses you suggested—Business Writing? Multicultural Communications? I plan to work in robotics, not marketing."

"Oh, really?" Dr. Woloshyn asked with a curious smile. Then he leaned forward on his desk. "Brett, didn't you tell me that you have an internship with a leading technology corporation this summer? Did anyone tell you what you would be doing there?"

"Not really," I said. "They just said I'd be helping out in different divisions of the company, depending on what they need."

"Right," said Dr. Woloshyn. "And is there a chance you might like to work there after you graduate?"

"Are you kidding? That would be my dream job."

"Good. So, let's think about it: Some divisions of the company might be working on new business proposals and will value a gifted writer. Some might be working on projects involving media companies, investment bankers, schools, or even foreign governments. They will need people who work well in a team structure. Some divisions might be working on new apps or software applications, which means—"

"Critical thinking," I cut in. We grinned at each other as I stood up. "Thanks, Professor. I guess I'll go register now."

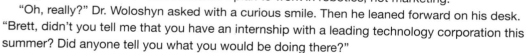

As Brett's story shows, college students should keep in mind how they plan to use their degree and begin building the skills that employers seek. What is your ideal job? How can you develop yourself as the ideal employee for that job? What kinds of skills do you need to develop as a college student? Can expertise in writing, critical thinking, and teamwork help you achieve your goals?

Careers and the New Economy

For some people, the reason for attending college is to get a good job. For others, the reason is to fulfill the dream of getting a college education, which helps students not only get better jobs but also become effective leaders.

Over the past few years, the global economy has experienced extreme ups and downs. Economic uncertainty is a reality, and although earning a college degree is one of the best ways for you to increase your chances of being employed, it is important to make decisions about your major and career path based on information about yourself and the long-term demands of the job market.

The following characteristics define today's economy:

- **It's global.** Many corporations are multinational; they look for cheap labor, capital, and resources both within and outside the United States. Competition on a global level presents challenges for American workers. College graduates in the United States now compete for jobs with others around the world, particularly in industries that involve science, technology, engineering, and mathematics (STEM).

- **It's unstable.** In late 2008, the world economy began suffering from a series of events that led to bankruptcies, foreclosures, failing businesses, downturns in stock markets, and lost jobs. The nation's economic situation gradually improved in subsequent years, but that improvement may have halted or even begun to reverse by the time you graduate. Economic instability is troubling, but having a college education gives you a great advantage over those without a degree.

- **It's innovative.** The economy has always depended on creativity to generate consumer interest in new products and services around the world. As a leader in industry innovation, the United States needs college graduates who possess imagination and a desire to move forward.

- **It's boundaryless.** In almost every organization, teams of workers need to cooperate. You might be an accountant and find yourself working with the public relations division of your company, or you might be a nurse who does staff training. The ability to work outside of traditional boundaries while expanding your skills, abilities, and knowledge will be essential to your professional success.

- **It's ever changing.** As we rebuild our economy, new jobs in nearly every industry will demand more education and training. As we have stated in this book, the most important skill you need to learn in college is how to keep learning throughout your life. To give yourself the best chance at avoiding a negative employment situation, it's important that you adapt your skills to the existing job market. Doing so requires flexibility and the desire to continue to develop yourself.

- **It's social.** Technology has allowed us to stay more connected than ever in our personal lives and in business; however, it has also decreased our need for face-to-face social interactions (or so we think—the long-term

▽ **Stiff Competition**
The information and strategies in this chapter will help you prepare for job interviews, so that when it's your turn to be interviewed, you can walk in with confidence. © Lynne Sladky/AP/Corbis.

effects of having less face-to-face contact have not been definitively measured yet). Employers rank the following abilities as the most important skills or qualities they look for in job candidates: the ability to work in a team structure; the ability to make decisions and solve problems; the ability to plan, organize, and prioritize work; and the ability to verbally communicate with people inside and outside the organization.[1] In this world of ever-increasing technology advancements, the ability to be a team player is the top asset organizations look for when hiring new employees.

These characteristics of the economy—that it is global, unstable, innovative, boundaryless, ever

[1]National Association of Colleges and Employers, *Job Outlook 2014* (Bethlehem, PA: National Association of Colleges and Employers, 2013).

changing, and social—should provide a roadmap for you as you make decisions throughout your college experience.

Building the Right Mind-Set for the Future

Even after you have landed a job, you will be expected to continue learning and developing yourself. Whether you are preparing to enter a career for the first time or to change careers after many years on the job, keep in mind the following:

- **A college degree does not guarantee employment.** Consider what it will be like competing for jobs with hundreds of other men and women earning the same degree as you and graduating from college at the same time! With a college degree, however, more

Working with an Academic Adviser

Academic planning is a vital step in your college career, and it should be an ongoing process that starts on your first day of school. Students who engage in academic planning are more likely to stay in college. Before you register for classes next term, sit down for a strategy session with your academic adviser. On most campuses, you are assigned an adviser (an instructor or staff person in your field or a professional adviser). A good adviser can help you choose courses, decide on a major, weigh career possibilities, and map out your degree and certificate requirements. He or she can also recommend instructors and help you simplify the different aspects of your academic life. Here are a few ways to make sure that your first meeting with your adviser is a valuable experience.

- **Prepare by looking at the course catalog, thinking about the available majors, and familiarizing yourself with campus resources.** If you haven't already decided on a major, ask your adviser about opportunities for taking an aptitude test or a self-assessment to help you narrow down your options. (Read more about self-assessments and self-exploration below.)
- **Prepare materials to bring to the meeting. Even if you submitted your academic transcript with your**

application, bring a copy of the transcript to the meeting. The transcript—your complete high school record—is an important tool; it shows your academic adviser where you've been, what your academic strengths are, and where your interests lie.
- **Make a list of majors that appeal to you.** Academic advisers love it when students come prepared—it shows that they're passionate and are taking their future seriously.
- **Map out your time frame and goals.** Do you plan to enroll full-time or part-time? If you're at a four-year college or university, when do you plan to graduate, and with what degree? Are you planning to go on to graduate school to finish your studies? If you are at a two-year college, do you want an associate's degree? A certificate? Do you plan to transfer to a four-year institution?
- **Know the right questions to ask.** Once you've chosen a major, you'll need to understand how to move forward in your academic program to meet the necessary requirements. You will have *prerequisites*—the basic core courses you need to take before you can enroll in upper-level classes in your major. Your major may also have *corequisites*: courses you have to take in conjunction with other courses during the same term (a chemistry lab alongside your chemistry class, for

opportunities, financial and otherwise, will be available to you than if you did not have a degree. For those who start an associate's degree and complete it, the reward is considerable. If you transfer to a four-year college or university after earning your associate's degree, the payoff is even greater. Just because you want to work for a certain organization or in a certain field, though, doesn't mean that a job will always be available for you there.

- **You are more or less solely responsible for your career.** Career development is a lifelong process, controlled only by you! Many employers offer some degree of training, and some might also offer assessments and information on available positions in the industry. However, the ultimate task of creating a career path is yours. Students who realize they are responsible for managing their

Even after you have landed a job, you will be expected to continue learning and developing yourself.

careers actively throughout their lifetime will be more successful and more satisfied than those who think someone else will come along to manage things for them.

- **To advance your career, you must accept the risks that accompany employment and plan for the future.** Organizations grow or downsize in response to economic conditions, so you must do your best to prepare for the unexpected. As we have stated at several points in this book, perhaps the most vital

---

instance). So, with this knowledge under your belt, here is what you need to find out:

- How many credits must I take each term to graduate on time? (Note: If you are on financial aid, are doing a work-study, or are a college athlete, you may have to take a minimum number of credits per term.)
- What are the prerequisites for my major? What are the corequisites?
- If I have any AP credits or have taken any placement exams, can I use them to fulfill some of my major's requirements?
- What career opportunities will I have once I graduate? What will the salary potential look like?
- **Know what to take away from your meeting.** When you leave the meeting, have in hand a printout of your current course schedule and plans for classes you might take in the next term and beyond. At many institutions, you and your adviser will set up a five- to seven-term plan online.
- **Know these rules of thumb about selecting your classes:**
  - Most full-time students take four to six courses a term. Decide which classes you want to take, find out which days and times they meet, and make sure they don't overlap.

- To get the classes you want, make sure to register as early as possible—in person or online.
- Resist the temptation to cram all of your classes into one or two days. It's better to aim for a manageable workload by spreading your classes throughout the week.
- Go for a mix of hard and easy classes. Especially at the beginning, you might not realize how challenging college classes can be or how much outside work they entail. If you load up on organic chemistry, Russian 101, and advanced thermodynamics, your grades and general well-being could suffer.
- **Know what to do if your academic adviser isn't very helpful.** If you think you and your adviser are not a good match, go to the admissions office and ask to be assigned to a different adviser. But whatever you do, don't throw in the towel. Academic planning is so critical to your success in college that it's worth persevering until you find an adviser with whom you feel comfortable.
- **Set up subsequent meetings with your academic adviser.** Check in with your adviser at least once a term, if not more often. It's important to stay connected and make sure you're on a positive track, especially if you plan to transfer or apply to graduate school. Programs change requirements occasionally, so it's smart to touch base with your adviser periodically in case you need to make any necessary adjustments.

△ **Thinking Things Through**

When you're asked about your plans for employment after college, do you have a response? Do you feel clueless? If so, you're not alone. Many students come to college without firm career plans. This chapter will give you some new ways to think about your career choices. Your experiences in college will help you make thoughtful decisions about your future. Blend Images/Getty Images.

skill you can gain in college is learning how to learn. Lifelong learning will help keep you employable and can provide you with many opportunities, regardless of the economy.

- **A first career choice might not be permanent.** College students often view the choice of a career as a big and permanent decision. However, a career is based on your professional development decisions over a lifetime. In fact, many students with jobs attend community colleges to get training for a new career. There is no one right occupation just waiting for you to discover it. Rather, there

are many career choices you might find satisfying. The question to consider is this: What is the best choice for me right now?

Now the good news: Hundreds of thousands of graduates find jobs every year, even in difficult economic times. It might take them longer to get where they want to be, but persistence pays off. If you start preparing now and continue to do so while in college, you'll have time to build a portfolio of academic and other learning experiences (e.g., on-campus clubs and groups, internships, work-study jobs) that will begin to add to your career profile. ■

Self-Exploration in Career Planning

Are you confident in your skills and abilities? Do you know what you want or can accomplish? How well you know yourself and how effectively you can do the things you need to do are central to your success not only as a student but also as a person. Self-assessment is the process of gathering information about yourself in order to make informed decisions.

Self-assessment is a good first step in setting your academic and career goals. While you might know what you like to do and what you are good at doing, you may lack a clear idea of how your self-knowledge can help you explore different career possibilities. Factors that can affect your career choices include your values, skills, aptitudes, personality, life goals and work satisfaction, and interests.

Values

Your values, formed through your life experiences, are those things you feel most strongly about. For career planning, values generally refer to what you most want in a career in relation to how you want to live. For example, some people value job security, money, and a regular schedule. Others value flexibility, excitement, independence, variety, and particular work environments, such as the outdoors. Some career choices pay higher salaries than others but may require hard work and long hours.

Thus, knowing your personal wishes and needs in relation to your values is important. You might find that what you value most is not money but rather the chance to work for a specific cause or the opportunity to have a particular lifestyle. In general, being aware of what you value is important because a career choice that is closely related to your core values is likely to be the best choice.

Skills

The ability to do something well can usually be improved with practice. You may bring different skills to different situations, and it is important to know both your strengths and

Self-assessment is a good first step in setting your academic and career goals.

your weaknesses. Skills typically fall into three categories:

1. **Personal.** Some skills come naturally or are learned through experience. Examples of these are honesty, punctuality, teamwork, self-motivation, and conflict management.

2. **Workplace.** Some skills can be learned on the job; others are gained through training designed to increase your knowledge or expertise in a certain area. Examples include designing Web sites, bookkeeping, and providing customer service.

▽ **A Passion for the Outdoors?**
Are you interested in American history? Do you enjoy talking with the public? Do you value education? Do you value the preservation of our natural resources and historical landmarks? People who answer yes to these questions might find that a career as a park ranger suits them. How does the career you are planning to pursue align with your values, interests, and personality? If you're coming up empty, you might want to reconsider your plans. The Washington Post/Getty Images.

3. **Transferable.** Some skills gained through your previous jobs or hobbies or through everyday life can be transferred to another job. Examples include planning events, motivating others, paying attention to detail, and organizing workspaces.

By identifying your skill set, you can turn your current skills into career possibilities.

Aptitudes

Aptitude is your natural or acquired proficiency in a particular area, which makes it easier for you to learn or to do certain things. Shine a light on your aptitudes and discover a path in which your strengths become your best intellectual assets.

Personality

Your personality makes you who you are and can't be ignored when you make career decisions. The quiet, orderly, calm, detail-oriented person will probably make a different work choice than the aggressive, outgoing, argumentative person will. Chapter 3, Understanding How You Learn, included discussion of the Myers-Briggs Type Indicator, one of the best-known and most widely used personality inventories. This assessment can help you understand how you make decisions, perceive the world, and interact with others.

TRY IT!

SETTING GOALS ▷
No Time like the Present to Plan for the Future

Do you plan for the future, or are you focused on the here and now? As you are thinking about what you have to do today or this week, set a goal to begin thinking for the longer term. Even if you haven't decided on a specific career, you probably know whether you're leaning toward the sciences, the arts, business, or some other field. When you next meet with your academic adviser, ask for advice on how to link both your required and your elective courses to the career direction that most interests you.

Life Goals and Work Satisfaction

Every person defines success and satisfaction in his or her own way. The process of defining them is complex and personal. Two factors can change how we feel about our success and satisfaction: knowing that we are achieving the life goals we've set for ourselves and finding that we gain satisfaction from what we're receiving from our work. If your values are not in line with the values of the organization where you work, you might be in for trouble.

Interests

From birth, we develop interests. These interests help shape our career paths and might even define them. Good career exploration begins with considering what you like to do and relating that to your career choices. For example, because you enjoyed writing for your high school paper, you might be interested in writing for the college newspaper with an eye on entering a career in journalism. On the other hand, you might enroll in Psych 101 because of your interest in human behavior and realize halfway through the course that psychology is not what you imagined and that you have no desire to become a psychologist. Because your interests are unique to you, you are the only person who should determine what you want to do in the future.

Exploring Your Interests

Most students want their major to lead directly into a career, although this doesn't always happen. You might be encouraged to select a major in a subject about which you are really passionate. Most academic advisers would agree with this decision-making advice: Try a major you think you'll like and that makes sense given the attributes described above—your values, strengths, aptitudes, skills, personality, goals, and interests—and see what develops. Take advantage of available self-assessments to help you learn more about yourself.

John Holland, a psychologist at Johns Hopkins University, developed a number of tools and concepts that can help you organize the various dimensions of yourself so that you can identify potential career choices (see Table 13.1).

Table 13.1 ▽ Holland Personality and Career Types

Category	Personality Characteristics	Career Fields
Realistic (R)	These people describe themselves as concrete, down-to-earth, and practical doers. They exhibit competitive/assertive behavior and show interest in activities that require motor coordination, skill, and physical strength. They prefer situations involving action solutions rather than tasks involving verbal or interpersonal skills, and they like taking a concrete approach to problem solving rather than relying on abstract theory. They tend to be interested in scientific or mechanical areas rather than the arts.	Environmental engineer, electrical contractor, industrial arts teacher, navy officer, fitness director, package engineer, electronics technician, Web designer
Investigative (I)	These people describe themselves as analytical, rational, and logical problem solvers. They value intellectual stimulation and intellectual achievement, and they prefer to think rather than to act and to organize and understand rather than to persuade. They usually have a strong interest in physical, biological, or social sciences. They are less apt to be people oriented.	Urban planner, chemical engineer, bacteriologist, flight engineer, genealogist, laboratory technician, marine scientist, nuclear medical technologist, obstetrician, quality-control technician, computer programmer, environmentalist, physician, college professor
Artistic (A)	These people describe themselves as creative, innovative, and independent. They value self-expression and relating with others through artistic expression and are also emotionally expressive. They dislike structure, preferring tasks involving personal or physical skills. They resemble investigative people but are more interested in the cultural or the aesthetic than the scientific.	Architect, film editor/director, actor, cartoonist, interior decorator, fashion model, graphic communications specialist, journalist, editor, orchestra leader, public relations specialist, sculptor, media specialist, librarian, reporter
Social (S)	These people describe themselves as kind, caring, helpful, and understanding of others. They value helping and making a contribution. They satisfy their needs in one-to-one or small-group interaction using strong speaking skills to teach, counsel, or advise. They are drawn to close interpersonal relationships and are less apt to engage in intellectual or extensive physical activity.	Nurse, teacher, social worker, genetic counselor, marriage counselor, rehabilitation counselor, school superintendent, geriatric specialist, insurance claims specialist, minister, travel agent, guidance counselor, convention planner
Enterprising (E)	These people describe themselves as assertive, risk taking, and persuasive. They value prestige, power, and status and are more inclined than other types to pursue such objectives. They use verbal skills to supervise, lead, direct, and persuade rather than to support or guide. They are interested in people and in achieving organizational goals.	Banker, city manager, FBI agent, health administrator, judge, labor arbitrator, salary and wage administrator, insurance salesperson, sales engineer, lawyer, sales representative, marketing manager
Conventional (C)	These people describe themselves as neat, orderly, detail oriented, and persistent. They value order, structure, prestige, and status and possess a high degree of self-control. They are not opposed to rules and regulations. They are skilled in organizing, planning, and scheduling and are interested in data and people.	Accountant, statistician, census enumerator, data processor, hospital administrator, insurance administrator, office manager, underwriter, auditor, personnel specialist, database manager, abstractor/indexer

Holland suggests that people are separated into six general categories based on differences in their interests, skills, values, and personality characteristics—in short, their preferred approaches to life. Holland's system organizes career fields into the same six categories. Career fields are grouped according to what they require of a person (the skills and personality characteristics most commonly associated with success in those fields) and what rewards they provide (the interests and values most commonly associated with satisfaction). As you view Table 13.1, highlight or note characteristics that you believe you have as well as those that are less closely matched.

Your career choice ultimately will involve a complex assessment of the factors that are most important to you. To display the relationship between career fields and the potential conflicts people face as they consider them, Holland's model is commonly presented in a hexagonal shape (Figure 13.1). The closer the types, the closer the relationships among the career fields; the farther apart the types, the more conflict between the career fields. Holland's model can help you address the questions surrounding career choice in two ways. First, you can begin to identify many career fields that are consistent with what you

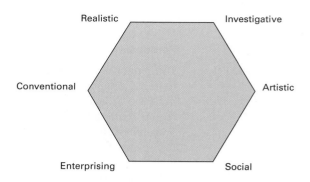

Figure 13.1 △ **Holland's Hexagonal Model of Career Fields**

Reproduced by special permission of the Publisher, Psychological Assessment Resources, Inc., 16204 N. Florida Ave., Lutz, FL 33549. From *The Self-Directed Search Professional User's Guide* by John L. Holland, PhD. Copyright © 1985, 1987, 1994, 1997. Further reproduction is prohibited without permission from PAR, Inc.

know about yourself. Once you have identified potential fields, you can use the career center at your college to get more information about those fields, such as the daily activities for specific jobs, the interests and abilities required, the preparation required for entry, the working conditions, the salary and benefits, and the employment outlook. Second, you can begin to identify the harmony or conflicts in your career choices. Doing so will help you analyze the reasons for your career decisions and help you be more confident as you make choices.

This book will introduce you to a variety of self-assessments designed to provide a clearer picture of who you are as an individual. These assessments are meant to be used as tools to assist the career exploration process. Never think that you have to make a decision based on the results of only one assessment. Career choices are complex and involve many factors; furthermore, these decisions are reversible. It is important not only to take time to talk your interests over with a career counselor but also to shadow individuals in the occupations that interest you. Obtaining a better understanding of what an occupation entails in terms of skills, commitment, and opportunity will help you make informed decisions about your own career choices. ■

TRY IT!

FEELING CONNECTED ▷
Where Do You Fit in the Holland Model?

After you have read about and discussed the Holland model, decide where you belong: Which of the six types is most like your personality? After you decide whether you are mostly realistic, investigative, artistic, social, enterprising, or conventional, find others in your class who have the same type. Get together in a small group and talk about your characteristics and how they link to your career goals. Share ideas about part-time jobs or campus clubs and organizations that will give you an opportunity to expand your interests.

Planning for Your Career

The process of making a career choice begins with creating a career plan, and college is a good time to start, if you haven't already. Here are some important steps to take:

- **Take a variety of classes.** You'll want to get exposure to various knowledge areas.

- **Visit your college's career center in person, and explore its Web site.** You'll find listings for part- and full-time positions, internships, cooperative (co-op) programs, and seasonal employment. You'll also find on-campus interviewing opportunities for internships and for full-time employment after graduation. Attend workshops on advanced résumé writing, internship placement, interviewing, and other job search skills. Participate in mock interview activities to improve your interviewing skills.

- **Take as many self-assessments as possible.** Talk to a career counselor about your skills, aptitudes, interests, and career plans. Research possible occupations that match your skills, interests, and academic major.

- **Prepare a draft of your résumé and have it reviewed by a career counselor or a professional in your desired field.** Create profiles on professional sites such as LinkedIn to share your skills and experience with potential employers and to make professional connections.

- **Get involved in clubs and organizations.** Take on a leadership role in clubs and organizations.

- **Attend your college's career fair.** Employers in the area visit your campus to hire students. Get to know more about the employers who hire graduates in your major. Some career fairs may be specific to disciplines such as health care, information technology, or business.

- **Build on your strengths and develop your weaker skills.** Whether in or out of class, find ways to practice what you are good at doing and get help with what you need to improve.

- **Network.** Connect with instructors, family members, and friends to find contacts in your fields of interest so that you can learn more about those areas. If possible, participate in mentor programs hosted by alumni (past graduates of your college). Spend the summer completing internship, service-learning, and co-op experiences.

- **Volunteer.** Whether you give your time to a nonprofit organization, a school, or a business, volunteering can help you explore careers and get some experience in an area that interests you.

- **Do occupational and industry research for your field or for geographic areas that interest you.** Look for other options within and beyond those fields.

- **Visit work environments in person.** Explore career options through informational interviews (interviewing to find out more about a career) and job shadowing (observing someone at work—with his or her permission).

- **Get a job.** Many students already have jobs when they enter college. Holding a job, especially one related to your major or to a course you are taking, can enhance your classroom learning. Even a part-time job will develop your skills and might help you to make decisions about what you like—and don't like—in a work environment. In any job, you learn essential skills such as teamwork, communication, and time management—all important to employers!

- **Conduct a social media audit of your own online presence.** Make sure nothing inappropriate is posted about you on Facebook, Instagram, Twitter, or any other social media sites.

Develop your qualifications, make good choices, and take advantage of opportunities on and off campus.

Diving into Industry Research

Throughout this text, you've been encouraged to explore your own strengths and interests, and you've obtained information on how to be a successful college student. Similarly, the more knowledge you have, the better your chances of making a good career decision. You can gain an edge over other job seekers by doing industry research.

Steps to Doing Industry Research	
Step 1.	Figure out what industries interest you.
Step 2.	Continue your research to identify your desired role within your chosen industry. Large industries offer many career possibilities.
Step 3.	Identify companies or organizations of interest within a larger industry. The federal government alone, for example, has approximately 575 departments and agencies! Because you have so many choices, this part of your research depends on your own expectations and wants.
Step 4.	Do research on each individual employer of interest. How well does a particular organization pay compared to others in the same industry? Does a job with this employer require long hours or frequent travel? Set up an informational interview to talk to people who are already working within the organization.

Finding out all you can early on about organizations you think you want to work for can help you make a career decision based on fit.

You might complete these steps at a different pace or in a different order than your friends do, and that's OK. What you want is to develop your qualifications, make good choices, and take advantage of opportunities on and off campus to learn more about your career preferences. Keep your goals in mind as you select courses and look for employment, but also keep an eye out for special opportunities. The route you think you want to take might change as you do. ■

Getting Experience

Now that you have developed a career plan, gotten a handle on your interests, and done your industry research, it's time to test the waters. College students often face a dilemma: Employers prefer to hire people with experience, but how can you gain experience if you can't find a job? The answer is that there are several ways to gain some experience while you are in college: Experiential learning opportunities include service-learning, volunteer activities, internships and co-op programs, and competitions and projects designed for students.

Experiential Learning Opportunities

Gaining experience in your field while you're in college can help you meet people who may later serve as important references for employment. That experience can also teach you things you won't learn in the classroom.

Here are a number of ways to pursue this experience:

- **Service-learning/volunteer activities.** Service-learning allows you to apply what you learn in class to actual practice. Some instructors build service-learning into their courses, but if this option isn't available, consider volunteering! A little time spent each week can provide many personal and professional rewards and will allow you to continue learning about yourself, your interests, and your abilities.
- **Internships and co-ops.** What you learn in the classroom can be applied to the real world through internships and co-ops. An *internship* is a short-term, structured method of on-the-job training. As an intern, you are not likely to be paid, but you might be able to receive academic credit. Check with your academic department and your career center to find out what internships are available in your major. Remember that if you have one or more internships on your résumé, you'll be a step ahead of students who ignore this

valuable experience. A *co-operative (co-op) program* allows you to alternate work experience and classes. As a co-op student, you can also have paid work assignments that provide you with an opportunity to apply what you've learned in college to the workplace.

- **Student projects/competitions.** In many fields, students engage in competitions based on what they have learned in the classroom. They might compete against teams from other colleges. In the process, they learn teamwork, communication, and problem-solving skills.

△ **Trash or Treasure?**
This student intern in the campus recycling department empties a bin of food into a container that will be sent to an off-campus composting center. Imagine what he is learning about the business of recycling, composting, and food waste reduction that he can apply to an academic area like environmental studies. MCT via Getty Images.

Working in College

Among the many benefits of holding down a job while taking classes are the following:

- Gaining professional experience
- Earning money for tuition, books, and living expenses
- Networking/making connections
- Learning more about yourself and others
- Developing key skills and attributes, such as communication, teamwork, problem solving, work ethic, and time management

Your first decision will be whether to work on campus or off. If you choose to work on campus, look for opportunities as early in the semester as you can. You might be pleasantly surprised to learn how varied on-campus opportunities are, such as tutoring in the writing or math center, being an attendant in the fitness center, or serving as a student ambassador for the admissions office or career center. Often you will see students on campus who are studying while they work. This is one benefit of on-campus employment. Another benefit is that the schedules are often flexible. Still another is that you might be able to connect with instructors and administrators whom you later can consult as mentors or ask for reference letters. In addition, your boss will understand that you occasionally need time off to study or take exams. Finally, students who work on campus are more likely to graduate from college than are students who work off campus; keep this fact in mind as you think about mixing college and work.

Some on-campus jobs are reserved for work-study students. The federal work-study program is a form of government-sponsored financial aid that provides part-time employment to help students with college expenses. Once you accept the work-study award on your financial aid notification, you will be sent information regarding the steps you should take for getting a job within the program. Keep in mind that your work-study award will be limited to a certain amount of money each term; once you reach your earnings limit, you can no longer work until the next term begins. Most work-study jobs are on campus, but some nonprofit organizations in your community may be able to accept work-study students as well. Generally, you will have to interview for a work-study position whether on or off campus. Check with your college's financial aid office or career center to get a list of available jobs and to get help preparing your application materials and getting ready for the interview.

An off-campus job might pay better than an on-campus one, or be closer to your home, or be in an organization where you want to continue working after you finish college. The best places to start looking for off-campus jobs are your campus career center and your financial aid office. Feel free to speak to a career counselor for suggestions.

Whether you choose to work on or off campus, keep in mind that overextending yourself can interfere with your college success and your ability to attend class, do your homework, and participate in many other valuable parts of college life, such as group study. Determine how involved you are able to be, and stay within reasonable limits. Students who work in paid jobs more than fifteen hours a week have a lower chance of success in college. ∎

TRY IT!

MAKING DECISIONS ▷
College Jobs and Your Career

At this point in your college experience, you probably have at least tentative plans for the major and/or the career you will pursue. If you must take a job while going to school, think about what jobs might be available on campus and in the outside community that could provide valuable experience with respect to your goals. Look at your campus Web site and your local newspaper (either the print or the online version). Make two lists—one for on-campus jobs that you discover on the campus Web site and the other for off-campus jobs listed in the paper that relate to your intended major. Make a decision to investigate the availability of the jobs you identify.

Job Search Strategies

It may be hard to imagine yourself searching for a job—after all, you've just begun college. But we want to give you some job search strategies that can be applied to an internship or a co-op program while you are in college as well as to a career-level job once you graduate. Additionally, some preparation requires you to plan early. Here are a few things to consider:

- Learn the names of the major employers in your college's geographic area: manufacturers, service industries, resorts, and so on. Once you know who the major employers are, check them out and visit their Web sites. If you like what you see, visit your career center to arrange an informational interview or a job-shadowing opportunity.

- Visit online job boards, and look at the classified ads in the local newspaper, either in print or online.

- Check your college's student newspaper. Employers who favor hiring college students (such as UPS) often advertise there. Be cautious about work opportunities that seem unrealistic, such as those offering big salaries for working at home or those that ask you to pay an up-front fee for a job. When in doubt, ask your career center for advice.

- Be aware that many job openings are never posted. Employers usually prefer to hire people who are recommended to them by current employees, friends, or the person leaving the position. Realize that who you know is important. Your friends who already work on campus or who have had an internship can be the best people to help you when you are ready to search for your job.

Market Yourself

Some people think that marketing yourself is what you do when you need a job, but in fact that's not the case at all. Marketing yourself is actually about developing a presence at your college and within your industry. If you can create a name and reputation for yourself, you can shape your own future. Here are a few points to consider:

Taking control of your own image is your responsibility.

- **If you don't do it, no one else will.** Taking control of your own image is your responsibility. There is no one who can portray you as accurately as you. Remember to share your career goals with instructors, advisers, friends, and family—they can't help market you if they don't know you! The more others know about your professional goals, the more they are able to help you make professional connections.

- **Get an edge over your competition.** You need to stand out from your peers if you want to go far in your career. Think carefully about what you are doing to advance yourself professionally outside the classroom, such as becoming a co-op student, an intern, or a volunteer.

Build a Résumé

A good résumé is an excellent and necessary way of marketing yourself. Before you finish college, you'll need a résumé, whether it's for a part-time job, an internship, or a co-op position, or to show to an instructor who agrees to write you a letter of recommendation. There are two résumé formats: chronological and skill focused. Generally, choose the chronological format if you have related job experience (listing your jobs and other experiences, starting with those that are the most recent). Choose the skill-focused résumé if you can group skills from a number of jobs or projects into several meaningful categories. Your career center can help you choose the format that is right for you based on your experience and future goals.

The average time an employer spends screening a résumé for the first time is 7 to 10 seconds. Many employers also use résumé-scanning software to identify key terms and experiences that are most highly prized by the employers. If you are a new professional, a one-page résumé is appropriate. Add a second page only if you have truly outstanding skills or work experiences that won't fit on the first page, but consult with your career center for guidance on this point. If you are in college to get retrained and change your career, make sure to update the information on your résumé.

Write a Cover Letter

A cover letter is *more important* than a résumé and much harder to write well. When composing a cover letter, think about who will receive it. Different organizations will have different requirements. Your career counselor can help you address your letter to the right person; so can the Internet. Never write, "To whom it may concern." Use the proper formats for date, address, and salutation (Dear _____:). These are details that hiring managers pay attention to, and a mistake in your letter may cost you an interview. And make sure to ask someone whose writing ability you trust to proof your cover letter.

A cover letter written to explain how hiring you will benefit the organization is an excellent way of marketing yourself to a potential employer. It is important to review the organization's Web site and find out what skills and experience its current employees have. Use the cover letter to highlight your skills for every requirement of the position. Your career center can help you write a cover letter that talks about your education and your experience related to the position. Spending time on writing an excellent cover letter also prepares you for the interview by allowing you to think about how your background matches the needs of that position and the organization.

Know How to Interview

The first year of college might not seem like a time to be concerned about interviews. However, students often find themselves in interview situations soon after arriving on campus. You might be looking for a position in student government, searching for an on-campus job, competing for a second-year scholarship, choosing a summer job opportunity, or applying for an internship. Your preparation for an interview begins the moment you arrive on campus because, as a first-year student, the interview will be about you and how college is changing you. Students who have taken only a little time to think about who they are and how they have changed can feel lost in an interview. Luckily, the chapters in this book have begun preparing you for the interview process.

Interview preparation. The purpose of the interview is to exchange information. The interviewer's goal is to assess your abilities and competencies. For you, the interview is an opportunity to learn more about the employer and to determine whether the job would be a good fit with your abilities and preferences. Ideally, you want to find a match between your interests and abilities and the position or experience you are seeking. It is important to research the organization and the people you may be working with prior to any interview. Doing so will help prepare you for the interview and help you know what questions to ask. Here's how you can get started:

1. **Start with the company Web site.** This is usually the single best resource. Scroll through the entire site. Note details you can use to develop good interview questions to ask in your interview and to prepare relevant answers to anticipated interview questions. If the company does not have its own Web site, go to other sites, such as Hoovers.com, that provide extensive information about companies and industries.

2. **Review competitor Web sites.** Gather information on developments in the company's industry or sector.

3. **Ask for advice.** Ask your instructor or your career center about the organization.

4. **Use your library.** Find articles in business publications and industry trade magazines.

5. **Note the employer's goals and values.** These tell you about the organizational culture. Use this information to decide whether you would be a good fit.

6. **Research details on the employer's products and services.** Being able to talk a firm's language shows that you have prepared yourself for the interview.

7. **Take your research with you to the interview.** It is recommended that you show how you have taken the time to find out about the organization prior to the interview.

After you've done your research, the next step is to practice interviewing *before* the actual interview. Check with your career center to find out whether you can participate in a mock interview. Mock interviews help students feel comfortable in real interview situations. Your counselor might ask you for a position description, your résumé, and an organizational profile prior to the interview—career counselors use these materials to create a situation similar to an actual interview. Many career centers also have practice interview software. InterviewStream is a popular program that allows you to record answers to interview questions asked by the computer for replay and review. You can record your answers multiple times as you aim to perfect your response; you can send your recorded interview to instructors or others for feedback; and, because the interview is recorded using a webcam, you can review not only your words but also your body language! Nonverbal communication is often more important that what you actually say in the interview. Even if a mock interview session is not available, the career center can offer tips on handling an interview situation. Check your career center Web site for sample interview questions so that you can practice before an interview.

If you are changing your career and have been interviewed before, make sure to think about the best and worst interviews you have had and try to avoid repeating the mistakes you made before; more important, build on the positive interview strategies you used in previous successful interviews.

Appropriate interview conduct. In an interview situation, any of the following might make the difference in whether you are hired for the position:

- **Dress appropriately.** First impressions matter, so always dress neatly and appropriately. You can be somewhat casual for some types of employers, but it is better to dress too professionally than too informally. Check with your career center to get advice about proper dress. Also, many community colleges have interview clothing to loan to students who cannot afford to buy expensive clothes.

- **Arrive on time to the interview.** If your interview is off campus, determine how long it will take you to travel to the interview site before the day of your interview. Be mindful of traffic volume at certain times of the day, and if you are driving, make sure you know where to park. The interviewer expects you to be on time, regardless of the weather or the morning commute.

- **Follow up.** It is important to follow up any interview with a thank-you e-mail or a signed card. Many times, the person to whom you addressed your cover letter is not the person with whom you actually interview. Prior to leaving the interview, ask for the business cards of the professionals you've met so that you have their contact information. Send a thank-you to every person who interviewed you. In your follow-up, you can highlight how your skills and experience match with the organization's goals. ■

△ **First Impressions**
A critical step on the way to any job is the personal interview. This is your chance to put your best foot forward. Remember to be on time, dress professionally, offer a firm handshake, answer questions honestly, and smile!

Skills Employers Seek

△ **Making Connections**
Some career fairs may be specific to fields such as health care, information technology, or business. Others may be specific to the audience, such as this career fair for military veterans. Attending events like these is part of planning for your career. Career fairs give job candidates the opportunity to make a strong first impression with potential employers. © Sandy Huffaker/Corbis.

One of the many important purposes and outcomes of your college experience is gaining a combination of knowledge and skills. Two types of skills are essential to employment and to life: content skills and transferable skills.

Content Skills

Content skills are intellectual, or "hard," skills you gain in your academic field. They include writing proficiency, computer literacy, and foreign language skills. Computer literacy is now a core skill like reading, writing, and mathematics. You can apply content skills to jobs in any field or occupation.

Certain types of employers expect you to have extensive knowledge in your academic major before they will consider hiring you; for example, to get a job in accounting, you must have knowledge of QuickBooks or of Microsoft Excel's advanced features. Employers will not train you in basic applications or knowledge related to your field, so remember to be prepared to speak of your qualifications during the interview process.

Job Candidate Skills/Qualities Ranked as Very Important by Employers

- Work in a team structure
- Make decisions and solve problems
- Plan, organize, and prioritize work
- Verbally communicate with persons inside and outside the organization
- Obtain and process information
- Analyze quantitative data
- Technical knowledge related to the job

Therefore, the ideal candidate is a team player and good communicator who can make decisions, solve problems, and prioritize.

Source: National Association of Colleges and Employers, *Job Outlook 2014* (Bethlehem, PA: National Association of Colleges and Employers, 2013).

For most college students, it's sufficient to have some fundamental knowledge. You will learn on the job as you move from entry-level to advanced positions.

Transferable Skills

Transferable skills are general abilities that can be applied in a lot of settings. Some transferable skills are listed and described in the table below.

Transferable skills are valuable to many kinds of employers. They give you flexibility in your career planning. For example, volunteer work, involvement in a student professional organization or club, and personal hobbies or interests can all build interpersonal awareness and teamwork, leadership, and effective communication abilities. Internships and career-related work can offer you valuable opportunities to practice these skills in the real world. ■

Skills	Abilities
Communication	Being a clear and persuasive speaker Listening attentively Writing well
Presentation	Justifying Persuading Responding to questions and serious critiques of presentation material
Leadership	Taking charge Providing direction
Teamwork	Working with different people while maintaining control over some assignments
Interpersonal	Relating to others Motivating others to participate Easing conflict between coworkers
Personal traits	Showing motivation Recognizing the need to take action Being adaptable to change Having a work ethic Being reliable and honest Acting in an ethical manner Knowing how to plan and organize multiple tasks Being able to respond positively to customer concerns
Critical thinking and problem solving	Identifying problems and their solutions by combining information from different sources and considering options

Staying on the Path to Success

Because so much research has been done on first-year students like you, we can confidently tell you that successful completion of this course is a good predictor for overall success in college. When you finish any of your courses in college, take some time to step back, think, ask yourself the following questions, and perhaps even record your answers:

- What did I learn in this course?
- How can I apply what I have learned to other courses or to my current job?
- How will I use what I learned both in and out of class?
- What did I learn that I am most likely to remember?
- Do I want to stay in touch with this instructor?

- Did I improve my basic skills?
- How do I feel about what I accomplished?
- Did I do better than I thought I would?
- What did I do that helped me progress, and how can I repeat those kinds of successful efforts in other courses?
- What challenges do I still face?

Whether you are finishing this course at the end of your first term or at the end of your first year in college, you have learned many success strategies that can help you throughout your entire college experience. For many students, the first year is by far the most challenging, especially in terms of adjusting or readjusting to college life. Once you complete your first year, you will have many decisions and opportunities, and you need a set of strategies to succeed beyond the first year. ∎

△ **Celebrate!**
Before you know it, you'll be a college graduate. © Corbis.

Chapter Review

Steps to Success:
Considering Majors & Careers

○ **Understand the nature of the new economy that you will be entering.** It is global, unstable, innovative, without boundaries, customized, ever changing, and social.

○ **Be responsible for planning your own career.** No one else is going to plan your career for you, but plenty of people on your campus are willing to help *you* do it. Think seriously about your major. You eventually have to get a degree in something, and you want to feel confident and comfortable about the major that you select. Use the insights into yourself that you have gotten from this course as motivation, now and in the future.

○ **Take academic planning seriously.** Once you lay a foundation for your studies, you'll save time and money, avoid missing credits, and take ownership of your curriculum. You'll also stay motivated with a clear sense of how each step in your academic plan contributes to your purpose for being in college.

○ **Enhance your employability by getting different kinds of work and travel experience during college.** You can get different experiences while taking classes— or better yet, consider maintaining your momentum during the summer. Continuous enrollment is a good thing. See your adviser and career center to learn about experiences that your college offers: volunteer or service learning, study abroad, internships and co-ops, employment on campus, and student projects and research.

○ **Learn which of your characteristics could and should affect your career choices.** Strive to define your interests, skills, aptitudes, personality, life goals, and work values. Talk them through with a career counselor. It's a normal thing for college students to do.

○ **Get professional help from your career center.** Advisers can help you with writing your résumé and cover letters, learning and practicing interview skills, and much more. For example, you can learn how your personality characteristics have been shown to have an affinity with particular career fields.

○ **Keep in touch with your instructors.** Consider keeping in touch with the instructor of this course and with other instructors. Later in college you may need to ask them to write letters of reference for you as you seek employment or admission to graduate school. When an instructor becomes part of your larger support group, it is a form of networking.

○ **Make a commitment to yourself.** You may think that you are not yet ready for a high level of commitment because too many things are still uncertain about your major and your future life. That's perfectly natural. But at the very least, we urge you to make a commitment to return to college next term and next year and to get as much as you can out of this often unpredictable but life-changing experience.

Applying what you've learned . . .

Now that you have read and discussed this chapter, consider how you can apply what you have learned to your academic and personal lives. The following prompts will help you reflect on the chapter material and its relevance to you both now and in the future.

1. Sometimes the best way to learn about a career is to talk to someone who is working or teaching in that field. Set up an appointment to talk with a professor who teaches in the area in which you are interested. Find out as much as possible about the education required for a specific career in that field.

2. Choosing a major is a big decision, one that should include consideration of your personal learning style, your personality, and your goals and values. Review what you learned in Chapter 3 about how you learn and about your emotional intelligence. How will those insights guide your exploration of majors and careers?

Create Community

GO TO ▷ The career center: If you need help learning about specific jobs and careers, about preparing an effective résumé and cover letter, and about preparing for an interview.

GO TO ▷ Academic advisers/first-year counselors: If you need help finding supportive networks to connect academic learning to co-curricular and extracurricular learning.

GO TO ▷ Your instructors: If you need help connecting your academic interests to careers.

GO TO ▷ The library: If you need help finding information on careers.

GO TO ▷ Upper-class students: If you need help navigating courses and finding important resources.

GO TO ▷ Student organizations: If you need help finding leadership development opportunities.

GO ONLINE TO ▷ The Occupational Information Network (O*NET) Resource Center (http://www.onetcenter.org): If you need help getting information on occupations, skill sets, and links to professional sites for selected occupations.

GO ONLINE TO ▷ Mapping Your Future (http://www.mappingyourfuture.org): If you need help exploring careers.

GO ONLINE TO ▷ The Riley Guide (http://www.rileyguide.com): If you need help finding tips for interviewing and job search strategies.

NOW... **How do you measure up?**

1. The world economy is changing, and how it changes will probably affect job prospects.
   - ○ Agree
   - ○ Don't Know
   - ○ Disagree

2. There is no guarantee that anyone's first career choice will be permanent.
   - ○ Agree
   - ○ Don't Know
   - ○ Disagree

3. I know my strengths and interests and how they might influence my career choice.
   - ○ Agree
   - ○ Don't Know
   - ○ Disagree

4. There are advantages and disadvantages to working while going to college.
   - ○ Agree
   - ○ Don't Know
   - ○ Disagree

How do your answers here compare to your responses to the quiz you took at the start of the chapter? Which sections of this chapter left a strong impression on you? What strategies for selecting your major and planning for your career have you started to use? Are they working? What other strategies will you commit to trying?

Index

A

Abstract of article, reading, 77
Academic advisers, working with, 200–1
Academic articles/journals. *See* Scholarly articles/journals
Academic databases, 124
Academic freedom, 153
Academic honesty, 99–101
Academic planning, 200–1
Active class participation, 55–56
Active reading, 67–84
    of different kinds of textbooks, 75–78
    four-step plan for, 69–74
    improving, 79–81
Adaptability, emotional intelligence and, 42–43
Advisers, working with, 200–1
Aerobic exercise. *See* Exercise
Age diversity on campus, 160
Alcohol use, 192–93
Analysis, as fourth level of learning, 112
Analytical information, 128
Annotations, making while reading, 71–72
Anorexia nervosa, 189
Anxiety
    public speaking and, 144
    while taking tests and exams, 95
APA documentation style, 142
Appealing to false authority, 110–11
Application, as third level of learning, 112
Appointments, making with instructors, 152
Arguments, thinking critically about, 116
Artistic personality type, 205, 206
Asking questions. *See* Questions, asking
Assertiveness, emotional intelligence and, 42
Assigned reading, doing for class preparation, 53
Assuming truth, as faulty reasoning, 111
Assumptions, challenging, 115–16
Attainable goals, setting, 10
Attention deficit disorder, 46
Attention deficit hyperactivity disorder, 46
Attention level
    improved memory and, 92
    study time and, 27
Audience
    public speaking and, 144
    writing for, 140–41
Aural learners
    critical listening and, 55
    methods for, 40
    preferences of, 36
    remembering information and, 64
Authority
    appealing to false, 110–11
    evaluating sources for, 130

B

Bar-On, Reuven, 42
Bar-On Model of Emotional Intelligence, 42
Begging, as faulty reasoning, 110

Bias, evaluating sources for, 130
Binders, for each course, 53, 62
Binge eating disorder, 189
Birth control, 190–91
Block scheduling, 27
Blogs, 129
Blood alcohol content, 192–93
Bloom, Benjamin, 112–13
Bloom's taxonomy, 112–13
Borrowing funds, balancing with working, 176–77
Brainstorming, critical thinking and, 109
Branch mapping, 70
Breathing, stress management and, 185
Budgeting, 169–71
Bulimia, 189

C

Caffeine, stress management and, 186
Calendars, 23–24
Campus career centers, 207
Campus learning centers, 88
Campus library resources, 125–27
Campus organizations and groups, getting involved in, 4
Campus tutoring centers, 88
Career centers, 207
Career fairs, 207, 214
Career planning, 197–219
    getting experience and, 209–10
    job search strategies and, 211–13
    new economy and, 197–202
    process of, 207–08
    self-exploration in, 203–6
    setting goals for, 8, 15–18
    skills employers seek and, 200, 214–15
    staying on path to success by, 216
Carnegie Commission on Higher Education, 6
Cheating, 99. *See also* Plagiari sm
Checkcards, 180
Choosing topic, 123–24
Chronological résumés, 211
Cigarette smoking, 193
Citing sources, 142–43
Class discussion. *See* Discussion
Classes, dropping, 22
Class participation, 55–56
Class preparation, 53
Class schedule, 26, 202
Clubs on campus, getting involved in, 4, 163
Cognitive learning disabilities, 46–48
Collaboration, critical thinking and, 109
Collaborative learning teams, 34–35
College Board PROFILE form, 173, 174
College education, advantages of, 6
College instructors. *See* Instructors
College librarians, assistance from, 126
College library resources, 125–27
College success courses, 3
Communicating, 135–48
    citing sources and, 142–43
    speaking and, 144–46
    writing and, 137–41
Community, creating. *See* Connecting with others
Community involvement, 163–64
Community service, 164

Competitions, career planning and, 209
Comprehension
    monitoring while reading, 73
    as second level of learning, 112
Comprehensive information, 128
Computer literacy, 121. *See also* Internet entries
Concentrating
    to improve memory, 92
    while reading, 72–73
Conclusions, drawing, 108
Condoms, 190–91
Conflict with others, 153, 154
Connecting with others. *See also* Relationships
    by finding niche on campus, 4
    by getting to know instructors, 5
    learning disabilities and, 47
    by participating in class, 55–56
    through tutors and study groups, 89
    through VARK learning styles, 39
Content skills, sought by employers, 214–15
Contraceptives, 190–91
Conventional personality type, 205, 206
Cooperative education, 173, 209
Cornell format for note taking, 57
Corporate Web sites, 129
Cost cutting, 170–71
Courses, dropping, 22
Course schedule, 26, 201
Course syllabus, 53, 88
Cover letter, writing, 213
Credibility of sources, 128–30
Credit cards, 178–80
Credit report, obtaining, 179
Credit score, 178–80
Critical listening, 55
Critical thinking, 105–18
    Bloom's taxonomy and, 112–13
    in college and life, 114–16
    faulty reasoning and, 110–12
    strategies for, 107–9
Cultural literacy, 121
Cultural views of time, 15
Currency of information, 128

D

Daily planners, 23
Databases
    researching with, 124
    for scholarly articles, 126
    subscription, 126–27
Dating relationships, 154
Debit cards, 179, 180
Definitional information, 128
Delayed gratification, 45
Delivery of speeches, 146
Developmental arithmetic disorder, 47
Developmental writing disabilities, 47
Diet. *See* Nutrition
Digital technology, communicating with, 157–58
Discussion
    assigned readings and, 53
    critical thinking and, 109
    note taking from, 62
    participating in, 56
Distractions
    avoiding while studying, 28
    dealing with, 20–21
    procrastination and, 20

Diversity on college campus, 159–61
Drafting
    steps for, 138–39
    of texts and e-mails, 158
Dressing appropriately
    for interviews, 213
    for speeches, 146
Drinking alcohol, 192–93
Dropping courses, 22
Dyslexia, 46

E

Earnings, future, college education and, 6
Eating disorders, 189
Eating healthy. *See* Nutrition
Economic diversity on campus, 160
Economy, today's, 197–202
Editing, 139
EI. *See* Emotional intelligence
Electronic planners, 23
E-mail
    appropriate use of, 157–58
    etiquette for, 141
Emergencies, credit card for, 178
Emotional intelligence, understanding, 41–43
Emotions
    effect on success, 44–45
    emotional intelligence and, 41–45
    self-awareness of, 42
    test preparation and, 90
Empathy, emotional intelligence and, 42
Employment after college
    job search strategies for, 211–13
    setting goals for, 15–18
Employment during college
    balancing with borrowing, 176–77
    benefits of, 210
    on campus, 163–64
    career planning and, 207
    work-study and, 172–73
Encyclopedias, topic overviews in, 123
Engaged learning, 31–50
    benefits of, 33
    collaborative learning teams and, 34–35
    emotional intelligence and, 41–45
    learning disabilities and, 46–48
    learning styles and, 36–39
English as a second language, 81
Enterprising personality type, 205, 206
Entertainment, cutting costs of, 171
E-readers, pros and cons of, 76
ESL, 81
Essay questions on tests/exams, 95–96
Ethnic diversity on campus, 159–60
Evaluating sources, 128–30
Evaluation, as sixth level of learning, 112
Evidence, examining, critical thinking and, 116
Exam plan, 87
Exams, 85–104
    academic honesty and misconduct on, 99–101
    preparing for, 87–90
    strategies for taking, 95–98
    studying for retention and, 91–94
Exercise
    scheduling, 25
    stress management and, 186–87
    test preparation and, 90

Expenses, budgeting for, 169
Experiential learning opportunities, 209
Expressive language disorders, 47

F

Facebook, 157–58
Face-to-face communication, versus online, 157–58
FAFSA, 173–74
Faith diversity on campus, 161
Fallacies, logical, 110–12
False authority, appealing to, 110–11
False cause, 111
Family relationships, 155–56
Faulty reasoning, 110–12
Federal loans, subsidized and unsubsidized, 176–77
Federal work-study, getting experience from, 210
Feeling connected. See Connecting with others
Fifty-minute study blocks, 27
Fill-in-the-blank questions on tests/exams, 97
Finances, personal. See Money management
Financial aid, 172–75
Financial aid office, 173
Fixed expenses, 170
Flash cards, 74, 92–93
Flexibility, emotional intelligence and, 42
Focusing
    to improve memory, 92
    while reading, 72–73
Forgetting curve, 62
Formal style of writing, 140–41
Franklin, Benjamin, 36
Free Application for Federal Student Aid, 173–74
Freewriting, 137

G

Gardasil, 190
Generalizations, hasty, 111
Global economy, 199
Goal setting
    importance of and methods for, 8–10
    for study time, 27, 72
    time management and, 15–18
Google, 128
Google Scholar, 127
Government Web sites, 124, 129
Grades, emotional intelligence and, 44
Graduate school, planning for, 177
Grants, 172
Gratification, delayed versus instant, 45
Group discussion. See Discussion
Group study. See Study groups

H

Happiness, emotional intelligence and, 43
Harassment, 161
Hasty generalizations, 111
Hate crimes, 161
Healthy living, 183–96
    alcohol use and, 192–93
    nutrition and weight management and, 188–89
    sexual health and, 190–91
    stress management and, 185–87
    test preparation and, 90
Highlighting, while reading, 71–72
Holland Personality and Career Types, 205–6
Homework, class notes for, 62–63

Honesty, academic, 99–101
HPV (human papillomavirus), 190
Humanities textbooks, reading, 77

I

Identify theft, 179, 180
Impulse control, emotional intelligence and, 43, 45
Income, budgeting and, 169
Independence, emotional intelligence and, 42
Industry research, career planning and, 207, 208
Informal style of writing, 140–41
Informational Web sites, 129
Information literacy, 119–33
    choosing, narrowing, researching topic and, 123–24
    evaluating sources and, 128–30
    synthesizing information and ideas and, 131
    understanding, 121–22
    using library and, 125–27
Instant gratification, 45
Instructors
    building relationships with, 5
    connecting with, 151–53
    preparing for tests with, 87
    writing e-mails to, 141
Interactive learners, 63
Interests, personal
    career choice and, 9
    career planning and, 204–6
Internet
    collaboration and critical thinking and, 109
    evaluating sources from, 128
    searching on, 123–24
    type of sites on, 129
    using to improve memory, 92
Internships, 209
Interpersonal skills, emotional intelligence and, 42
Interviewing, 212–13
InterviewStream, 213
Intrapersonal skills, emotional intelligence and, 42
Introductory sources, 128
Investigative personality type, 205, 206
Involvement
    in campus organizations and groups, 4
    community, connecting with others through, 163–64

J

Jobs. See Employment after college; Employment during college
Journals/journal articles. See Scholarly articles/journals
Jumping on bandwagon, 111

K

Kadison, Richard, 44
Key terms, vocabulary development from, 79
Key words, Internet search with, 123
Kinesthetic learners, 36
Knowledge, as first level of learning, 112
Kolb Learning Styles Inventory, 36

L

Late payments/fees, on credit cards, 178–80
Learning, engaged. See Engaged learning

Learning, lifelong, career planning and, 200–2
Learning, six levels of, 112–13
Learning centers, tutors and, 88
Learning challenges/disabilities
    learning with, 46–48
    meeting people with, 161
Learning styles
    engaged learning and, 33
    questionnaire to determine, 36–39
    types of, 36
Learning teams, 35
Levels of learning, six, 112–13
Librarians, assistance from, 126
Library catalog, 127
Library research, learning teams and, 35
Library resources, 125–27
Life connections, using to improve memory, 92
Life goals, career planning and, 204
Lifelong learning, career planning and, 200–2
Listening, 54–56
List format for note taking, 60
Living expenses, budgeting for, 169
Loans, balancing with working, 176–77
Logical fallacies, 110–12
Long-term goals
    prioritizing, 17
    setting, 8–10
Love relationships, 154

M

Magazines, researching with, 124
Main idea, identifying while taking notes, 61
Majors. See also Career planning
    choosing, 200
    exploring interests and, 204
    linking interests to, 4
    making decisions about, 8
Managing money. See Money management
Mapping, while previewing, 70
Margin notes, writing while reading, 71–72
Marketing Web sites, 129
Marketing yourself, 211
Marking textbooks while reading, 71–72
Marriage, during college, 155
Marshmallow study, 45
Matching questions on tests/exams, 98
Math courses, note taking in, 62
Math exams, preparing for, 89–90
Math textbooks, reading, 75–76
Measurable goals, setting, 9
Media literacy, 121
Memory, improving, 91–92
Merit scholarships, 172
Mind mapping, 92, 93
Misconduct, academic, 99–101
MLA documentation style, 142
MLA Handbook for Writers of Research Papers, 142
Mock interviews, 214
Money management, 167–82
    balancing working and borrowing and, 176–77
    budgeting and, 169–71
    financial aid and, 172–75
    managing credit and, 178–80
Moods, emotional intelligence and, 41–45
Motivation, maintaining, 22
Multiple-choice questions on tests/exams, 96–97
Multitasking, avoiding while studying, 27

Myers-Briggs Type Indicator, 36, 204
MyPlate eating guidelines, 188

N

Napping, stress management and, 187
Narrowing topic, 123–24
Needs
    scholarships based on, 172
    versus wants, 171
Newspapers, researching with, 124
Newspaper Web sites, researching with, 124
News Web sites, description of, 129
Notes, creating for speeches, 146
Note taking, 54–64
    adjusting for different classes, 61
    learning teams and, 35
    methods for, 57–60
    in quantitative courses, 62
    reviewing after, 63–64
    while listening, 56
    while reading, 72
Nutrition
    paying attention to, 188–89
    stress management and, 185–87
    test preparation and, 90

O

Off-campus employment, versus on-campus, 177, 210
Office hours, meeting with instructors during, 152
On-campus employment, versus off-campus, 177, 210
Online communication, 157–58
Online tests, strategies for taking, 98
Optimism, emotional intelligence and, 43
Organization
    class preparation and, 53
    of schedule, 23–26
    using to improve memory, 92
Organizations on campus, getting involved in, 4, 162
Outlining
    for essay tests/exams, 96
    for note taking, 58
    for science textbooks, 77
    for speeches, 146
    studying from, 90
    while previewing, 70
    writing process and, 138
Overlearning, to improve memory, 92
Overscheduling, 22

P

Paragraph format for note taking, 59
Parenting, during college, 155
Parent Loan for Undergraduate Students, 177
Parents, relationships with, 156
Participating in class, 54–56
Passwords
    identity theft and, 179
    online communication and, 158
Paul, Richard, 107
Paying attention, 54–55
Peer review, of first draft, 139
Peer-reviewed scholarly articles/journals. See Scholarly articles/journals
Periodicals
    evaluating, 130
    information time line for, 124
    researching with, 126–27
Personal attacks, 110
Personal bias, evaluating sources for, 130

Personal finance. *See* Money management
Personal identification number, debit cards and, 180
Personalities, career planning and, 204
Personal relationships, managing, 154
Personal skills, career planning and, 202
Phaup, Tricia, 191
Physical activity. *See* Exercise
Physical challenges/disabilities, 161
Physical health. *See* Healthy living
PIN, debit cards and, 180
Plagiarism, 100, 142–43
Planners, daily or weekly, 23
PLUS loans, 177
Points of view. *See* Viewpoints
Portals, Internet, 129
Positive self-talk, test preparation and, 90
Posting online, appropriate use of, 157–58
PowerPoint, 144
Pregnancy, safe sex and, 190–91
Prejudice, 159–60
Preparing for class, 53
Presentations, 135, 144–46
Previewing, before reading, 69
Prewriting, 137
Prezi, 144
Primary sources, value of, 77
Priorities, setting, 17, 25
Private student loans, 177
Problem-solving ability, emotional intelligence and, 42
Procrastination, 19–20
Pronunciation, in speeches, 146
Publication Manual of the American Psychological Association, 142
Public speaking, 135, 144–46
Punctuality
  instructor's expectations of, 151
  for interviews, 215
  as sign of respect, 18

Q

Quantitative courses, note taking in, 62
Questions, asking
  critical thinking and, 107–8
  to overcome procrastination and distractions, 20

R

Racial diversity on campus, 159–60
Rape, protecting against, 191
Reading, active. *See* Active reading
Reading, assigned, 53
Reading disabilities, 46–47
Read/write learners, 36
Realistic personality type, 205, 206
Reality testing, emotional intelligence and, 42
Reasoning, faulty, 110–12
Reciting, to remember information, 63
Relationships, 149–65. *See also* Connecting with others
  digital technology and, 157–58
  diversity on campus and, 159–62
  with family members, 155–56
  with instructors, 151–53
  personal, 154
  through community involvement, 163–64
Relevance of sources, 128–30
Relevant goals, setting, 10

Reliability of sources, 128–30
Religious diversity on campus, 161
Research, 123–24
  learning teams and, 35
  online, 123–24
  setting aside time for, 25
Respectfulness, time management and, 18
Résumé
  building, 211–12
  drafting, 207
Returning students, challenges and advantages for, 6
Reviewing, while reading, 74
Reviewing notes, 63–64
Review sheets, 92
Revising, 139
Rewards, for meeting goals, 28
Romantic relationships, 154
Roommates, 154

S

Safe sex, 190–91
Safety, online communication and, 158
Salary, future, college education and, 6
SaVE legislation, 191
Savings account, establishing, 177
Scams, identity theft and, 179
Schedule of classes, 26, 201
Scheduling time, 23–26. *See also* Time management
Scholarly articles/journals
  evaluating, 130
  information time line for, 124
  researching with, 126–27
Scholarships, 172
Science courses, note taking in, 62
Science exams, preparing for, 89–90
Science textbooks, reading, 76–77
Search operators, 124
Self-actualization, emotional intelligence and, 42
Self-assessment, for career planning, 203–6
Self-awareness, emotional intelligence and, 42
Self-regard, emotional intelligence and, 42
Self-talk, positive, test preparation and, 90
Service-learning, 209
Sessums, Christopher D., 109
Setting goals. *See* Goal setting
Sexual assault, protecting against, 191
Sexual diversity on campus, 160–62
Sexual health, 190–91
Sexually transmitted infections, 190
Short-term goals, 8–10, 15
Six levels of learning, 112–13
Skill-focused résumés, 211
Skills
  career planning and, 203–4
  sought by employers, 200, 214–15
Sleep
  stress management and, 187
  test preparation and, 90
Slippery slope, 111
SMART goals, 9–10
Smoking, 193
Social networking sites, appropriate use of, 157–58
Social personality type, 205, 206
Social responsibility, emotional intelligence and, 42
Source citation, 142–43
Source evaluation, 128–30
Speaking, 135, 144–46
Steel, Piers, 19–20

Stereotyping, 159–60
STIs, 190
Strengths, personal, career choice and, 6
Stress management
  emotional intelligence and, 43
  healthy living and, 185–87
  to improve memory, 92
Student loans, 176–77
Study groups, 35, 87–88
Studying
  avoiding distractions while, 20–21
  improving concentration during, 72–73
  learning teams and, 35
  maximizing time for, 27–28
  preparing notes for, 61
  2-for-1 rule for, 23–25
Study location, 27, 72
Subscription databases, 126–27
Subsidized federal student loans, 176–77
Success, setting goals for, 8–10
Summaries, writing, for test preparation, 93–94
Supplemental Instruction classes, note taking from, 61
Syllabus, 53, 88
Synthesis, as fifth level of learning, 112
Synthesizing information and ideas, 131

T

Tablets, digital, pros and cons of, 76
Taking notes. *See* Note taking
Talent, scholarships based on, 172
Teachers. *See* Instructors
Teamwork, critical thinking and, 109
Technology, communicating with, 157–58
Ten-year plan, 16
Test files, 100
Tests, 85–104
  academic honesty and misconduct on, 99–101
  preparing for, 87–90
  strategies for taking, 95–98
  studying for retention and, 91–94
Textbooks
  getting most from, 73
  reading different types of, 75–78
Texting, appropriate use of, 157–58
Thank-you notes, to interviewers, 213
Thesaurus, 79–80
Thesis statements, 138–39
Thinking critically. *See* Critical thinking
Time, cultural views of, 15
Time management, 13–30
  campus activities and, 163
  employment and, 164, 176
  goal setting and, 15–18
  maximizing study time and, 27–28
  organizing time and tasks for, 23–26
  pitfalls of poor time management, 19–22
  punctuality and, 151
  for reading assignments, 78
  setting priorities and, 16–17
  stress management and, 187
  while taking tests and exams, 95–96
  for writing process, 139
To-do list, creating, 25
Topic, choosing, narrowing and researching, 123–24
Transferable skills
  career planning and, 204
  sought by employers, 215

Transportation, cutting costs of, 171
Travel time, using wisely, 28
True/false questions on tests/exams, 98
Truth, critical thinking and, 107. *See also* Critical thinking
Turnitin's Originality Check, 143
Tutoring centers on campus, 88
Tutors, preparing for tests with, 88
2-for-1 study rule, 23–25

U

Underlining, while reading, 71–72
Unemployment rate, college education and, 6
Unsubsidized federal student loans, 177

V

Values, personal
  career planning and, 203
  time management and, 15
Variable expenses, 170
VARK Learning Styles Inventory, 36–40
Verbal harassment, 161
Viewpoints
  considering, critical thinking and, 108
  of different instructors, 152, 153
  evaluating sources for, 130
Visual aids, for speeches, 144–45
Visual learners
  mapping and, 70
  methods for, 36
Vocabulary, developing, 79–80
Volunteering
  career planning and, 207, 209
  connecting with others by, 164

W

Wants, versus needs, 171
Web sites, evaluating, 128. *See also* Internet entries
Weekly planning, 23–24
Weight management, 188–89
Wheel mapping, 70
Wikipedia, 123
Wikis, 123, 129
Williams, Juan, 142
Word choice, in speeches, 146
Word games, for vocabulary development, 80
Word lists, reviewing, 80
Working. *See* Employment after college; Employment during college
Workplace skills, career planning and, 203–4
Work satisfaction, career planning and, 204
Work-study
  as financial aid, 172–73
  getting experience from, 210–11
Writing
  basics of, 137–41
  importance of doing well, 135
  to remember information, 63
Writing disabilities, 47

Z

Zakaria, Fareed, 142